VK
555
T87
1986

CELESTIAL
for
the
CRUISING
NAVIGATOR

by Merle B. Turner

Cornell Maritime Press
Centreville, Maryland

Copyright © 1986 by Cornell Maritime Press, Inc.

All drawings and photographs are by the author except as indicated.

Library of Congress Cataloging in Publication Data

Turner, Merle B.
Celestial for the cruising navigator.

    Bibliography: p.
    Includes index.
    1. Nautical astronomy.   I. Title.
VK555.T87 1986   527   85-47837
ISBN 0-87033-341-0

Manufactured in the United States of America
First edition, 1986; fourth printing, 1994

To Marjorie, fellow navigator

Contents

Preface

Another book on celestial navigation? The student of navigation has many choices running from how-to-do-it primers to those venerable volumes renowned at the Naval Academy, *Dutton* and *Bowditch*. But the primers are far too simplistic to give the student an understanding of the relation of celestial to terrestrial position, and *Dutton* and *Bowditch* are too comprehensive and encyclopedic to serve as handy manuals of instruction. The present volume attempts to capture the practical directness of the primer yet build upon something more than a superficial treatment of nautical astronomy.

Doubtless there are those who have learned the mechanics of plotting a sun line in an hour or two, such being the ritual of utilizing an almanac and tables. But without background and understanding, that ritual becomes a cloak for truly arcane matters. The ritual conceals the essential relations of time, celestial position, latitude, and longitude. It leaves one wondering, if not bewildered, how sextant observation at sea can result in a unique determination of position.

Typically the student is introduced to the rudiments of time, nautical astronomy, and the celestial triangle without so much as a mention of that mathematical vehicle of inference, spherical trigonometry. Methods of sight reduction (the mechanical utilization of tables of altitudes and azimuths) obviate the mathematics. However, there is good reason to resurrect the basic trigonometric equations from technical source books: today the availability of inexpensive hand calculators makes it possible to compute altitude and azimuths as readily as they can be obtained from the volumes of sight reduction tables. Furthermore, once the basic operations are mastered, the calculator offers convenience, precision, and generality not to be found in any of the rituals of tabular solution. Not only does it handle sight reduction with dispatch, but it is readily adapted to compass checks, passage planning, chartwork, sailings, and individual determinations of latitude and longitude.

Though making use of mathematical formulae, the present work is not in a strict sense mathematical. No attempt is made to derive fundamental formulae. Rather the trigonometric formulae are presented simply as instructional guides for carrying out a sequence of operations on a hand calculator.

Although this book is directed toward the small boat navigator, the treatment is comprehensive, going well beyond the basic rituals of sight reduction. Indeed, the reader who masters the details will be familiar with all such topics in celestial navigation as may be brought forth to test the competence of the professional mariner.

It gives me great pleasure to express debts of gradditude to the late Capt. Henry H. Shufeldt for his critical reading of the manuscript, and for his comments and generous sharing of expertise; and to Mr. John Luykx for helpful comments and suggestions concerning the glossary and Chapters 9 and 10. I am also indebted to Barbara Land for converting an illegible hand into typescript.

I wish also to acknowledge my gratitude for permission to use the following material:

Figure 9.3. From *Dutton's Navigation and Pilotage,* 12th ed. by G. D. Dunlap and Capt. H. H. Shufeldt. Copyright © 1969, U.S. Naval Institute, Annapolis, Maryland.

Quotation, Chapter 3. Joshua Slocum, *Sailing Alone Around the World.* New York: Macmillan Publishing Co., 1970. By permission of the literary heirs.

I am indebted to Piotr Kiedron for pointing out an error in the version of Figure 5.9 that appeared in earlier printings of this book.

CELESTIAL FOR THE CRUISING NAVIGATOR

CHAPTER ONE

Introduction

Celestial navigation is the practical art of getting from one place to another with heavenly assistance. Contrary to the testimony of seafaring novices, it has nothing to do with theology. And contrary to the way it is introduced into some popular accounts of cruising, it does not stand apart from basic navigational practice as something to learn only when the intrepid skipper ventures out of sight of land. Rather, celestial navigation is as old as navigational practice itself.

The practice of celestial navigation goes back at least to Babylon and the Phoenicians who were credited with carrying commerce through the Mediterranean, the Red Sea, out to India, and around the whole of Africa. These early maritime adventurers possessed nothing of the modern paraphernalia of pilotage or dead reckoning. The compass, for example, can be regarded as a fairly modern invention, coming out of China or the Mediterranean in the thirteenth century. And logs of even the simplest design did not come into general use until the end of the sixteenth century. Columbus and his pilots, for example, were reported to have eyeballed their speeds.

Essentially the only early navigation was celestial navigation. Not only were stars the guide to direction, but in a very loose way they told the navigator something about his latitude. Sophisticated inferences as to position came along much later. Early sailors depended upon the observation and description of the regularities in celestial motion, descriptions that required the application of mathematics to celestial and terrestrial position. As early as 160 B.C., Hipparchus, the great astronomer of antiquity, attempted to correlate celestial and terrestrial positions. That done, then it was only a matter of time, considerable as it was, before man could utilize the altitude of a celestial body to tell him of his terrestrial position.

Nowadays one is not likely to begin a study of navigation with a course in nautical astronomy. Rather, one learns basic pilotage, chart work, and dead reckoning, all with the customary accoutrements of keeping course and distance by means of compass, log, clock, and bearing compass or pelorus. To be sure, many recreational boaters have no need for celestial navigation. Pilotage, dead reckoning, and electronic assistance, if the yachtsman can afford the many options, will suffice. But once the sailor ventures out of sight of his familiar shores, celestial navigation becomes indispensable.

This handbook of celestial navigation is addressed to the cruising navigator who, like myself, a sailboater, will have more time than paraphernalia to determine position at sea. There may be a time, of course, when modern technology will enable us to clutter up our navigation stations with consoles of electronic lasagna which will blink out positions like a digital watch blinks out the time. But by then, something will have been lost in the challenge and excitement of navigation. And unless our electronic navigator is also something of an expert repairman, he will still face the necessity of casting a knowing eye at the telltale skies.

It is assumed that the reader has a basic knowledge of pilotage and dead reckoning, and of course-keeping and tracking. Our purpose here is to describe the celestial aids for establishing and checking position. There are, to be sure, aspects of celestial navigation other than the plotting of a fix. For example, we check the compass by celestial bearings; we make separate determinations of latitude and longitude; and we plot great-circle courses by the same trigonometric means we use in finding the altitude and bearing of a celestial body. All of these applications of celestial navigation (or nautical astronomy, as it is sometimes called) depend upon the close, unambiguous ties of celestial position to terrestrial position.

It is no accident that early astronomy and navigation developed hand in hand. Nearly every development in observational astronomy had relevance for navigation. The mathematics of positional astronomy (spherical trigonometry) is that of navigation. The treatments of time are interchangeable. Latitude and longitude are fundamental concepts for both. The promise of celestial navigation is straightforward: if we can describe accurately the position of some conspicuous celestial object at any given instant of time (nautical astronomy), and if we can orient ourselves to that body in terms of its altitude and its true bearing from us, then we can make an inference from that information as to our own position.

Thus we begin the presentation of celestial navigation in Chapter 2 with a rather detailed description of the coordinate systems that enable us to relate terrestrial and celestial positions. From this foundation we move on to a discussion of time. Time is the inseparable element in celestial motion; it is also an indispensable element in our concept of longitude. Our modern concept of time, "that abstract of irreversible sequences," as Herbert Spencer defined it, has become integral with the description of apparent celestial motion.

The relating of time to celestial motion (Chapter 3) enables us to establish the fundamental connections between celestial and terrestrial positions. Timekeeping on earth and celestial motion—these two, conjointly, conspire to tell the navigator where he is. However, in the general case, the procedure for inferring position is not a simple one. We start with an approximation of our position, and that, compared with the coordinates of a celestial body positioned above earth according to time, enables us to construct a spherical triangle, some of whose parts are known and some unknown. From the position of the star, and from our assumed position, we can calculate what altitude the celestial body should have. Comparing an actual sextant observation of altitude with that computed altitude will enable us to move from an assumed to an actual position.

In Chapter 4, we move on to setting up the structure and coordinates of the venerable celestial triangle. Here we bring our knowledge of position, motion, and time to focus upon the basic structure of navigational astronomy. The celestial triangle, or the nautical or navigational triangle as it is variously called, is crucial to our finding course and position by celestial means. Its vertices are a terrestrial pole, our own assumed position, and the position of the observed celestial body. Its sides are arcs or portions of great circles interchangeably projected between the earth's surface and the celestial sphere. Both description and analysis are done with the tools of spherical trigonometry, tools incidentally that can be readily applied without our having to master the formal structures of the mathematics.

In Chapter 5 we turn our attention to the computational details, to the procedures traditionally known as *sight reduction*. We need not be proficient in spherical trigonometry to carry out the celestial calculations. Until fairly recently, both professional and recreational navigators have relied upon tabular solutions, that is, upon volumes of precomputed solutions, for most of the conceivable situations. But nowadays, with inexpensive calculators within the reach of all, there is good reason to return to the computing of the basic trigonometric formulae. With no more skill than that required to read a formula as an instructional unit, the navigator can now compute the original navigational formulae for altitude and azimuth as quickly as he can find the solution in sight reduction tables.

It has been said that the many tables and rituals of sight reduction were invented to keep weak-minded navigators from having to use their heads. It is true that solutions by logarithms are cumbersome and, on occasion, subject to ambiguity, but the simple operating mechanics of the modern calculator have all but eliminated these difficulties. Sight reduction tables may always be kept on hand as backup aids, but it is very likely that in the near future most computations and sight reductions will be done by the hand calculator.

Chapter 6 discusses the description and utilization of the modern sextant. Modern? Well, perhaps not. The sextant is one of the oldest in design of all the still-current instruments of navigation. Although there have been modest optical improvements in recent years, many old instruments are still in use today. However, there is more to observation than a good sextant. There is the practice of observation and also a panoply of errors that the observer must compensate for in order to get an accurate reading of altitude.

While on the subject of observation we move on in Chapter 7 to star identification. Most all of us know a few stars, but this short discussion points out a few more ways for developing a more intimate familiarity with constellations and configurations.

Not all of celestial navigation deals with obtaining the classic noonday fix. The remaining chapters of the book enlarge on these other areas. Chapter 8 covers the subject of finding latitude and longitude—practices, incidentally, which individually preceded any systematic efforts to establish a definitive position, as such. In Chapter 9 we cover the sailings, the procedures for planning and plotting ocean passages. And we use the occasion to introduce various checks on course, distance, and compass that are now accessible through the use of the calculator. In the final chapter we undertake an overall review of navigational practice, the routines, and the preparation that will distinguish a person as being competent beyond just being capable of finding some reasonable approximation of position.

This book is written for the cruising navigator, the small boat sailor, although the basic materials are appropriate for all navigators. What is distinctive about our focusing upon the small boat navigator is the realization that he has a limited navigation station, limited equipment, and limited time to carry out navigational chores. The book is not intended as an encyclopedia; for that, one is referred to a work that should be in the hands of every serious student of navigation—*Bowditch: American Practical Navigator.* On the other hand, it is not a how-to-do-it primer ignoring the mathematical underpinnings. It is hoped the treatment will generate an interest and appreciation of the subject such that navigation becomes more than a perfunctory chore that one would leave to a machine if that were possible (*cf.* Note 1.1).

The writer, incidentally, has had an academic background. Consequently it is with the trepidation of a reformed alcoholic confronting a drink that he promises not to indulge in footnotes. However, the temptations—historical asides, mathematical embellishments, and details not entirely germane to the ongoing argument—remain. These he remands as Notes to the ends of the chapters, a tease for those happy masochists who sense that there is more to a subject than meets the casual eye.

NOTES

Note 1.1
Two important references for any serious student of navigation are Dutton's *Navigation and Piloting* and Bowditch's *American Practical Navigator*. Dutton, however, is too much the manual for the naval officer to be of uniform relevance to the recreational navigator. And Bowditch, blessed Bowditch, is too much the encyclopedic and historical reference to be the handy textbook.

In addition to the above two books, the writer has relied heavily upon, and wishes to acknowledge his indebtedness to, H. R. Mills' *Positional Astronomy and Astro-Navigation Made Easy* and Charles H. Cotter's *The Complete Nautical Astronomer*. And for historical background, Charles H. Cotter's *A History of Nautical Astronomy,* W. E. May's *A History of Maritime Navigation,* and E. G. R. Taylor's *The Haven-Finding Art.*

CHAPTER TWO

Position: Terrestrial and Celestial

Where are we? In our conventional world of space there are any number of ways of specifying position. Mail, as we know, is distributed by a relatively simple code: street address, city, state, country. This, however, is not the simplest of positional systems. We could do better, and be more efficient and less ambiguous, by merely specifying latitude and longitude.

COORDINATE SYSTEMS

Consider ideal two-dimensional Euclidean space, the kind that is assumed in the construction of our coastal charts. There are two systems of coordinates that we might utilize to specify position. One is the (x, y) set as given to us in the classical Cartesian algebra of space. The other is that of polar coordinates as given in the direction-distance set. Figure 2.1 demonstrates the two. The point p has the Cartesian coordinates (x, y) and polar coordinates (α, a) or, namely, the angle α on the vertical N with a distance from the origin (o, o) of a. Both systems of specification, it should be noted, are utilized in navigation. For the (x, y) system we have longitude, latitude; for the polar system we utilize course and distance to determine a position, as in routine dead reckoning.

We do not, of course, live in that simple ideal space so neatly projected by our charts. Rather than flat Euclidean space we have a two-dimensional spherical surface to contend with. But so far as this surface is concerned, we can still use a Cartesian set and a polar set of coordinates. Adjustments do have to be made, however, when the cartographer is faced with the problem of flattening a section of spherical surface onto a simple Euclidean plane (*cf.* Note 2.1).

Terrestrial Surface

Any point on the earth's surface can be specified by a given latitude-longitude set. And any point on the celestial sphere above us can be specified by an analogous set of coordinates. Hence the two positional sets, terrestrial and celestial, can be interrelated.

For sake of simplicity we assume the earth to be a perfect sphere rotating on its north-south polar axis. Any plane passing through the earth's center will inscribe a *great circle* on the earth's surface. Such a great-circle inscription constitutes the straight or shortest distance line (geodesic) on the spherical surface (*cf.* Note 2.2).

In general the coordinate systems for representing space are arbitrarily specified. For the familiar Cartesian (x, y) set, the origin (o, o) can be anywhere. And so also for a spherical surface. However, the earth is a rotating sphere. Hence we take the equatorial plane and its great circle as one of our origins and the prime meridian passing through

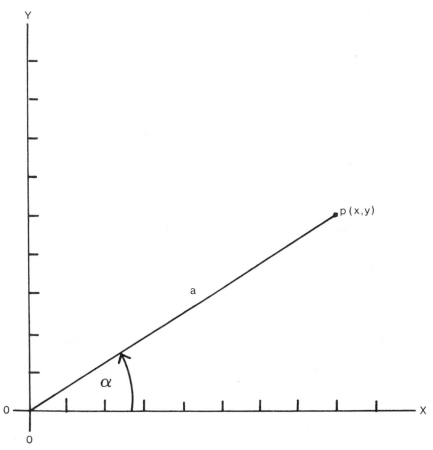

Figure 2.1 Cartesian and polar coordinates

Greenwich as the other (*cf.* Note 2.3). A *meridian* is a great circle intersecting both terrestrial poles. The plane of any meridian passes through the two poles and the center of the earth and necessarily cuts the equatorial plane at right angles.

For our system of coordinates we have two sets of circles: meridians of longitude measured east and west from the prime meridian of Greenwich, and circles of latitude, those small circles cut by planes parallel to the equatorial plane and measured north and south from the equator. Among parallels of latitude only the equator, or zero latitude line, is a great circle. Figure 2.2 shows the constructional details. G is the prime meridian through Greenwich, M is the latitude circle of the observer at M. Angle L in the plane of the meridian through M is the latitude of M. Angle λ in the equatorial plane between G and M is the longitude of M.

Finding Terrestrial Position

For the navigator, terrestrial position is found in one of several ways: by pilotage, by dead reckoning, by electronic means such as radio bearings, and by celestial observations. Although the subject of this book is celestial navigation, the taking of bearings is

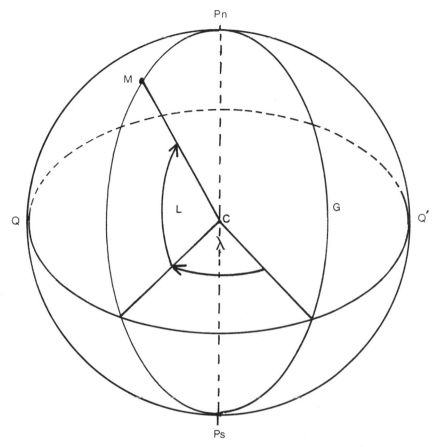

Figure 2.2   Latitude and longitude

basic to all navigational practice. It will be helpful, therefore, to review some basic principles of determining position by the observing and plotting of bearings.

The reciprocal of the true bearing of an object from the observer on a boat is the bearing of the boat from the object. Such a bearing is a line of position (LOP), and if two such bearings are plotted, the intersection of the two fixes our position.

According to the fundamentals of coastal pilotage, position can be found in one of three ways: one, by crossing bearing lines; two, by advancing a bearing line for a running fix; and three, by timing changes of bearing on a given object.

In Figure 2.3 we have an example of a position fixed by crossing bearing lines. A bearing is obtained on object A, another on object B, and the plot of their reciprocal angles yields a position P.

Figure 2.4 presents the example of a running fix. B1 is the first bearing, B2 is the second, and B1' is the first bearing advanced distance D, the distance the vessel has run on its track between the two obervations. Any track will serve, providing it represents an accurate DR record between the initial and final bearings.

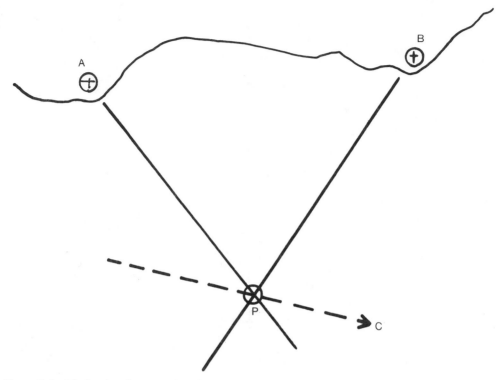

Figure 2.3   Fix by simultaneous bearings

Figure 2.5 illustrates the situation whereby some basic trigonometric relation enables us to determine a position by virtue of changes in bearing on the same object. The vessel is proceeding on course C. At the time the object A bears relatively 45° (i.e., relative to course) the navigator marks the time. When the object bears relatively 90°, time is taken and distance D computed. Because the triangle in the figure is an isosceles one, the distance out from A on the true bearing, as determined on B2, is equal to the distance D.

There are, of course, other trigonometric relations that we can use. All make use of relative bearings of an object A, distance run between bearings, and position when the vessel is abeam A.

Of the methods reviewed here, that most widely used is the simple intersection of two or more distinct bearings. It would appear, now, that if we could determine the substellar positions of stellar objects, and take bearings on these objects, we could then find our position by celestial bearings. This would be straightforward application of the principles of pilotage. However, the distances involved from the observer to the substellar position are so great that we would need to measure bearings to an accuracy far beyond the means of anything but the finest of astronomical observatories. Rather than relying on bearings, we find that the combination of observed altitude and computed azimuth will afford us the accuracy we require.

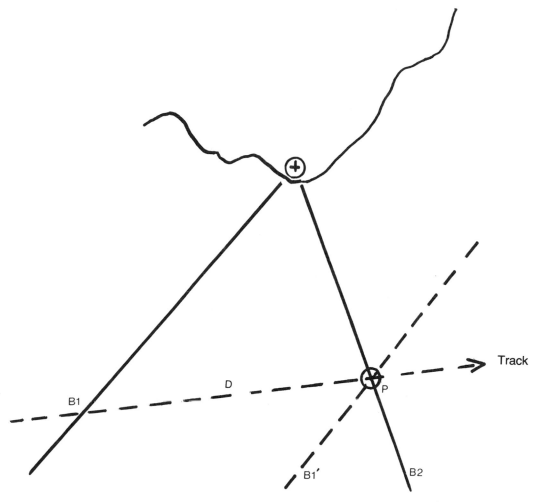

Track

Figure 2.4   Running fix

Celestial Sphere

To map celestial bodies by means of a coordinate system we follow a tradition as old as astronomy itself. We consider the stars to be fixed on a sphere that rotates about the center of the earth. The sun, moon, and planets, however, stand apart. They travel their separate ways across the celestial canopy.

As in the case of terrestrial globes, we now adopt a system of latitude and longitude for the celestial sphere. By projecting the equatorial plane outward from the earth we inscribe the celestial equator (QQ′) on the celestial sphere. This celestial equator is known as the *equinoctial*. Projections of lines of latitude inscribe circles of equal *declination* on the celestial sphere. Thus declination, like latitude, is measured north and south of the equator, in this case, the celestial equator. Figure 2.6 shows that declination d of the star ☆ corresponds to a latitude X on the earth's surface.

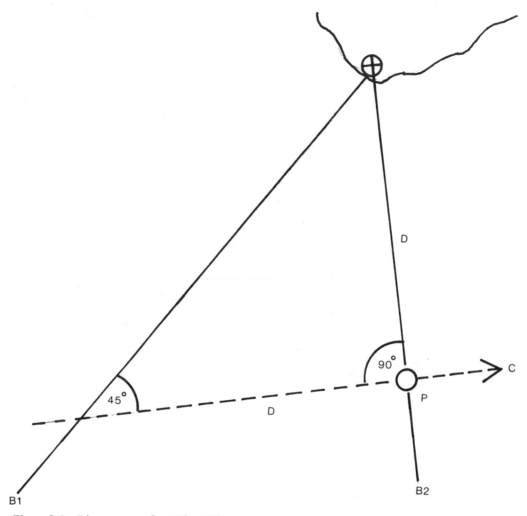

Figure 2.5   Distance-run fix: 45° to 90°

Designating longitude in the heavens is a more complicated matter. The earth spins on its own polar axis, thereby imparting relative motion to the celestial sphere. But the celestial sphere is actually stationary. Thus, if we were to project earth's Greenwich meridian onto the celestial sphere, it would sweep through the entire sphere in diurnal rotation. We can also give the celestial sphere a set of fixed meridians as in the case of the earth, but, in order to relate longitude in the heavens to that on earth, we need to relate the fixed meridians in the celestial sphere to the prime meridian of earth that undergoes diurnal rotation.

Now it is clear that the appearance of motion of the prime meridian can be generated in one of two ways, either by assuming rotation of earth on its polar axis, or by assuming rotation of the celestial sphere on its projected polar axis. From the terrestrial observer's point of view it is the heavens that appear to move. To relate the two systems of longitude we establish a prime meridian in the celestial sphere and relate its motion

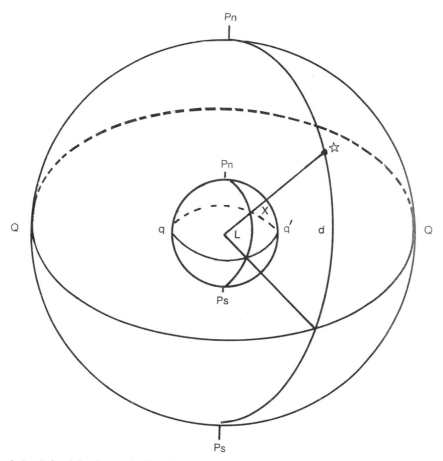

Figure 2.6 Celestial sphere, declination

to the prime meridian of earth, i.e., to Greenwich, that apparent motion being a function of the earth's diurnal rotation.

As the prime meridian in the celestial sphere we take the first point of Aries (symbolized ♈) so named for its location in the constellation of the same name. What is more important, this is the point at which the *ecliptic*, the sun's apparent path against the fixed background of stars, passes from the southern hemisphere across the equator into the northern hemisphere. This point, also known as the vernal equinox, marks the first day of northern spring. Keep in mind that this is a fixed point of reference in the celestial sphere. Always on the first day of spring the sun will be at this point. And all positions of stars can be located with respect to this point of reference.

The meridian passing through the first point of Aries is thereby taken as the prime celestial meridian. The fixed longitude, as it were, of any given star is the angle measured at the center of the celestial sphere (i.e., the earth) between the first point of Aries and the meridian through the star. Unlike longitude on the earth, this angle is always measured west through 360°. This angle is known as the *sidereal hour angle* (SHA) of the body.

To relate our celestial longitude to terrestrial longitude we now establish the angular (time) relationship between the Greenwich meridian on earth and the meridian or *hour circle* through Aries. This angle is known as the *Greenwich hour angle* of Aries (GHA♈), and it is always measured westerly from Greenwich. If we can determine the GHA♈ for any given instant of time, as indeed we can by consulting the *Nautical Almanac,* then we can determine the GHA of the given star by the fundamental equation:

GHA☆ = GHA♈ + SHA☆ (Formula 2.1)

The SHA of a star and its declination are relatively fixed quantities that change very little over the year (due to the great distances of the stars from the earth). Therefore, for any instant of time, the quantities SHA and declination for a given star and the GHA of Aries enable us to locate the star with respect not only to its celestial coordinates, but to its substellar coordinates on earth as well.

For the sun, moon, and planets the situations are specific to the body, not general as in the case of the stars. That is to say, each of these bodies has its own unique motion against the background of fixed stars. As we shall see, the *Nautical Almanac* provides information as to the GHA's of the sun, moon, navigational planets, and Aries. This information, coupled with that of declination, enables us to determine the positions of any of these bodies *at any given instant of time.*

In review, then, the GHA and the declination of a celestial body locate the body in the celestial sphere and also locate its substellar position on the earth's surface, the substellar position (known also as the *geographical position,* or GP) being the point on the earth's surface directly beneath the star. For the sun, moon, and planets, GHA and declination are provided individually in the *Nautical Almanac* (see Chapter 3). For stars, on the other hand, GHA is obtained via Formula 2.1.

Example: Find the latitude and longitude (i.e., the declination and GHA) of the sun, moon, Jupiter, and Arcturus at 1200 GMT on May 16, 1982. (Data are from the appropriate pages of the *Nautical Almanac,* Figure 3.7 of this text.)

Body	GHA	Dec.
Sun	0°55.5′	19°05.2′ N
Moon	81°52.6′	15°20.3′ S
Jupiter	202°37.8′	11°10.3′ S
Arcturus	200°09.5′	19°16.5′ S
GHA♈	53°52.4′	
SHA Arcturus	146°17.1′	
GHA Arcturus	200°09.5′	

Time Diagram

The concept of the hour angle and its role in celestial location is closely related to the treatment of time, Chapter 3. However, the basic relations can be demonstrated by a simple time diagram. In Figure 2.7 the circle represents the equinoctial, P is the north celestial pole, and G is the standard projection of Greenwich onto the celestial equator. The symbols ☉, ♈, and ☆ indicate the sun, Aries, and a given star, respectively. And all GHA's are measured westerly from the hour circle or meridian through Greenwich.

Diagrams such as these are known as *time diagrams* since all hour angles, even though expressed in terms of angles and arc, are a function of time. For example,

GHA$\odot$ shows the position of the sun with respect to the Greenwich meridian at a given instant of time. And so also for the hour angles of Aries and the star ☆. Such diagrams can be utilized to include the observer's position. Since the Greenwich meridian is the projected standard for all GHA's, then we can easily plot the observer's longitude east and west from G as well. In this way, we can make graphic comparisons of an observer's longitude to that of some celestial body. There is one difference between the GHA's we assign to celestial bodies and the longitudes we assign to the observer's position. GHA is always measured westerly through 360°, and longitude is measured east or west through 180°. Thus a longitude of 70°E would correspond to a GHA of 290°.

Mapping the Heavens

Star maps are both informative and useful. The highest degree of conformity is obtained by mapping the stars onto the surface of a transparent sphere as, in fact, manufacturers of star globes do. But such globes are both expensive and awkward to use. Therefore, we rely on the cartographer's usual projections—stereographic maps, mercators, gnomonic charts, and the like. The star chart the writer has found most useful is that reproduced in Figure 2.8.

This chart from the *Air Almanac* is constructed on a simple rectangular grid. Although it affords a rather distorted picture of stars in the polar region, its overall representation of star patterns is quite good.

Take note, however, of the unconventional feature of this chart. North is at the top as we would expect, but west is to the right and east to the left, counter to the usual orientation on a terrestrial chart.

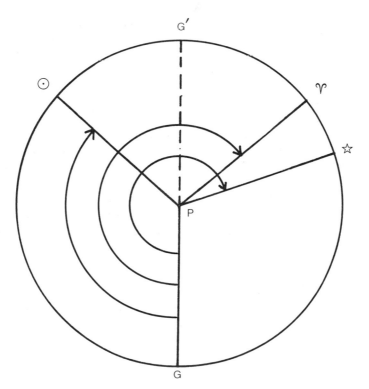

Figure 2.7 Time diagram

This is necessitated by the fact that the star chart maps what is overhead. However, if we hold this chart overhead with its top facing north, the westerly direction of the chart is properly oriented. Thus, we see that Capella is north and west of Pollux, Aldebaran is north and west of Betelgeuse, and so on. The apparent motion of stars is westerly, the stars rising in the east, setting in the west. Thus, from the chart we observe Regulus rising before Arcturus, and Procyon rising before Regulus, and so on.

The important navigation stars, those of first and second magnitude, are located according to declination and sidereal hour angle. The major constellations are shown in outline and include many stars of lesser magnitude. Since this is a chart of the entire celestial sphere, only roughly one half of the sky will be visible throughout a given night. In order to approximate the evening sky from a given location, the observer would determine the GHA of Aries and then by applying SHA (Formula 2.1) he would locate those stars which will cross his meridian throughout the evening hours. With experience, of course, one learns what constellations are in the summer and winter skies. In general, Orion dominates the northern skies in winter and Cygnus and Pegasus dominate the summer skies.

Note also the smooth sinusoidal line straddling the celestial equator. This, the ecliptic, maps the path of the sun's annual migration through the sky. This motion, however, is only apparent. It is due to the earth's annual revolution about the sun. Since the earth moves counterclockwise (i.e., easterly) in its orbit around the sun, the sun is seen to move easterly against the stellar background (*cf.* Note 2.4). Were we equipped observationally to see the sun against the stellar background, we would see it wander north and south of the equinoctial according to season. For example, as summer approaches in the north (actually early June) the sun is just north of the bright star Aldebaran. Later (about mid-July) it passes just to the south of Pollux. Still later (around August 20) it is nearly juxtaposed on Regulus. The vernal equinox is the point at which the sun passes from south declination to north declination. Seasonally this marks the beginning of spring, an event that takes place when the sun passes through the first point of Aries.

Position by Celestial Bearings

We have seen that there is a system of coordinates for locating objects in the celestial sphere that is conformal with our system of coordinates in the terrestrial sphere. For every star with a unique declination and GHA for a given time, there is a unique substellar point on the earth's surface with a corresponding latitude and longitude. Since the coordinates of both spherical surfaces are mappable, say, onto a Mercator chart, then we should be able to take bearings on celestial bodies and plot the reciprocals of such bearings to determine position in the same way we utilize terrestrial bearings to plot our position.

There are, however, two difficulties that prohibit such practice. One, the distances between observer and substellar point would be so great as to make chart work impracticable. (A star whose altitude is $50°$, for example, would have a substellar point 2,400 nautical miles from the observer.) And two, the accuracy required in taking a bearing would be beyond the observational means available to the nautical navigator (e.g., a $2°$ error in a bearing line 2,400 miles long would generate an error in position of 80 miles).

In principle, then, celestial bearings could be used to establish a terrestrial position. In practice they are not. This is not to say, however, that celestial bearings cannot be

Not only can the navigator steer by his star but his celestial bearings can be
ntly accurate to check true headings and compass error (*cf.* Note 2.5).

TIONS OF NONSTELLAR BODIES

The stars within our galaxy are in motion with respect to one another, but the intragalactic distances are so great as to make those motions negligible for the navigator.
This is not the case, however, with the sun, moon, and planets. All appear to have
unique diurnal motions. And all appear to have unique motions against the fixed stellar
background.

The Sun

The sun's apparent motion along the ecliptic is generated by two factors: one, the
earth's revolution about the sun, and two, the $23\frac{1}{2}°$ inclination of the earth's axis to the
orbital plane of its revolution. The inclination of the earth's polar axis is further
complicated by the precession of its axis of rotation. Under the influence of gravitation
rotating bodies tend to wobble about their axes rather than remaining upright. Were it
not for inclination and precession, the earth's geographic equator would coincide with
the plane of the ecliptic, the sun would not journey north and south of the equator, and
there would be no pronounced seasons.

The inclination of the earth's axis coupled with its annual revolution about the sun
account for the cyclical pattern of the seasons. It is the declination of the sun that tells
the story. The two solstices, summer and winter, as seen from the north occur when the
sun reaches its most southerly and northerly excursions (i.e., $23\frac{1}{2}°$ south and $23\frac{1}{2}°$
north declination). The two equinoxes, fall and spring, occur when the sun descends
and ascends across the equinoctial (i.e., when declination is zero) (*cf.* Note 2.4).

The Moon

The moon itself orbits about the orbiting earth. Its orbital plane is inclined about 5° to
the plane of the ecliptic. But since its orbital period, full moon to full moon, is a fraction
over 29 days we expect a full excursion, north to south declination, during that lunar
month.

The apparent excursion of the moon against the stellar background is a complex
affair. It is not a simple case of imposing the moon's orbit upon the ecliptic path. Rather
it is a matter of calculating how the lunar orbit crosses the ecliptic, that is to say, how the
moon's orbital excursion phases in with the earth's revolutionary orbit. As a result of the
complicated phasing, the north-south excursions of the moon's declination range from
$\pm 18.5°$ to $\pm 28.5°$ over a period of 18 years (*cf.* Note 2.4). The result of this is that the
range of north-to-south deviation in the moon's own monthly excursion varies from
month to month. One curious effect is notable. The visible moon tends to ride higher in
the northern winter sky than it does in the summer sky, lending moon glow comfort to
those tramping in the snows.

The Planets

There are four navigational planets, one orbitally inferior to the earth, Venus, and
three superior, Mars, Saturn, and Jupiter. Nearly all have orbital planes within 8° of the
ecliptic. Here, as with the moon, GHA of the body varies diurnally, but deviation varies
as a function of orbital position as viewed from the earth. But due to the size and period

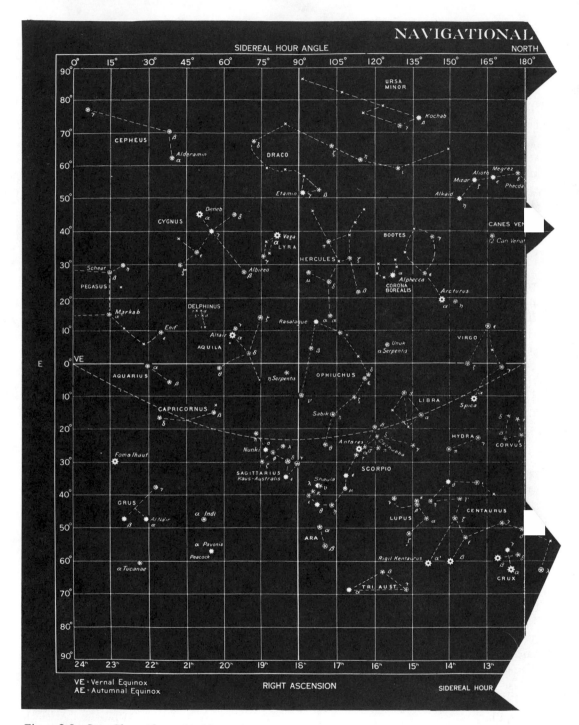

Figure 2.8   Star Chart (from *Air Almanac*)

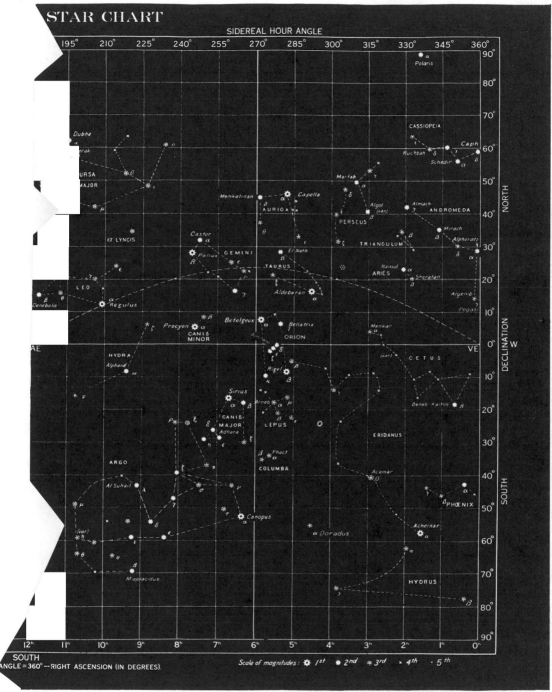

The American Nautical Almanac—The American Air Almanac

of orbital revolution, annual change or variation in declination is much greater for nearby Venus and Mars than it is for the more distant Saturn and Jupiter. The *Nautical Almanac* provides us the essential information for determining the GHA and declination for all navigational bodies. Before describing the *Almanac* and the nature of the entries we need to undertake a more detailed description of time. This we turn to in the next chapter.

NOTES

Note 2.1
Projective geometry involves taking objects mapped on one surface and projecting them onto a different surface while maintaining invariant relations. In terrestrial mapping the problem is to project the spherical world onto a flat surface in an unambiguous manner.

Ideally, of course, we could construct a spherical map upon the surface of a globe, but a globe is expensive, awkward to use, and would have to be cumbersomely large to be of use to the navigator. Obviously, projecting a spherical surface onto a flat surface or chart is going to involve distortion. Nevertheless, we can list certain properties we would like a chart to have:

1. Simplicity of use, most of all; ease of plotting course and distance with straightedge, dividers, and protractor.
2. Conformality, or the property of being orthomorphic (i.e., incorporating invariant angular relationships).
3. Constancy in areas and distance relationships.
4. Geodesics (shortest distance lines) as straight lines.
5. Rhumb lines, that is, lines of constant course, as straight lines.

No conventional chart possesses all of these properties. In fact for any given chart these properties may prove incompatible. Such is the case with properties 4 and 5.

Although there are many conceivable projections, there are only three that tend to dominate the construction of navigational charts. These are projections onto a cylinder (the Mercator), onto a cone (polyconic), and onto a plane (gnomonic).

Mercator Projection: By far the most popular of all cartographic projections in nautical navigation, Mercator projections are utilized almost exclusively for our coastal and harbor charts and for the large- and small-scale plotting sheets used in oceanic passages. Figure 2.9 shows the simple schema of the cylindrical projection. The Mercator projection is similar except that it is modified mathematically so as to reduce distortion in the higher latitudes and retain, through all latitudes, the property that a line between any two points is a rhumb line.*

For the cylindrical projection, a cylinder with a diameter equal to that of the earth is placed tangent to the earth at its equator. All points on the spherical surface are then projected linearly to the surface of the cylinder from a pinpoint source of light at the earth's center. As a result, the convergent great circles constituting the meridians of longitude on the earth's spherical surface are projected as parallel vertical lines on the cylinder. Also, all small-circle parallels of latitude are projected as parallel horizontal lines. For the Mercator, conformality is maintained throughout the projection, and all course lines are straight rhumb lines cutting all meridians at a constant angle. However, two distortions should be noted: one, the latitudinal (hence distance) scale expands the farther we move from the equator; and two, the great-circle course, the shortest distance on a sphere, will appear to be longer on the chart than the rhumb line course.

One can easily construct a Mercator chart from scratch. This is done by use of a table of meridional parts (to be found in *Bowditch*, along with a description of the procedure). In brief, a

---

*I am grateful to Forrest Meiere for pointing out the need to distinguish between the Mercator and the simple cylindrical projection.

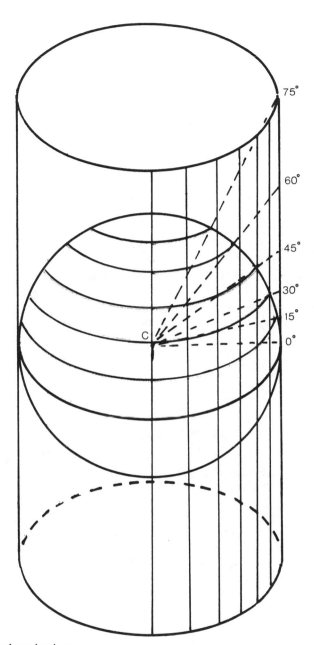

Figure 2.9 Cylindrical projection

table of meridional parts gives the number of proportional parts between the equator and any specified degree of latitude. First, we establish some standard distance for difference of longitude; and then we determine the expanding scale of latitude as a function of meridional parts. The overall effect is this: although longitudinal difference remains graphically constant over the range of latitude, the latitude scale itself is an expanding one. Since a minute of arc wherever taken on a meridian of the earth is one nautical mile, then the distance scale on the Mercator chart varies with latitude and must be picked off with a pair of dividers at the appropriate latitude.

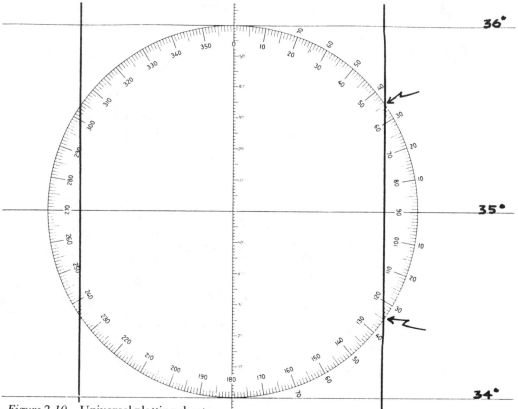

Figure 2.10   Universal plotting sheet

The most easily constructed Mercator charts, so-called, make use of universal plotting sheets. Figure 2.10 reproduces an example. Available in pad form, these are printed with equidistant parallels of latitude, a compass rose, and a fixed scale of distance. To construct meridians of longitude, one first selects the mid-latitude for the chart area desired and then pinpoints the angle of that latitude on the compass rose. There will be two such points, one above and one below the mid-latitude line. A line of longitude is then drawn to intercept the two points, thereby determining the scale for longitudinal difference for the other meridians. The procedure is a simple one and these plotting sheets are used routinely in celestial and dead reckoning work.

They are also useful for copying salient features of printed charts.

Lambert's Polyconic Charts: These charts are generally used in mapping land expanses for the air navigator. They are constructed by projecting details of the earth's surface onto a secant cone that intersects that surface at two standard parallels of latitude. See Figure 2.11.

These charts are highly conformal: great circles appear on them nearly as straight lines, making the charts ideal for the use of radio bearings; and area relationships and configurations are easily identified, making the charts ideal for air pilotage. Lambert charts covering coastal areas contain greater topographic and structural detail than nautical charts and include greater detail for radio bearings; in these respects they can be very useful to the small boat navigator.

Gnomonic Charts: These charts are constructed by projecting the earth's surface onto a plane tangent to the earth's sphere at an arbitrary point. They are used primarily in overall passage planning. Great-circle courses plot as straight lines. These course lines will intersect the convergent nonparallel meridians at different angles. Therefore, the navigator can determine a comprehensive set of course changes that will enable him to keep his vessel's track approximating a true great-circle course.

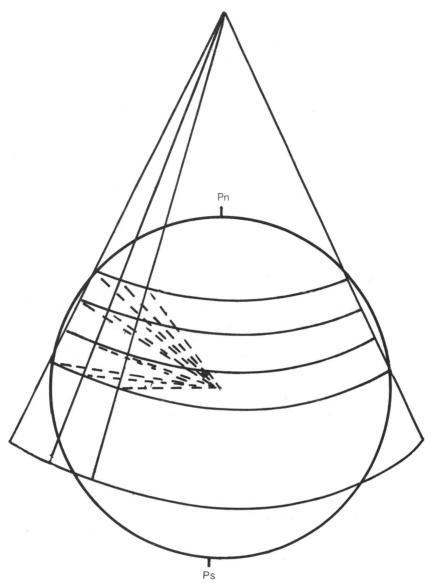

Figure 2.11 Conic projection

As we shall see in Chapter 9, there are easy computational procedures for determining a great-circle course by trigonometric means. Gnomonic planning charts are therefore not essential. Also, we must confess, great-circle sailing becomes rather an academic matter for the cruising sailor. Hampered by limited crew, fickle and sometimes fearsome winds, and recalcitrant self-steering devices, the navigator must be content, as often as not, to track his vessel's wanderlust rather than compel its adherence to a preplanned course.

Note 2.2
The concept of a straight line is intuitively obvious when we consider conventional Euclidean two-dimensional space. On a spherical surface, however, it is less obvious. A geodesic is a shortest-distance line as defined within spatial constraints. For a spherical surface this line is

generated by passing a plane through the center of the sphere so as to intersect the departure and destination points on the sphere's surface. Such geodesics are known as great circles and play an important part in navigational practice.

As an aside, there are many other possible spaces, other geometrics, wherein spatial constraints (e.g., tunneling is disallowed, as in nautical navigation for surface vessels) determine the nature of the geodesic. In the history of non-Euclidean geometry two such spaces were of special interest. In one, which we owe to the Russian mathematician Lobachevsky and the Hungarian Bolyai, the surface of constraint is hyperbolic or saddle-shaped. From our Euclidean vantage, straight lines on such a saddle surface appear curved. In Euclidean geometry there is a well-known postulate which asserts that through a given point one and only one line can be drawn parallel to a given line. Furthermore, parallel lines do not intersect. In our Lobachevskian space we find a curious deviation. If we take a given straight line and a point external to that line, we can draw not one but an infinity of straight lines that will not intersect the given line.

In another space, a spherical one explored by the German mathematician Riemann, one finds a contrary result. With a spherical restraint on drawing straight lines, it is not possible to draw any two straight lines such that they will not intersect.

Note 2.3

Why Greenwich? Mapping the world by a rectangular grid goes back at least as far as Democritus (460 B.C.). Since time was conceived as relative to the meridian passage of various celestial bodies it was necessary to specify "datum lines" or reference meridians. From Greek antiquity to the Renaissance, the prime meridian was defined as that passing through the Fortunate Isles (the Canaries). When Europe later turned to sea adventure and map-making, cartographers became provincial, often making their respective capitals the base for the prime meridian (e.g., London, Paris, Amsterdam). At one time an attempt was made to make Washington, D.C., a prime meridian candidate. By international agreement in 1884, the Greenwich observatory was established as the reference point for the prime meridian. This was done out of deference to the great observational work accomplished there that led to the publication of the *Nautical Almanac* in 1767.

Note 2.4

The most difficult feature of descriptive astronomy is the matter of relative or apparent motion. Were it not for the fact that the sun, moon, and planets introduce nonuniform motion into the heavens, it would have been difficult for man to have transcended the idea of a fixed earth surrounded by a rotating celestial sphere.

As it was, systemic thinking in astronomy moved from the geocentric system of Ptolemy (the fixed earth surrounded by concentric orbits of nonstellar objects, all within an outer rotating celestial sphere) to the heliocentric system of Copernicus. It is no doubt surprising to would-be scientific realists to learn that even in Copernicus' time, hypotheses to account for irregular motions (such as the apparent retrogression of Mars) were introduced as computational devices rather than as descriptions of what the universe was really like. In the philosophy of science such a pragmatic approach to scientific thinking is called "instrumentalism."

The Copernican revolution was brought to maturity largely through the works of Kepler and Newton, Kepler giving us the laws of orbital motion, and Newton deducing these from his own laws of motion and universal gravitation. Although Einstein's theories of special and general relativity have introduced major systemic changes into astrophysics, the earthbound navigator gets by quite well on the classical Newtonian model of the universe.

Consider now some conspicuous apparent motions as being generated from the earth's rotational and orbital motions. The earth revolves in an eliptical orbit about the sun which is fixed at one of the two foci of the ellipse, as in Figure 2.12. The earth's axis of rotation is inclined at $23\frac{1}{2}°$ to the ecliptic plane. The broken line on the earth's surface indicates the cut of the ecliptic plane, the solid line the equator. If we start with the earth in the April position (northern spring) we observe that the sun is directly over the intersection of the ecliptic line and the equator.

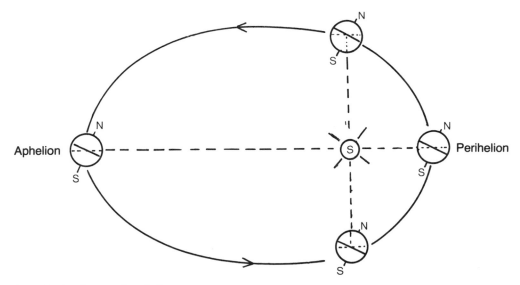

Aphelion   Perihelion

Figure 2.12   Seasonal variations

Where the sun's position is projected onto the celestial sphere this intersection represents the vernal equinox (♈), the intersection of the ecliptic and the equinoctial. As the earth revolves to the summer position the sun is directly over the Tropic of Cancer (latitude 23½°N). In its autumnal position it is again over the intersection of the equator and the ecliptic line, the corresponding autumnal equinox on the celestial sphere. And at perihelion we have the sun over the Tropic of Capricorn (latitude 23½°S) marking the northern winter. It is obvious here that the sun's rays are most direct in summer, and most oblique in winter. The outer perimeter presents segments of the celestial sphere. Viewed from the earth the sun is projected to the ecliptic, the path cut by projecting the earth's orbital plane to the celestial sphere. Therefore, as the earth revolves in its orbit west to east, the sun is seen as moving west to east against the stellar background. For example, in late August the sun's position is seen as being very near the bright star Regulus; in mid-October it has moved to a position near Spica.

Retrograde Motion: One of the most difficult problems for the astronomers of antiquity was to account for the retrograde motion of Mars. We observe Mars wandering across the skies within the ecliptic zone, or zodiac, and moving in an easterly direction against the stellar background. Suddenly Mars reverses itself, moves westerly for a spell and then resumes its easterly ways. Geocentric astronomers in the tradition of Ptolemy accounted for this by giving Mars epicyclical as well as orbital motion (i.e., orbital motion around a point itself in orbit). However, the apparent retrograde motion of Mars and that of all the other superior planets can be easily accounted for by the heliocentric model as refined by Johannes Kepler. In Figure 2.13 the earth's orbit is inferior with respect to that of Mars. Also the earth's orbital velocity is greater than that of Mars. Thus Mars' motion coupled with that of the earth conjointly generate the retrograde motion of Mars as seen by the observer on earth.

Morning and Evening Stars: Whereas planets having orbits superior to that of the earth are subject to retrograde motion, those with inferior orbits, Venus and Mercury, are subject to an oscillation that results in their appearing as morning stars for a spell, then as evening stars. Mercury's orbit is so near to the sun that it limits the availability of that planet as a navigational body. With Venus the situation is different. Next to the sun and moon, Venus is the brightest object in the sky. And through much of the year it is seen either just before sunrise or just after sunset.

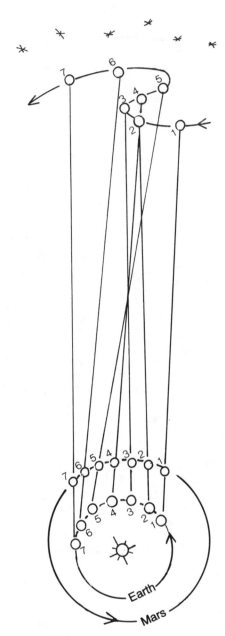

Figure 2.13   Retrograde motion of Mars

As in all planetary motion, that of Venus is generated by the orbital differences between the earth and the observed planet. In Figure 2.14 the period of revolution (sidereal period) for Venus is 225 days, that for earth is 365.25 days. However, as seen from the earth and with the sun as reference, the period for two successive conjunctions with the sun, the so-called *synodic* period, is 584 days. At point A, Figure 2.14, Venus and the sun are aligned (first conjunction); 584 days later they will again be seen aligned (second conjunction) after Venus has undergone 2.59 revolutions by sidereal reckoning and the earth, 1.59 revolutions.

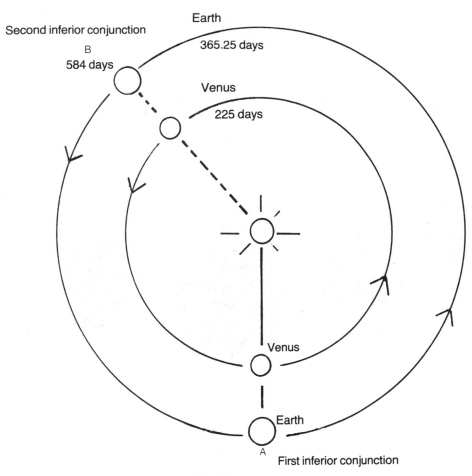

Figure 2.14 Synodic period: Venus and Earth

At one time during the synodic period Venus will be at superior conjunction (i.e., in line with the sun, the sun interposed), and at one time at inferior conjunction. Since the mean radii of the orbits of Venus and earth are 67 and 97 million miles, respectively, differences separating the two planets vary considerably between inferior and superior conjunctions (160 million miles to 26 million miles). Therefore, as seen from the earth, Venus varies considerably in apparent size and will show conspicuous phases as in the case of the moon.

Aside from the moon, Venus appears to be the brightest object in the night sky. As it emerges from superior conjunction (Figure 2.15), it is seen in its full nonoccluded phase. It is also seen emerging as an evening star. Because of the distance factor, however, Venus will appear brightest about 36 days before and after inferior conjunction. Observed through binoculars, Venus will appear crescent shaped and will be about 2½ times as bright as it appears in its full phase.

The synodic period, that 584-day period that it takes Venus to complete an orbit as seen from the earth, can be broken into three parts. As Venus emerges it takes 220 days to reach east elongation, that point at which Venus reaches its most easterly appearing distance. All through this time Venus is seen as moving away (easterly from the sun). At elongation it changes course and turns westerly toward the sun. During inferior conjunction, Venus is not seen for approximately 20 days. Where it emerges from inferior conjunction it will be seen as the morning star.

Galileo, the first great scientist to put the telescope to scientific use, discovered Venus' phases, as well as Jupiter's moons, and did much to establish modern planetary mechanics. The Greeks, it

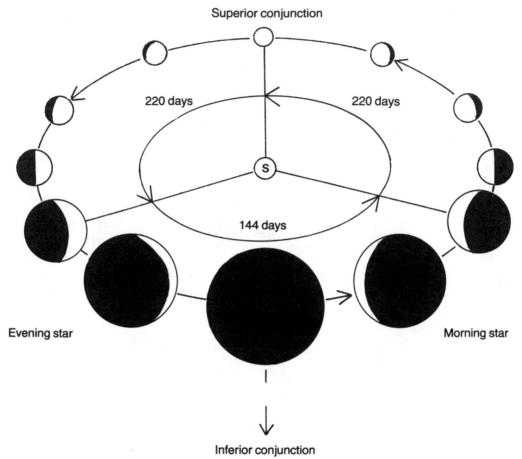

Figure 2.15   Phases of Venus from Earth

is reported, were slow in recognizing that the morning and evening appearances of Venus could both be of the same star. Alas, the writer knows of a sailor who bought a boat with the understanding that he could not retain its name, *Evening Star.* However, when he proposed to change the name to *Morning Star,* that was quite all right with the seller.

The Moon: The moon orbits the earth in a plane inclined at 5° to the ecliptic. Its sidereal period, as measured on successive conjunctions with a given star as seen from the earth, is about $27\frac{1}{3}$ days. However, the synodic period between successive conjunctions of sun-moon-earth is approximately $29\frac{1}{2}$ days. This is the observational period from full moon to full moon. During this period the moon passes through its familiar phases while undertaking its full excursion from north to south deviation. However, the pattern is not a rigidly repetitious one, lunar month to lunar month. The intersection of the moon's orbit and the ecliptic plane form nodal points which themselves regress in a westerly direction. These nodal points follow the ecliptic as in Figure 2.16.

When the ascending node is at the vernal equinox then the moon's orbit reaches points $28\frac{1}{2}°$ above and below the celestial equator $(23\frac{1}{2} + 5)$. However, when the ascending node is at the autumnal equinox the range is from $18\frac{1}{2}°$N to $18\frac{1}{2}°$S $(23\frac{1}{2} - 5)$. It takes 18 years to complete the regression of nodes; thus the extreme north-south excursions of the moon occur but once in the 18-year cycle.

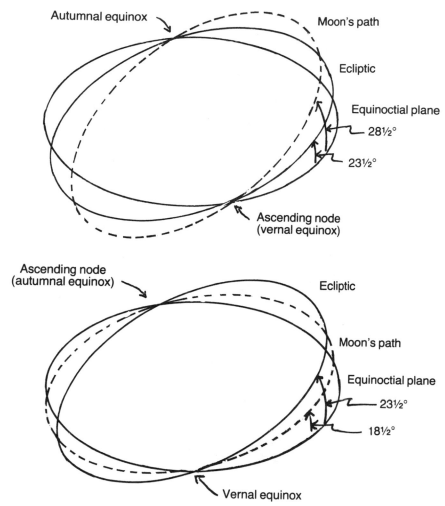

Figure 2.16　Moon's orbit and the ecliptic

Note 2.5

The use of celestial observations clearly antedates the practice of dead reckoning. Early navigators of the Mediterranean and Polynesia relied primarily on stellar observations. In the Mediterranean the circumpolar stars were especially useful; they remained in view throughout the year. In Book V of the *Odyssey* Homer writes of how Calypso gave sailing instructions to Ulysses, advising him to keep a watchful eye on Orion, Bootes, and the Pleiades which "setteth late," and to keep the Bear ever on the left.

　　In similar fashion early Polynesian explorers and navigators made use of the familiar patterns and motions of stars to keep course. A common tactic was to keep course on stars known through experience to be, at given times of the night, in the direction of one's destination. Distance was measured by crude estimates of altitude. Strangely, Polynesians were not known to have invented or utilized any instruments for measuring altitude.

　　The gnomon, or shadow stick, was borrowed from the Phoenicians. As forerunner of the sundial, it was used to tell time and keep one oriented with the diurnal passage of the sun. It also figured in early efforts to measure distance and latitude, and to estimate the size of the earth. Eratosthenes' (275–195 B.C.) early estimate of the earth's diameter was based on the comparison of sun shadows in different locales, and his estimate was within 50 miles of the earth's true polar diameter.

The date of the invention of the magnetic compass is unknown. By the thirteenth century compasses were utilized to supplement the navigator's reliance on the polar star. However, since it is likely that the Canary Islands and Iceland were discovered much earlier by Mediterranean and Nordic mariners, it is safe to conjecture that these early oceanic navigators relied on solar and stellar observations for determining latitude and course.

CHAPTER THREE

Time

The determination of one's latitude and longitude should be quite straightforward. All that is required are the proper observational tools. What are these tools? For latitude one needs an accurate instrument for measuring the altitude of a celestial body—a sextant or a transit. But for longitude one needs, in addition, an accurate timepiece. Instruments for measuring altitude date from antiquity, but reliable chronometers came relatively late in the history of navigation. Thus, determining latitude was never a serious problem for the early navigators, but finding longitude was a different matter. Knowledge of longitude depends on good clocks and a sophisticated treatment of time.

Time is all-important to the navigator. What is it? Or, more to the point, how do we measure it? According to the English philosopher, Herbert Spencer, time is a matter of "irreversible sequences" as measured by periodic phenomena.

The earth's daily rotation and yearly revolution about the sun are periodic phenomena of great consistency. So are the oscillations of a pendulum, or a tuning fork, or a resonating crystal, all of which have been utilized in the works of fine clocks.

Among celestial motions, the earth's rotation, the earth's revolution, and the moon's orbital revolution about the earth have all been utilized in the defining and keeping of time. The earth's rotation is the basis for defining the 24-hour day. Its revolution about the sun is the basis for defining the year. The moon's orbital pattern gives us the lunar month.

Even though all of the above are motions of remarkable regularity there are both long-term and transient effects that generate aberrations. For example, there are both a slight fluctuation and a slowing down of the earth's rotation. These very small irregularities can be detected by the finest of atomic clocks that are kept in bureaus of standards throughout the world. So far as navigation and nautical astronomy are concerned the main function of our overseers of time is to keep our clocks in tune with celestial phenomena.

For the earth's motions there can be different points of reference. To measure the rotation of the earth we need to go outside the earth for a point of reference. Thus, we can measure the earth's rotation against some object in the stellar background. And so, also, for the earth's period of revolution. In similar fashion we can measure rotation and revolution with the sun as the point of outside reference. With stars as reference we have sidereal time; with the sun as reference, solar time. Solar time is the base of all timekeeping in navigational work. However, sidereal time is of use to the astronomer in his observational work and is relevant to the navigator in his understanding and comparing differences in apparent motions between the fixed stars and other celestial objects—the sun, the moon, and the planets.

SIDEREAL TIME

We can think of all time as being measured by successive transits of celestial objects. Consider a standard meridian on the earth's surface, say, that passing through the observatory at Greenwich, England. In Figure 3.1a the star S is considered fixed and the earth with Greenwich meridian G rotates in an easterly direction. Therefore, the star will appear to move in a westerly direction. A transit of the star S occurs at G the moment the star appears to cross the meridian at G.

A sidereal day is then defined as the period between successive transits of a reference star S. More specifically we regard the stars as fixed in the celestial canopy and and the standard point of stellar reference is taken as the first point of Aries (Υ), that point at which the ecliptic crosses the celestial equator. Another way of visualizing this (Figure 3.1b) is to consider the hour circle locating the first point of Aries as sweeping through the equinoctial plane. Then one rotation of the hour circle of Aries as seen from the observer's fixed position determines the sidereal day. As we shall see, a sidereal day is a few seconds shorter than a solar day.

A sidereal year is the time it takes the earth to complete an orbit of the sun with a fixed stellar object being the point of outside reference. With regard to apparent motion it is the interval of time it takes the sun to complete its seasonal revolution with reference to a fixed stellar point such as the vernal equinox (the first point of Aries). This period is equal to 365.25 mean solar days, that is to say, the sidereal year is measured in standard solar time.

SOLAR TIME

A solar day is the period between successive transits of the sun as observed from a fixed meridian on earth. Again, we may utilize Figure 3.1 to visualize how the measure of transit is taken, with S designating the sun.

Keep in mind that all motions, stars' or sun's, are apparent. In the case of the stars, the apparent motion between transits is due to the earth's rotation. But in the case of the

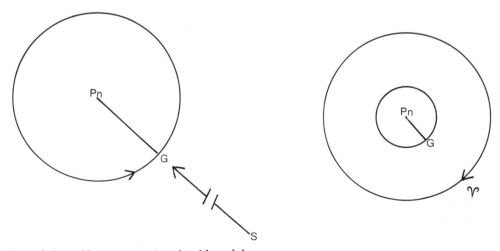

Figure 3.1a and b   Determining the sidereal day

sun there is an additional factor, namely, that due to orbital motion of the earth along the trajectory of revolution. As the earth progresses from one day to the next in its orbital revolution it must rotate through slightly more than 360° for an observer to detect successive transits of the sun.

In Figure 3.2, D approximates the distance the earth moves in its orbit between successive transits of the sun, and Δx is the increment of additional rotation that is required for the observation of successive transits of the sun. The result of this is that the solar day will be somewhat longer than a sidereal day. Compared to the conventional solar day, a sidereal day is 23h 56m 4s, i.e., approximately 4 minutes shorter than the 24-hour solar day. This is reflected in the fact that against the stellar background the sun appears to move in an easterly direction at approximately one degree per day.

Our solar year, sometimes called the *tropical* year, is the time in solar days that it takes for the earth to complete one orbit of the sun. On first impression the sidereal and solar years would appear to be identical, but that is not the case. For the solar year, we consider the apparent motion of the sun along the ecliptic. A solar year would then be the period between successive intersections of the vernal equinox. However, due to the precession of the earth's axis the vernal equinox appears to move westerly against the stellar background. The motion is slow, but the difference between the two years is significant. The sidereal year is 365.256 days, the solar year is 365.242 days. It is the latter upon which calendar time is based and which serves as the base for making our periodic leap year adjustments.

Solar Mean Time

We mark the solar day by successive transits of the sun as seen from the earth. We have seen also, in Figure 3.2, that the orbiting earth must rotate through more than 360° to achieve successive transits of the sun. Now, if the orbit of the earth were circular and orbital velocity constant, the amount of rotation to complete the solar day would be

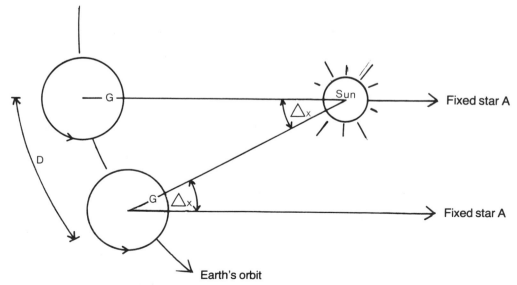

Figure 3.2   Difference between solar and sidereal day

constant throughout the year. That, however, is not the case. The earth's orbit is elliptical (see Figure 2.12) and since, according to one of Kepler's laws, the earth sweeps out equal areas in the orbital plane in equal times, the earth moves more rapidly when it is closest to the sun (perihelion) than it does when it is farthest away (aphelion). The effect of this is that successive solar transits take comparatively more time at perihelion than they do at aphelion. Observe again in Figure 3.2 that the earth rotates by an amount Δx in excess of 360° on successive transits. As the distance D between these transits increases so does Δx.

To compensate for these irregularities, our timekeepers have invented a fictitious sun, the so-called *mean sun,* that follows a code of strict conformity. It is an imaginary or ideal sun traveling at a uniform rate. Thus, there is the true sun which we actually observe and there is the fictitious *mean sun* for keeping time. The arc differences between the two can be expressed as a factor of time, namely, as the equation of time (*cf.* Note 3.1).

STANDARDS OF TIME

Let us now be more explicit about keeping time. By international agreement the meridian through the Greenwich observatory in England is taken as the prime meridian for measuring longitude. It thereby becomes the standard meridian for measuring time. The relation between angular measure and time should be obvious. Noon to noon, the sun sweeps around the earth in 24 hours. Thus, there would be 15° of angular sweep for every 60 minutes of time.

To facilitate our understanding of time let us resort to the traditional time diagram. In Figure 3.3, the center of the circle, Pn, represents the north celestial pole. All radii represent the meridians of the celestial sphere and since angle and arc are interchangeable the circumference of the circle designates arc along the celestial equator. Note, however, our angle-arc schema does not provide for locating latitudes.

In our diagram, then, Pn designates the north celestial pole at which all angular measure is made; GG', the prime meridian through Greenwich, is the fixed reference meridian, and ⊙ designates the mean sun. Since the earth rotates from west to east, the sun and its meridian are visualized as moving in a westerly or clockwise direction. The solid segment PnG represents the upper branch of the Greenwich meridian (i.e., it is that segment of the meridian between the two poles which intersects Greenwich itself). PnG' represents the lower branch of Greenwich, also known as the international date line.

In Figure 3.3., the mean sun ⊙ is shown approaching Greenwich in a westerly direction. At the moment the mean sun coincides with the upper branch of Greenwich it will be noon Greenwich time. The mean sun then continues to move in a westerly direction until it intersects G', the international date line. At that instant it will be midnight at Greenwich, and the starting of the new day.

In general, then, the sun, or rather the upper branch of its hour circle, rotates through Greenwich every 24 hours so that, for the 360°, each hour represents 15° of rotation. Greenwich mean time, therefore, is always a matter of the location of the mean sun with respect to the Greenwich meridian, arc and time being interchangeable.

Greenwich Mean Time
GMT is solar mean time as measured at the Greenwich meridian. This is the standard time that is the basis for the navigator's observations and computations. It is the time for

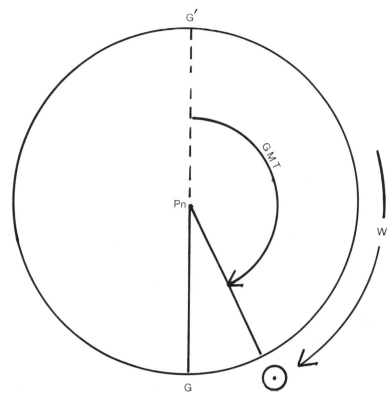

Figure 3.3   HA of sun for GMT

all entries in the *Nautical Almanac*. And it is the time that the navigator keeps on his chronometer (*cf.* Note 3.2). Specifically, GMT is determined by the angle (hour angle) between the lower branch of Greenwich and the hour circle or meridian through the mean sun, that angle converted to time on the basis of 15° of angular rotation for every 60 minutes.

Local Time and Hour Angle
Although GMT is the basic time for celestial navigation there are occasions when the navigator needs to work with local time. Indeed, the ship's clock is continually adjusted to local, or zone, time during a passage.

For local time we need to build on the concept of hour angle. Traditionally an *hour angle* is the angular difference between any two celestial meridians. Such angles are convertible to arc on the celestial equator. Since 15° equals one hour of time, then any so-called hour angle is convertible precisely to time, and vice versa. For the navigator, hour angles generally involve the observer's meridian and the meridian or hour circle of some celestial body. *Local hour angle* (LHA) of a celestial body is the hour angle measured in a *westerly* direction up to 360°. However, it is often convenient to measure hour angle east or west from the observer's meridian up to 180°. In such cases the hour angle is known as *meridian angle* (t). In general, throughout the text hour angle is used interchangeably with meridian angle, t, whereas LHA is always measured westerly through 360°.

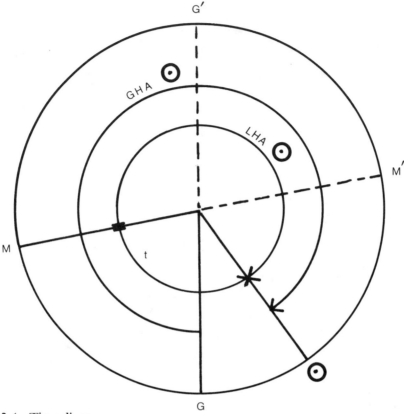

Figure 3.4   Time diagram

In Figure 3.4 we add an observer's meridian MM′ to the diagram presented in Figure 3.3. The hour angle from M to ☉ is the meridian angle between the observer and the mean sun. The LHA of ☉, on the other hand, is measured in a westerly direction from M and, in this case, is greater than 180°. Greenwich hour angle (i.e., GHA☉), it will be recalled from Chapter 2, is measured always in a westerly direction.

Both longitude and GHA are measured from the upper branch of the Greenwich meridian. Greenwich time, on the other hand, is measured from the international date line or lower branch of Greenwich (G′). GMT, then, is no more than the LHA☉ as measured from G′, that LHA being converted to time. (A table for converting arc to time is to be found in the *Nautical Almanac.*)

Local mean time (LMT) is equal to the LHA of the mean sun as measured from the lower branch of the observer's meridian (i.e., from M′), that arc converted to time. Thus, if the observer were located at Greenwich then LMT would be identical to GMT.

If the observer's longitude is known then it is a relatively simple matter to determine LMT. The simplest procedure is to convert the longitude of the observer to hour angle and apply the equivalent in time as a correction to GMT.

Suppose, for example, at 1430 GMT the observer is at 80°W longitude. An hour angle of 80° is equivalent to 5h 20m of time. All longitude west of Greenwich is locally earlier than Greenwich. Hence, LMT would be 0910. This can be verified by locating

M' and ☉ precisely at 1430 GMT and determining the LHA☉ (see Figure 3.5). Since at 1430 GMT, GHA☉ is, by conversion of time to arc, 37°30', then the LHA☉ from M' will be 137°30', which converts to 9h 10m. Suppose, on the other hand, the observer is at 80°E longitude. All east longitude is later than Greenwich. Therefore, the time equivalent of the hour angle of 80° would be added. Hence at 1430 GMT, LMT at 80°E would be 1950.

The relationship between GMT and LMT can be expressed as follows:

$$GMT = LMT \begin{array}{l} + \text{ W Longitude} \\ - \text{ E Longitude} \end{array}$$

or

$$LMT = GMT \begin{array}{l} - \text{ W Longitude} \\ + \text{ E Longitude} \end{array}$$

where the angle of longitude is converted to time.

Local apparent time (LAT) follows the argument for LMT except that LHA is measured from the lower branch of the observer's meridian M' to the true or apparent sun. The difference between local mean time and local apparent time is known as the *equation of time*. This is also the difference in arc between the true or apparent sun and

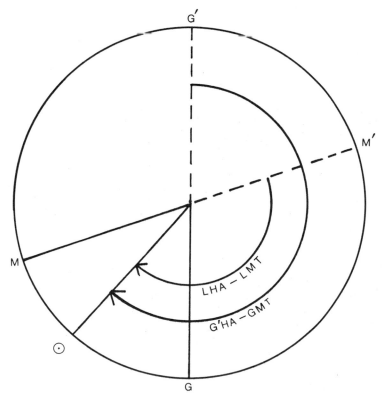

Figure 3.5 Time diagram: LMT

the mean sun, the arc converted to time (*cf.* Note 3.1). There are occasions when the navigator wishes to determine the time of meridian passage, in other words, the time at which, locally, the sun reaches its highest altitude. Noon LMT will give the time of meridian passage for the mean sun. To obtain the time of meridian passage of the true sun, i.e., noon LAT, we would apply the equation of time as a correction. The procedure for determining meridian passage is more fully discussed in Chapter 8.

Zone Time
Local time, whether by virtue of the mean or the apparent sun, is not a time we would carry on a watch or a chronometer. Our familiar local standard time is based on time zones with the Greenwich meridian taken as the center of the prime time zone. Since the mean sun revolves about the earth in 24 hours, the earth's day can be divided into 24 time zones, each having a longitudinal span of 15°. Since the Greenwich meridian is the standard, zonal time at Greenwich is simply Greenwich time. The boundaries of the zero time zone center on the 0° meridian and range from 7.5°E longitude to 7.5°W. For all subsequent time zones the midmeridian of the time zone will be a multiple of 15, and the corresponding limits will be the midmeridian of the time zone ±7.5° of longitude.

With Greenwich as the prime meridian we can infer zone time according to longitude. As an example, the longitude of Victoria, B. C., is 120°20'W; the nearest whole multiple of 15° is 120°, the meridian 8 hours slow on Greenwich. As the sun appears to move westerly from Greenwich it carries local noon with it, so to speak, so that in the time zone in which Victoria is located 120°±7.5° local standard time is 8 hours slow on Greenwich. Knowing this, we can always ascertain Greenwich mean time in Victoria by adding 8 hours to local standard time.

International Date Line
One of the more confusing aspects of time occurs at the international date line where, if we cross it going west, we advance the calendar (lose a day) or if we cross it going east we set back the calendar (gain a day). The international date line, 180°E or W longitude, is located within the time zone running from 172°30'W longitude to 172°30'E longitude. This is a time zone 12 hours different from that of Greenwich. On entering this time zone traveling westerly we are 12 hours slow on Greenwich in the region of 172°30'W to 180°W. Then suddenly as we cross the date line we are twelve hours fast on Greenwich. Since local time on our watch remains the same as we transit the time zone of the international date line, crossing the date line itself entails our advancing or retarding the date.

To explain more fully, let us visualize ourselves in a supersonic jet keeping apace of the mean sun. For simplicity's sake consider the sun at zero declination and the course of the jet westerly along the equator. (What will be its speed?) As we cross the Greenwich meridian, 0° longitude, the time is necessarily noon GMT. (Remember, we are traveling with the mean sun.) As we proceed around the world GMT will coincide with the GHA of our position (i.e., the GHA of the mean sun plus 180°, that arc being converted to time). As we enter the first time zone to the west of Greenwich (i.e., 7°30'W longitude) GMT will be 1230, but local zone time will be 1130 since this, the first zone to the west of Greenwich, is 1 hour slow on Greenwich. As we fly through the zone 1 hour of time will elapse and the difference between local zone time and GMT will always be 1 hour. As we enter the second time zone, the difference between the two will be 2 hours. And so on through the time zones. Now let us enter the twelfth time zone straddling the international date line and running from 172°30'W longitude to 172°30'E longitude. As our position (and the mean sun's) coincides with 172°30'W, GMT will be 2330 and local zone time will be 1130 indicating that local time is 12 hours slow on Greenwich. It will now take us 30 minutes to reach 180°E or W, the international date line. As we intersect that line, GMT is 2400. The old day at Greenwich has ended, the new day begins. Throughout our transit of this time zone, however, our watch carrying local time is 12 hours different from GMT. As we cross the date line west to east we move abruptly from 12 hours slow to 12 hours fast on Greenwich. And to achieve this sudden transposition of slow to fast we need to advance the current calendar 1 day. Were we to travel in the opposite direction, east to west, we would reverse the procedure, thereby setting back the date and gaining a day rather than losing it. It should be apparent from our solar jet ride that as we and the sun approach the international date line, the day is ending in Greenwich with the new day beginning just as we cross that line. Since we are locked into the sun in our jet ride we carry noon with us, so to speak. Thus, as we cross the international date line west to east, we go from noon of one day instantly to noon of the next day.

Navigator's Times

As a rule the navigator carries two times, standard or zone time for the convenience of ship's chores (maintaining watches, scheduling observations, etc.) and Greenwich time for the greater part of his celestial computations.

Zone time is not altogether helpful in determining times of meridian passage, but if the observer is aware of where he is in his time zone, he will know whether meridian passage of the sun will occur earlier or later than local noon.

A map of time zones does not rigidly adhere to the 15° interval. Local departures from the appropriate zonal boundaries are frequently introduced as a matter of geographic convenience. This is obvious from an inspection of the time zone boundaries across the United States. The *Nautical Almanac* offers a table of time zone corrections for various localities throughout the world.

Time Diagrams

In many navigational problems it is helpful to utilize time diagrams to establish arc and time relationships between terrestrial locations (meridians) and those of celestial objects (hour circles). In Figures 3.3, 3.4, and 3.5, we let the center of the circle designate the northern pole, the circle itself represents the equatorial perimeter, and the radii, various meridians and hour circles. The broken segments represent the lower branches of such meridians. Again, since GHA and longitude are measured from the Greenwich meridian, both terrestrial and celestial positions can be plotted and compared on the basis of hour angle.

Figure 3.6 represents a time diagram depicting the arc angle relationships between an observer at 120°W longitude (M) and the positions of three planets, Mars, Jupiter, Saturn, and the star Arcturus on May 17, 1982, 2300 hours local zone time. (For necessary information the appropriate pages from the *Nautical Almanac* are reproduced in Figure 3.7.)

Let us first determine the GHA's for the three planets so that we may plot them along with our own longitudinal position. At 120°W, 2300 LZT, we are 8 hours slow on Greenwich, hence GMT for the time of observation is 0700, May 18 (i.e., with respect to

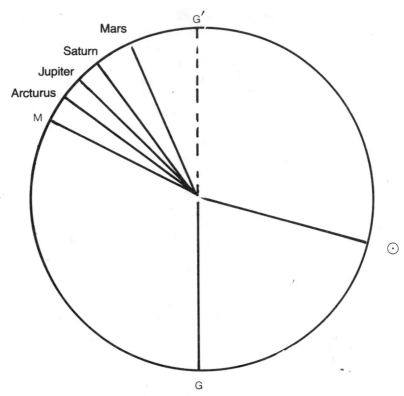

Figure 3.6   Time diagram: May 18, 1982, 0700 GMT

Greenwich the sun has already passed the international date line).

The three GHA's are:

Mars	159°37.3'
Jupiter	129°35.1'
Saturn	144°35.9'

These are given their appropriate plots along with our longitudinal position. The sun's GHA of 275°54.8' is also plotted to give the position with respect to the international date line. For the plot of Arcturus we utilize the formula:

$$GHA\star = GHA\Upsilon + SHA\star \qquad \text{(Formula 2.1)}$$

Since the GHAΥ is 340°38.3' and the SHA of Arcturus is 146°17.1', the GHA of Arcturus is 126°55.4'. Our time diagram, therefore, portrays this rather dramatic celestial display on this mid-May evening. The specimen pages from the *Almanac* also provide information on the positions of the moon and Venus. As an exercise, the reader can easily determine the relative positions of these bodies to ascertain whether they also were visible to the observer.

THE NAUTICAL ALMANAC

An almanac or ephemeris is essential to the navigator or an astronomer for all computational work. The mapping of the heavens and the recording of observations is as old as astronomy itself. The Babylonians studied the motions of the planets and the moon and were able to make predictions as to their future positions with considerable accuracy. It has been proposed that prehistoric Stonehenge (circa 1500 B.C.) was designed to window seasonal positions of celestial bodies. Later the astronomical theories of Ptolemy and Copernicus were generated by large quantities of observational data, and each theory in its way was able to predict planetary and solar motion with remarkable accuracy (*cf.* Note 3.3). One of the great observers of all time, Tycho Brahe (1546–1601) left such a comprehensive set of planetary observations that his one-time pupil, Johannes Kepler (1571–1630), was able to formulate the three classic laws of planetary motion.

By and large, our almanacs are compendia of data representing predictions of the positions of celestial bodies—the moon, sun, stars, and planets. The earliest almanac designed for the nautical navigator appears to have been the French *Connaissance des Temps*. Its publication began in 1679 and continues to this day. Our American *Nautical Almanac* derives from the British *Nautical Almanac* which was first published in 1767. Today the two are conjoined. The *Nautical Almanac* is jointly produced by the Royal Observatory of Great Britain and the U. S. Naval Observatory. A form of this almanac, amplified in special respects for the air navigator, is issued semiannually as the *Air Almanac*.

The main function of the *Almanac* is to provide information as to the location of the sun, moon, and selected planets and stars for any instant throughout the year.

In the sample pages represented in Figure 3.7 we find pertinent data for May 16, 17, 18, 1982, for the sun, the moon, the useful navigational planets, and Aries. The right-hand column, p. 100 in the figure, includes a list of nearly all the navigational stars with the SHA and declination of each.

The main entries are for hourly increments, GMT. To find the GHA for intervening minutes and seconds, we refer to a table of "Increments and Corrections." A page from this table is reproduced in Figure 3.8.

For the sun and planets the increments are the same. They are based on the assumption that GHA changes 15° per hour. However, each of the planets possesses its own unique orbital behavior. Thus, additional corrections for GHA and declination are sometimes required. Since the sidereal day is shorter than that of the sun, and the lunar day longer, separate columns are required for Aries and the moon.

Except for the v or d corrections the utilization of the data in the table of corrections is straightforward. We enter the appropriate odd minutes and seconds, find the increment of GHA, and add that to the GHA taken from the main tabular data. For example, what is the GHA of the sun, May 16, 1982, at 17h 46m 27s (i.e., 17 46 27) GMT?

$$1700 \text{ GMT, GHA} = 75°55.5'$$
$$\text{Increment } 46'27'', \quad 11°36.8'$$
$$17\ 46\ 27 \quad \text{GHA} = \quad 87°32.3'$$

Since declination changes relatively slowly we can easily interpolate for the odd minutes by visual inspection.

The Moon

Consider now a problem in determining GHA and declination (Dec.) of the moon. Under the entries for the moon, Figure 3.7, there are five columns of data, not only GHA and Dec. but also v, d, and HP. (HP designates horizontal parallax, and though

100   1982 MAY 16, 17, 18 (SUN., MON., TUES.)

G.M.T.	ARIES G.H.A.	VENUS −3.6 G.H.A.	Dec.	MARS −0.3 G.H.A.	Dec.	JUPITER −2.0 G.H.A.	Dec.	SATURN +0.7 G.H.A.	Dec.	Name	S.H.A.	Dec.
16 00	233 22.8	220 47.1 N 3 26.7		52 27.9 N 0 52.6		22 05.0 S11 11.3		37 13.9 S 3 56.7		Acamar	315 36.8	S40 22.6
01	248 25.3	235 46.9	27.7	67 30.3	52.5	37 07.8	11.3	52 16.5	56.6	Achernar	335 44.9	S57 19.6
02	263 27.7	250 46.8	28.8	82 32.7	52.3	52 10.5	11.2	67 19.1	56.6	Acrux	173 35.6	S63 00.2
03	278 30.2	265 46.6 ··	29.8	97 35.1 ··	52.2	67 13.2 ··	11.1	82 21.7 ··	56.5	Adhara	255 31.5	S28 57.0
04	293 32.7	280 46.4	30.8	112 37.4	52.0	82 16.0	11.0	97 24.2	56.5	Aldebaran	291 17.0	N16 28.3
05	308 35.1	295 46.2	31.9	127 39.8	51.9	97 18.7	10.9	112 26.8	56.5			
06	323 37.6	310 46.0 N 3 32.9		142 42.2 N 0 51.8		112 21.4 S11 10.8		127 29.4 S 3 56.4		Alioth	166 41.0	N56 03.6
07	338 40.0	325 45.8	33.9	157 44.6	51.6	127 24.2	10.7	142 32.0	56.4	Alkaid	153 17.1	N49 24.3
08	353 42.5	340 45.6	35.0	172 46.9	51.5	142 26.9	10.6	157 34.6	56.3	Al Na'ir	28 13.5	S47 02.7
S 09	8 45.0	355 45.4 ··	36.0	187 49.3 ··	51.3	157 29.6 ··	10.5	172 37.2 ··	56.3	Alnilam	276 10.8	S 1 12.9
U 10	23 47.4	10 45.2	37.0	202 51.7	51.2	172 32.3	10.5	187 39.8	56.3	Alphard	218 19.5	S 8 35.0
N 11	38 49.9	25 45.0	38.1	217 54.1	51.0	187 35.1	10.4	202 42.3	56.2			
D 12	53 52.4	40 44.9 N 3 39.1		232 56.4 N 0 50.9		202 37.8 S11 10.3		217 44.9 S 3 56.2		Alphecca	126 30.8	N26 46.5
A 13	68 54.8	55 44.7	40.1	247 58.8	50.7	217 40.5	10.2	232 47.5	56.1	Alpheratz	358 08.4	N28 59.3
Y 14	83 57.3	70 44.5	41.2	263 01.2	50.6	232 43.3	10.1	247 50.1	56.1	Altair	62 31.2	N 8 49.1
15	98 59.8	85 44.3 ··	42.2	278 03.5 ··	50.4	247 46.0 ··	10.0	262 52.7 ··	56.0	Ankaa	353 39.4	S42 24.1
16	114 02.2	100 44.1	43.2	293 05.9	50.3	262 48.7	09.9	277 55.3	56.0	Antares	112 55.1	S26 23.6
17	129 04.7	115 43.9	44.3	308 08.3	50.1	277 51.5	09.9	292 57.8	56.0			
18	144 07.2	130 43.7 N 3 45.3		323 10.6 N 0 50.0		292 54.2 S11 09.8		308 00.4 S 3 55.9		Arcturus	146 17.1	N19 16.5
19	159 09.6	145 43.5	46.3	338 13.0	49.8	307 56.9	09.7	323 03.0	55.9	Atria	108 17.8	S68 59.7
20	174 12.1	160 43.3	47.4	353 15.4	49.7	322 59.6	09.6	338 05.6	55.8	Avior	234 28.0	S59 27.4
21	189 14.5	175 43.1 ··	48.4	8 17.7 ··	49.5	338 02.4 ··	09.5	353 08.2 ··	55.8	Bellatrix	278 57.8	N 6 20.0
22	204 17.0	190 42.9	49.4	23 20.1	49.4	353 05.1	09.4	8 10.8	55.8	Betelgeuse	271 27.3	N 7 24.2
23	219 19.5	205 42.7	50.4	38 22.4	49.2	8 07.8	09.3	23 13.3	55.7			
17 00	234 21.9	220 42.6 N 3 51.5		53 24.8 N 0 49.0		23 10.6 S11 09.2		38 15.9 S 3 55.7		Canopus	264 07.1	S52 41.4
01	249 24.4	235 42.4	52.5	68 27.1	48.9	38 13.3	09.2	53 18.5	55.6	Capella	281 10.1	N45 58.9
02	264 26.9	250 42.2	53.5	83 29.5	48.7	53 16.0	09.1	68 21.1	55.6	Deneb	49 47.6	N45 12.7
03	279 29.3	265 42.0 ··	54.6	98 31.9 ··	48.6	68 18.7 ··	09.0	83 23.7 ··	55.6	Denebola	182 57.7	N14 40.4
04	294 31.8	280 41.8	55.6	113 34.2	48.4	83 21.5	08.9	98 26.3	55.5	Diphda	349 19.9	S18 05.1
05	309 34.3	295 41.6	56.6	128 36.6	48.3	98 24.2	08.8	113 28.8	55.5			
06	324 36.7	310 41.4 N 3 57.7		143 38.9 N 0 48.1		113 26.9 S11 08.7		128 31.4 S 3 55.4		Dubhe	194 20.5	N61 51.1
07	339 39.2	325 41.2	58.7	158 41.3	48.0	128 29.7	08.6	143 34.0	55.4	Elnath	278 43.0	N28 35.6
08	354 41.6	340 41.0	3 59.7	173 43.6	47.8	143 32.4	08.6	158 36.6	55.3	Eltanin	90 56.7	N51 29.3
M 09	9 44.1	355 40.8	4 00.8	188 46.0 ··	47.6	158 35.1 ··	08.5	173 39.2 ··	55.3	Enif	34 10.5	N 9 47.4
O 10	24 46.6	10 40.6	01.8	203 48.3	47.5	173 37.8	08.4	188 41.8	55.3	Fomalhaut	15 50.2	S29 43.0
N 11	39 49.0	25 40.4	02.8	218 50.6	47.3	188 40.6	08.3	203 44.3	55.2			
D 12	54 51.5	40 40.2 N 4 03.9		233 53.0 N 0 47.2		203 43.3 S11 08.2		218 46.9 S 3 55.2		Gacrux	172 27.1	S57 01.0
A 13	69 54.0	55 40.0	04.9	248 55.3	47.0	218 46.0	08.1	233 49.5	55.1	Gienah	176 16.6	S17 26.7
Y 14	84 56.4	70 39.8	05.9	263 57.7	46.8	233 48.7	08.0	248 52.1	55.1	Hadar	149 21.2	S60 17.4
15	99 58.9	85 39.6 ··	07.0	279 00.0 ··	46.7	248 51.5 ··	08.0	263 54.7 ··	55.1	Hamal	328 28.0	N23 22.5
16	115 01.4	100 39.4	08.0	294 02.3	46.5	263 54.2	07.9	278 57.2	55.0	Kaus Aust.	84 15.0	S34 23.6
17	130 03.8	115 39.2	09.0	309 04.7	46.4	278 56.9	07.8	293 59.8	55.0			
18	145 06.3	130 39.0 N 4 10.1		324 07.0 N 0 46.2		293 59.6 S11 07.7		309 02.4 S 3 54.9		Kochab	137 17.8	N74 13.8
19	160 08.8	145 38.8	11.1	339 09.4	46.0	309 02.4	07.6	324 05.0	54.9	Markab	14 02.1	N15 06.4
20	175 11.2	160 38.6	12.1	354 11.7	45.9	324 05.1	07.5	339 07.6	54.9	Menkar	314 40.3	N 4 01.1
21	190 13.7	175 38.4 ··	13.2	9 14.0 ··	45.7	339 07.8 ··	07.4	354 10.1 ··	54.8	Menkent	148 35.3	S36 17.1
22	205 16.1	190 38.2	14.2	24 16.3	45.5	354 10.5	07.4	9 12.7	54.8	Miaplacidus	221 44.9	S69 38.9
23	220 18.6	205 38.0	15.2	39 18.7	45.4	9 13.3	07.3	24 15.3	54.7			
18 00	235 21.1	220 37.8 N 4 16.3		54 21.0 N 0 45.2		24 16.0 S11 07.2		39 17.9 S 3 54.7		Mirfak	309 15.0	N49 47.8
01	250 23.5	235 37.6	17.3	69 23.3	45.1	39 18.7	07.1	54 20.5	54.7	Nunki	76 27.5	S26 19.1
02	265 26.0	250 37.4	18.3	84 25.7	44.9	54 21.4	07.0	69 23.0	54.6	Peacock	53 56.3	S56 47.4
03	280 28.5	265 37.2 ··	19.4	99 28.0 ··	44.7	69 24.2 ··	06.9	84 25.6 ··	54.6	Pollux	243 57.0	N28 04.3
04	295 30.9	280 37.0	20.4	114 30.3	44.6	84 26.9	06.9	99 28.2	54.6	Procyon	245 24.8	N 5 16.2
05	310 33.4	295 36.8	21.4	129 32.6	44.4	99 29.6	06.8	114 30.8	54.5			
06	325 35.9	310 36.6 N 4 22.5		144 35.0 N 0 44.2		114 32.3 S11 06.7		129 33.4 S 3 54.5		Rasalhague	96 28.2	N12 34.3
07	340 38.3	325 36.4	23.5	159 37.3	44.1	129 35.1	06.6	144 35.9	54.4	Regulus	208 08.8	N12 03.3
08	355 40.8	340 36.2	24.5	174 39.6	43.9	144 37.8	06.5	159 38.5	54.4	Rigel	281 35.2	S 8 13.4
T 09	10 43.3	355 36.0 ··	25.6	189 41.9 ··	43.7	159 40.5 ··	06.4	174 41.1 ··	54.4	Rigil Kent.	140 23.7	S60 45.7
U 10	25 45.7	10 35.8	26.6	204 44.2	43.5	174 43.2	06.3	189 43.7	54.3	Sabik	102 39.5	S15 42.2
E 11	40 48.2	25 35.6	27.6	219 46.6	43.4	189 45.9	06.3	204 46.3	54.3			
S 12	55 50.6	40 35.4 N 4 28.7		234 48.9 N 0 43.2		204 48.7 S11 06.2		219 48.8 S 3 54.2		Schedar	350 08.2	N56 26.1
D 13	70 53.1	55 35.2	29.7	249 51.2	43.0	219 51.4	06.1	234 51.4	54.2	Shaula	96 53.8	S37 05.4
A 14	85 55.6	70 35.0	30.7	264 53.5	42.9	234 54.1	06.0	249 54.0	54.2	Sirius	258 55.0	S16 41.7
Y 15	100 58.0	85 34.8 ··	31.8	279 55.8 ··	42.7	249 56.8 ··	05.9	264 56.6 ··	54.1	Spica	158-56.1	S11 04.2
16	116 00.5	100 34.6	32.8	294 58.1	42.5	264 59.6	05.8	279 59.2	54.1	Suhail	223 10.1	S43 21.9
17	131 03.0	115 34.4	33.8	310 00.4	42.3	280 02.3	05.8	295 01.7	54.0			
18	146 05.4	130 34.2 N 4 34.9		325 02.7 N 0 42.2		295 05.0 S11 05.7		310 04.3 S 3 54.0		Vega	80 54.7	N38 45.8
19	161 07.9	145 34.0	35.9	340 05.0	42.0	310 07.7	05.6	325 06.9	54.0	Zuben'ubi	137 31.5	S15 58.1
20	176 10.4	160 33.8	36.9	355 07.3	41.8	325 10.4	05.5	340 09.5	53.9			
21	191 12.8	175 33.6 ··	37.9	10 09.7 ··	41.7	340 13.2 ··	05.4	355 12.0 ··	53.9		S.H.A.	Mer. Pass.
22	206 15.3	190 33.4	39.0	25 12.0	41.5	355 15.9	05.3	10 14.6	53.9	Venus	346 20.6	9 17
23	221 17.7	205 33.2	40.0	40 14.3	41.3	10 18.6	05.3	25 17.2	53.8	Mars	179 02.9	20 23
										Jupiter	148 48.6	22 23
Mer. Pass. 8 21.2		v −0.2 d 1.0		v 2.3 d 0.2		v 2.7 d 0.1		v 2.6 d 0.0		Saturn	163 54.0	21 23

Figure 3.7   Specimen pages from *Nautical Almanac* (1982, pp. 100, 101)

1982 MAY 16, 17, 18 (SUN., MON., TUES.)

G.M.T.	SUN G.H.A.	Dec.	MOON G.H.A.	v	Dec.	d	H.P.
16 00	180 55.7	N18 58.3	267 36.4	12.3	S17 03.4	8.1	54.4
01	195 55.7	58.9	282 07.7	12.3	16 55.3	8.2	55.5
02	210 55.7	18 59.4	296 39.0	12.3	16 47.1	8.3	55.5
03	225 55.6	19 00.0	311 10.3	12.3	16 38.8	8.4	55.5
04	240 55.6	00.6	325 41.6	12.3	16 30.4	8.5	55.5
05	255 55.6	01.2	340 12.9	12.4	16 21.9	8.5	55.6
06	270 55.6	N19 01.8	354 44.3	12.3	S16 13.4	8.7	55.6
07	285 55.6	02.4	9 15.6	12.4	16 04.7	8.7	55.6
08	300 55.6	02.9	23 47.0	12.4	15 56.0	8.8	55.7
S 09	315 55.6	·· 03.5	38 18.4	12.4	15 47.2	8.9	55.7
U 10	330 55.6	04.1	52 49.8	12.4	15 38.3	8.9	55.7
N 11	345 55.6	04.7	67 21.2	12.4	15 29.4	9.1	55.7
D 12	0 55.5	N19 05.2	81 52.6	12.5	S15 20.3	9.1	55.8
A 13	15 55.5	05.8	96 24.1	12.4	15 11.2	9.3	55.8
Y 14	30 55.5	06.4	110 55.5	12.5	15 01.9	9.2	55.8
15	45 55.5	·· 07.0	125 27.0	12.4	14 52.7	9.4	55.9
16	60 55.5	07.6	139 58.4	12.5	14 43.3	9.5	55.9
17	75 55.5	08.1	154 29.9	12.5	14 33.8	9.5	55.9
18	90 55.5	N19 08.7	169 01.4	12.5	S14 24.3	9.6	56.0
19	105 55.5	09.3	183 32.9	12.5	14 14.7	9.7	56.0
20	120 55.4	09.9	198 04.4	12.5	14 05.0	9.8	56.0
21	135 55.4	·· 10.4	212 35.9	12.5	13 55.2	9.8	56.1
22	150 55.4	11.0	227 07.4	12.5	13 45.4	9.9	56.1
23	165 55.4	11.6	241 39.0	12.5	13 35.5	10.0	56.1
17 00	180 55.4	N19 12.1	256 10.5	12.5	S13 25.5	10.1	56.2
01	195 55.4	12.7	270 42.0	12.3	13 15.4	10.1	56.2
02	210 55.4	13.3	285 13.6	12.5	13 05.3	10.3	56.2
03	225 55.3	·· 13.8	299 45.1	12.6	12 55.0	10.3	56.3
04	240 55.3	14.4	314 16.7	12.6	12 44.7	10.3	56.3
05	255 55.3	15.0	328 48.3	12.5	12 34.4	10.4	56.3
06	270 55.3	N19 15.6	343 19.8	12.6	S12 24.0	10.6	56.4
07	285 55.3	16.1	357 51.4	12.6	12 13.4	10.5	56.4
08	300 55.3	16.7	12 23.0	12.5	12 02.9	10.7	56.4
M 09	315 55.2	·· 17.3	26 54.5	12.6	11 52.2	10.7	56.5
O 10	330 55.2	17.8	41 26.1	12.6	11 41.5	10.8	56.5
N 11	345 55.2	18.4	55 57.7	12.5	11 30.7	10.8	56.5
D 12	0 55.2	N19 18.9	70 29.2	12.6	S11 19.9	10.9	56.6
A 13	15 55.2	19.5	85 00.8	12.6	11 09.0	11.0	56.6
Y 14	30 55.2	20.1	99 32.4	12.6	10 58.0	11.1	56.6
15	45 55.1	·· 20.6	114 04.0	12.6	10 46.9	11.1	56.7
16	60 55.1	21.2	128 35.5	12.6	10 35.8	11.2	56.7
17	75 55.1	21.8	143 07.1	12.6	10 24.6	11.2	56.7
18	90 55.1	N19 22.3	157 38.7	12.5	S10 13.4	11.3	56.8
19	105 55.1	22.9	172 10.2	12.6	10 02.1	11.4	56.8
20	120 55.0	23.4	186 41.8	12.5	9 50.7	11.5	56.8
21	135 55.0	·· 24.0	201 13.3	12.6	9 39.2	11.5	56.9
22	150 55.0	24.6	215 44.9	12.5	9 27.7	11.5	56.9
23	165 55.0	25.1	230 16.4	12.5	9 16.2	11.6	57.0
18 00	180 55.0	N19 25.7	244 47.9	12.5	S 9 04.6	11.7	57.0
01	195 54.9	26.2	259 19.4	12.6	8 52.9	11.7	57.0
02	210 54.9	26.8	273 51.0	12.5	8 41.2	11.8	57.1
03	225 54.9	·· 27.3	288 22.5	12.4	8 29.4	11.9	57.1
04	240 54.9	27.9	302 53.9	12.5	8 17.5	11.9	57.1
05	255 54.9	28.5	317 25.4	12.5	8 05.6	12.0	57.2
06	270 54.8	N19 29.0	331 56.9	12.4	S 7 53.6	12.0	57.2
07	285 54.8	29.6	346 28.3	12.5	7 41.6	12.1	57.2
08	300 54.8	30.1	0 59.8	12.4	7 29.5	12.1	57.3
T 09	315 54.8	·· 30.7	15 31.2	12.4	7 17.4	12.2	57.3
U 10	330 54.7	31.2	30 02.6	12.4	7 05.2	12.2	57.4
E 11	345 54.7	31.8	44 34.0	12.4	6 53.0	12.3	57.4
S 12	0 54.7	N19 32.3	59 05.4	12.4	S 6 40.7	12.3	57.4
D 13	15 54.7	32.9	73 36.8	12.3	6 28.4	12.4	57.5
A 14	30 54.7	33.4	88 08.1	12.3	6 16.0	12.4	57.5
Y 15	45 54.6	·· 34.0	102 39.4	12.3	6 03.6	12.5	57.6
16	60 54.6	34.5	117 10.7	12.3	5 51.1	12.5	57.6
17	75 54.6	35.1	131 42.0	12.3	5 38.6	12.6	57.6
18	90 54.6	N19 35.6	146 13.3	12.2	S 5 26.0	12.6	57.7
19	105 54.5	36.2	160 44.5	12.2	5 13.4	12.6	57.7
20	120 54.5	36.7	175 15.7	12.2	5 00.8	12.7	57.7
21	135 54.5	·· 37.2	189 46.9	12.2	4 48.1	12.8	57.8
22	150 54.5	37.8	204 18.1	12.1	4 35.3	12.7	57.8
23	165 54.4	38.3	218 49.2	12.1	4 22.6	12.9	57.9
	S.D. 15.8	d 0.6	S.D. 15.2		15.4		15.7

Lat.	Twilight Naut.	Civil	Sunrise	Moonrise 16	17	18	19
N 72	□	□	□	04 42	04 01	03 37	03 18
N 70	□	□	□	03 58	03 39	03 25	03 13
68	////	////	01 38	03 28	03 21	03 15	03 09
66	////	////	02 16	03 06	03 06	03 06	03 06
64	////	00 55	02 42	02 48	02 54	02 59	03 03
62	////	01 44	03 02	02 33	02 44	02 53	03 00
60	////	02 14	03 19	02 21	02 35	02 47	02 58
N 58	00 50	02 36	03 32	02 10	02 28	02 43	02 56
56	01 34	02 54	03 44	02 01	02 21	02 38	02 54
54	02 01	03 08	03 55	01 52	02 15	02 34	02 53
52	02 22	03 21	04 04	01 45	02 09	02 31	02 51
50	02 39	03 32	04 12	01 38	02 04	02 28	02 50
45	03 11	03 55	04 29	01 23	01 53	02 21	02 47
N 40	03 34	04 13	04 43	01 12	01 44	02 15	02 45
35	03 53	04 27	04 55	01 01	01 37	02 10	02 43
30	04 08	04 39	05 06	00 52	01 30	02 06	02 41
20	04 32	05 00	05 23	00 37	01 18	01 58	02 38
N 10	04 50	05 16	05 39	00 23	01 07	01 51	02 35
0	05 05	05 31	05 53	00 10	00 58	01 45	02 32
S 10	05 19	05 45	06 07	24 48	00 48	01 38	02 29
20	05 32	05 58	06 22	24 37	00 37	01 31	02 27
30	05 44	06 13	06 39	24 25	00 25	01 24	02 23
35	05 51	06 21	06 49	24 18	00 18	01 19	02 22
40	05 58	06 31	07 00	24 10	00 10	01 14	02 20
45	06 05	06 41	07 13	24 01	00 01	01 08	02 17
S 50	06 13	06 53	07 29	23 49	25 01	01 01	02 14
52	06 17	06 58	07 36	23 44	24 57	00 57	02 13
54	06 21	07 04	07 45	23 38	24 54	00 54	02 11
56	06 25	07 11	07 54	23 32	24 50	00 50	02 10
58	06 29	07 18	08 05	23 25	24 45	00 45	02 08
S 60	06 34	07 27	08 17	23 16	24 40	00 40	02 06

Lat.	Sunset	Twilight Civil	Naut.	Moonset 16	17	18	19
N 72	□	□	□	08 18	10 37	12 40	14 42
N 70	□	□	□	09 01	10 58	12 51	14 43
68	22 20	////	////	09 29	11 15	12 59	14 44
66	21 40	////	////	09 51	11 28	13 06	14 45
64	21 13	23 06	////	10 08	11 39	13 11	14 46
62	20 52	22 12	////	10 22	11 48	13 16	14 47
60	20 36	21 41	////	10 33	11 56	13 20	14 48
N 58	20 22	21 19	23 11	10 43	12 02	13 24	14 48
56	20 10	21 01	22 22	10 52	12 08	13 27	14 49
54	19 59	20 46	21 54	11 00	12 14	13 30	14 49
52	19 50	20 33	21 32	11 07	12 19	13 33	14 50
50	19 42	20 22	21 15	11 13	12 23	13 35	14 50
45	19 24	19 59	20 43	11 27	12 33	13 41	14 51
N 40	19 10	19 41	20 19	11 38	12 40	13 45	14 52
35	18 58	19 26	20 00	11 47	12 47	13 49	14 52
30	18 47	19 14	19 45	11 55	12 53	13 52	14 53
20	18 30	18 53	19 21	12 09	13 03	13 58	14 54
N 10	18 14	18 37	19 03	12 22	13 12	14 03	14 54
0	18 00	18 22	18 47	12 33	13 20	14 07	14 55
S 10	17 46	18 08	18 34	12 44	13 28	14 12	14 56
20	17 31	17 54	18 21	12 56	13 37	14 17	14 56
30	17 14	17 39	18 08	13 10	13 47	14 22	14 57
35	17 04	17 31	18 02	13 18	13 52	14 25	14 58
40	16 53	17 22	17 55	13 27	13 59	14 28	14 58
45	16 39	17 11	17 47	13 37	14 06	14 33	14 59
S 50	16 23	16 59	17 39	13 50	14 15	14 38	14 59
52	16 16	16 54	17 35	13 56	14 19	14 39	14 59
54	16 07	16 48	17 31	14 02	14 23	14 42	15 00
56	15 58	16 41	17 27	14 09	14 28	14 44	15 00
58	15 48	16 34	17 23	14 17	14 33	14 47	15 00
S 60	15 35	16 25	17 18	14 26	14 40	14 51	15 01

Day	SUN Eqn. of Time 00h	12h	Mer. Pass.	MOON Mer. Pass. Upper	Lower	Age	Phase
16	03 43	03 42	11 56	06 22	18 45	23	
17	03 42	03 41	11 56	07 09	19 32	24	◑
18	03 40	03 39	11 56	07 56	20 20	25	

44^m   INCREMENTS AND CORRECTIONS   **45^m**

44	SUN PLANETS	ARIES	MOON	v or Corr^n d		v or Corr^n d		v or Corr^n d		45	SUN PLANETS	ARIES	MOON	v or Corr^n d		v or Corr^n d		v or Corr^n d	
00	11 00·0	11 01·8	10 29·9	0·0	0·0	6·0	4·5	12·0	8·9	00	11 15·0	11 16·8	10 44·3	0·0	0·0	6·0	4·6	12·0	9·1
01	11 00·3	11 02·1	10 30·2	0·1	0·1	6·1	4·5	12·1	9·0	01	11 15·3	11 17·1	10 44·5	0·1	0·1	6·1	4·6	12·1	9·2
02	11 00·5	11 02·3	10 30·4	0·2	0·1	6·2	4·6	12·2	9·0	02	11 15·5	11 17·3	10 44·7	0·2	0·2	6·2	4·7	12·2	9·3
03	11 00·8	11 02·6	10 30·6	0·3	0·2	6·3	4·7	12·3	9·1	03	11 15·8	11 17·6	10 45·0	0·3	0·2	6·3	4·8	12·3	9·3
04	11 01·0	11 02·8	10 30·9	0·4	0·3	6·4	4·7	12·4	9·2	04	11 16·0	11 17·9	10 45·2	0·4	0·3	6·4	4·9	12·4	9·4
05	11 01·3	11 03·1	10 31·1	0·5	0·4	6·5	4·8	12·5	9·3	05	11 16·3	11 18·1	10 45·4	0·5	0·4	6·5	4·9	12·5	9·5
06	11 01·5	11 03·3	10 31·4	0·6	0·4	6·6	4·9	12·6	9·3	06	11 16·5	11 18·4	10 45·7	0·6	0·5	6·6	5·0	12·6	9·6
07	11 01·8	11 03·6	10 31·6	0·7	0·5	6·7	5·0	12·7	9·4	07	11 16·8	11 18·6	10 45·9	0·7	0·5	6·7	5·1	12·7	9·6
08	11 02·0	11 03·8	10 31·8	0·8	0·6	6·8	5·0	12·8	9·5	08	11 17·0	11 18·9	10 46·2	0·8	0·6	6·8	5·2	12·8	9·7
09	11 02·3	11 04·1	10 32·1	0·9	0·7	6·9	5·1	12·9	9·6	09	11 17·3	11 19·1	10 46·4	0·9	0·7	6·9	5·2	12·9	9·8
10	11 02·5	11 04·3	10 32·3	1·0	0·7	7·0	5·2	13·0	9·6	10	11 17·5	11 19·4	10 46·6	1·0	0·8	7·0	5·3	13·0	9·9
11	11 02·8	11 04·6	10 32·6	1·1	0·8	7·1	5·3	13·1	9·7	11	11 17·8	11 19·6	10 46·9	1·1	0·8	7·1	5·4	13·1	9·9
12	11 03·0	11 04·8	10 32·8	1·2	0·9	7·2	5·3	13·2	9·8	12	11 18·0	11 19·9	10 47·1	1·2	0·9	7·2	5·5	13·2	10·0
13	11 03·3	11 05·1	10 33·0	1·3	1·0	7·3	5·4	13·3	9·9	13	11 18·3	11 20·1	10 47·4	1·3	1·0	7·3	5·5	13·3	10·1
14	11 03·5	11 05·3	10 33·3	1·4	1·0	7·4	5·5	13·4	9·9	14	11 18·5	11 20·4	10 47·6	1·4	1·1	7·4	5·6	13·4	10·2
15	11 03·8	11 05·6	10 33·5	1·5	1·1	7·5	5·6	13·5	10·0	15	11 18·8	11 20·6	10 47·8	1·5	1·1	7·5	5·7	13·5	10·2
16	11 04·0	11 05·8	10 33·8	1·6	1·2	7·6	5·6	13·6	10·1	16	11 19·0	11 20·9	10 48·1	1·6	1·2	7·6	5·8	13·6	10·3
17	11 04·3	11 06·1	10 34·0	1·7	1·3	7·7	5·7	13·7	10·2	17	11 19·3	11 21·1	10 48·3	1·7	1·3	7·7	5·8	13·7	10·4
18	11 04·5	11 06·3	10 34·2	1·8	1·3	7·8	5·8	13·8	10·2	18	11 19·5	11 21·4	10 48·5	1·8	1·4	7·8	5·9	13·8	10·5
19	11 04·8	11 06·6	10 34·5	1·9	1·4	7·9	5·9	13·9	10·3	19	11 19·8	11 21·6	10 48·8	1·9	1·4	7·9	6·0	13·9	10·5
20	11 05·0	11 06·8	10 34·7	2·0	1·5	8·0	5·9	14·0	10·4	20	11 20·0	11 21·9	10 49·0	2·0	1·5	8·0	6·1	14·0	10·6
21	11 05·3	11 07·1	10 34·9	2·1	1·6	8·1	6·0	14·1	10·5	21	11 20·3	11 22·1	10 49·3	2·1	1·6	8·1	6·1	14·1	10·7
22	11 05·5	11 07·3	10 35·2	2·2	1·6	8·2	6·1	14·2	10·5	22	11 20·5	11 22·4	10 49·5	2·2	1·7	8·2	6·2	14·2	10·8
23	11 05·8	11 07·6	10 35·4	2·3	1·7	8·3	6·2	14·3	10·6	23	11 20·8	11 22·6	10 49·7	2·3	1·7	8·3	6·3	14·3	10·8
24	11 06·0	11 07·8	10 35·7	2·4	1·8	8·4	6·2	14·4	10·7	24	11 21·0	11 22·9	10 50·0	2·4	1·8	8·4	6·4	14·4	10·9
25	11 06·3	11 08·1	10 35·9	2·5	1·9	8·5	6·3	14·5	10·8	25	11 21·3	11 23·1	10 50·2	2·5	1·9	8·5	6·4	14·5	11·0
26	11 06·5	11 08·3	10 36·1	2·6	1·9	8·6	6·4	14·6	10·8	26	11 21·5	11 23·4	10 50·5	2·6	2·0	8·6	6·5	14·6	11·1
27	11 06·8	11 08·6	10 36·4	2·7	2·0	8·7	6·5	14·7	10·9	27	11 21·8	11 23·6	10 50·7	2·7	2·0	8·7	6·6	14·7	11·1
28	11 07·0	11 08·8	10 36·6	2·8	2·1	8·8	6·5	14·8	11·0	28	11 22·0	11 23·9	10 50·9	2·8	2·1	8·8	6·7	14·8	11·2
29	11 07·3	11 09·1	10 36·9	2·9	2·2	8·9	6·6	14·9	11·1	29	11 22·3	11 24·1	10 51·2	2·9	2·2	8·9	6·7	14·9	11·3
30	11 07·5	11 09·3	10 37·1	3·0	2·2	9·0	6·7	15·0	11·1	30	11 22·5	11 24·4	10 51·4	3·0	2·3	9·0	6·8	15·0	11·4
31	11 07·8	11 09·6	10 37·3	3·1	2·3	9·1	6·7	15·1	11·2	31	11 22·8	11 24·6	10 51·6	3·1	2·4	9·1	6·9	15·1	11·5
32	11 08·0	11 09·8	10 37·6	3·2	2·4	9·2	6·8	15·2	11·3	32	11 23·0	11 24·9	10 51·9	3·2	2·4	9·2	7·0	15·2	11·5
33	11 08·3	11 10·1	10 37·8	3·3	2·4	9·3	6·9	15·3	11·3	33	11 23·3	11 25·1	10 52·1	3·3	2·5	9·3	7·1	15·3	11·6
34	11 08·5	11 10·3	10 38·0	3·4	2·5	9·4	7·0	15·4	11·4	34	11 23·5	11 25·4	10 52·4	3·4	2·6	9·4	7·1	15·4	11·7
35	11 08·8	11 10·6	10 38·3	3·5	2·6	9·5	7·0	15·5	11·5	35	11 23·8	11 25·6	10 52·6	3·5	2·7	9·5	7·2	15·5	11·8
36	11 09·0	11 10·8	10 38·5	3·6	2·7	9·6	7·1	15·6	11·6	36	11 24·0	11 25·9	10 52·8	3·6	2·7	9·6	7·3	15·6	11·8
37	11 09·3	11 11·1	10 38·8	3·7	2·7	9·7	7·2	15·7	11·6	37	11 24·3	11 26·1	10 53·1	3·7	2·8	9·7	7·4	15·7	11·9
38	11 09·5	11 11·3	10 39·0	3·8	2·8	9·8	7·3	15·8	11·7	38	11 24·5	11 26·4	10 53·3	3·8	2·9	9·8	7·4	15·8	12·0
39	11 09·8	11 11·6	10 39·2	3·9	2·9	9·9	7·3	15·9	11·8	39	11 24·8	11 26·6	10 53·6	3·9	3·0	9·9	7·5	15·9	12·1
40	11 10·0	11 11·8	10 39·5	4·0	3·0	10·0	7·4	16·0	11·9	40	11 25·0	11 26·9	10 53·8	4·0	3·0	10·0	7·6	16·0	12·1
41	11 10·3	11 12·1	10 39·7	4·1	3·0	10·1	7·5	16·1	11·9	41	11 25·3	11 27·1	10 54·0	4·1	3·1	10·1	7·7	16·1	12·2
42	11 10·5	11 12·3	10 40·0	4·2	3·1	10·2	7·6	16·2	12·0	42	11 25·5	11 27·4	10 54·3	4·2	3·2	10·2	7·7	16·2	12·3
43	11 10·8	11 12·6	10 40·2	4·3	3·2	10·3	7·6	16·3	12·1	43	11 25·8	11 27·6	10 54·5	4·3	3·3	10·3	7·8	16·3	12·4
44	11 11·0	11 12·8	10 40·4	4·4	3·3	10·4	7·7	16·4	12·2	44	11 26·0	11 27·9	10 54·7	4·4	3·3	10·4	7·9	16·4	12·4
45	11 11·3	11 13·1	10 40·7	4·5	3·3	10·5	7·8	16·5	12·2	45	11 26·3	11 28·1	10 55·0	4·5	3·4	10·5	8·0	16·5	12·5
46	11 11·5	11 13·3	10 40·9	4·6	3·4	10·6	7·9	16·6	12·3	46	11 26·5	11 28·4	10 55·2	4·6	3·5	10·6	8·0	16·6	12·6
47	11 11·8	11 13·6	10 41·1	4·7	3·5	10·7	7·9	16·7	12·4	47	11 26·8	11 28·6	10 55·5	4·7	3·6	10·7	8·1	16·7	12·7
48	11 12·0	11 13·8	10 41·4	4·8	3·6	10·8	8·0	16·8	12·5	48	11 27·0	11 28·9	10 55·7	4·8	3·6	10·8	8·2	16·8	12·7
49	11 12·3	11 14·1	10 41·6	4·9	3·6	10·9	8·1	16·9	12·5	49	11 27·3	11 29·1	10 55·9	4·9	3·7	10·9	8·3	16·9	12·8
50	11 12·5	11 14·3	10 41·9	5·0	3·7	11·0	8·2	17·0	12·6	50	11 27·5	11 29·4	10 56·2	5·0	3·8	11·0	8·3	17·0	12·9
51	11 12·8	11 14·6	10 42·1	5·1	3·8	11·1	8·2	17·1	12·7	51	11 27·8	11 29·6	10 56·4	5·1	3·9	11·1	8·4	17·1	13·0
52	11 13·0	11 14·8	10 42·3	5·2	3·9	11·2	8·3	17·2	12·8	52	11 28·0	11 29·9	10 56·7	5·2	3·9	11·2	8·5	17·2	13·0
53	11 13·3	11 15·1	10 42·6	5·3	3·9	11·3	8·4	17·3	12·8	53	11 28·3	11 30·1	10 56·9	5·3	4·0	11·3	8·6	17·3	13·1
54	11 13·5	11 15·3	10 42·8	5·4	4·0	11·4	8·5	17·4	12·9	54	11 28·5	11 30·4	10 57·1	5·4	4·1	11·4	8·6	17·4	13·2
55	11 13·8	11 15·6	10 43·1	5·5	4·1	11·5	8·5	17·5	13·0	55	11 28·8	11 30·6	10 57·4	5·5	4·2	11·5	8·7	17·5	13·3
56	11 14·0	11 15·8	10 43·3	5·6	4·2	11·6	8·6	17·6	13·1	56	11 29·0	11 30·9	10 57·6	5·6	4·2	11·6	8·8	17·6	13·3
57	11 14·3	11 16·1	10 43·5	5·7	4·2	11·7	8·7	17·7	13·1	57	11 29·3	11 31·1	10 57·9	5·7	4·3	11·7	8·9	17·7	13·4
58	11 14·5	11 16·3	10 43·8	5·8	4·3	11·8	8·8	17·8	13·2	58	11 29·5	11 31·4	10 58·1	5·8	4·4	11·8	8·9	17·8	13·5
59	11 14·8	11 16·6	10 44·0	5·9	4·4	11·9	8·8	17·9	13·3	59	11 29·8	11 31·6	10 58·3	5·9	4·5	11·9	9·0	17·9	13·6
60	11 15·0	11 16·8	10 44·3	6·0	4·5	12·0	8·9	18·0	13·4	60	11 30·0	11 31·9	10 58·6	6·0	4·6	12·0	9·1	18·0	13·7

xxiv

Figure 3.8   Specimen pages from *Nautical Almanac* (Table of Increments and Corrections, p. xxv)

INCREMENTS AND CORRECTIONS

46^m — **47^m**

46^m	SUN PLANETS	ARIES	MOON	v or d Corrⁿ	v or d Corrⁿ	v or d Corrⁿ	47^m	SUN PLANETS	ARIES	MOON	v or d Corrⁿ	v or d Corrⁿ	v or d Corrⁿ
s	° ′	° ′	° ′	′ ′	′ ′	′ ′	s	° ′	° ′	° ′	′ ′	′ ′	′ ′
00	11 30·0	11 31·9	10 58·6	0·0 0·0	6·0 4·7	12·0 9·3	00	11 45·0	11 46·9	11 12·9	0·0 0·0	6·0 4·8	12·0 9·5
01	11 30·3	11 32·1	10 58·8	0·1 0·1	6·1 4·7	12·1 9·4	01	11 45·3	11 47·2	11 13·1	0·1 0·1	6·1 4·8	12·1 9·6
02	11 30·5	11 32·4	10 59·0	0·2 0·2	6·2 4·8	12·2 9·5	02	11 45·5	11 47·4	11 13·4	0·2 0·2	6·2 4·9	12·2 9·7
03	11 30·8	11 32·6	10 59·3	0·3 0·2	6·3 4·9	12·3 9·5	03	11 45·8	11 47·7	11 13·6	0·3 0·2	6·3 5·0	12·3 9·7
04	11 31·0	11 32·9	10 59·5	0·4 0·3	6·4 5·0	12·4 9·6	04	11 46·0	11 47·9	11 13·8	0·4 0·3	6·4 5·1	12·4 9·8
05	11 31·3	11 33·1	10 59·8	0·5 0·4	6·5 5·0	12·5 9·7	05	11 46·3	11 48·2	11 14·1	0·5 0·4	6·5 5·1	12·5 9·9
06	11 31·5	11 33·4	11 00·0	0·6 0·5	6·6 5·1	12·6 9·8	06	11 46·5	11 48·4	11 14·3	0·6 0·5	6·6 5·2	12·6 10·0
07	11 31·8	11 33·6	11 00·2	0·7 0·5	6·7 5·2	12·7 9·8	07	11 46·8	11 48·7	11 14·6	0·7 0·6	6·7 5·3	12·7 10·1
08	11 32·0	11 33·9	11 00·5	0·8 0·6	6·8 5·3	12·8 9·9	08	11 47·0	11 48·9	11 14·8	0·8 0·6	6·8 5·4	12·8 10·1
09	11 32·3	11 34·1	11 00·7	0·9 0·7	6·9 5·3	12·9 10·0	09	11 47·3	11 49·2	11 15·0	0·9 0·7	6·9 5·5	12·9 10·2
10	11 32·5	11 34·4	11 01·0	1·0 0·8	7·0 5·4	13·0 10·1	10	11 47·5	11 49·4	11 15·3	1·0 0·8	7·0 5·5	13·0 10·3
11	11 32·8	11 34·6	11 01·2	1·1 0·9	7·1 5·5	13·1 10·2	11	11 47·8	11 49·7	11 15·5	1·1 0·9	7·1 5·6	13·1 10·4
12	11 33·0	11 34·9	11 01·4	1·2 0·9	7·2 5·6	13·2 10·2	12	11 48·0	11 49·9	11 15·7	1·2 1·0	7·2 5·7	13·2 10·5
13	11 33·3	11 35·1	11 01·7	1·3 1·0	7·3 5·7	13·3 10·3	13	11 48·3	11 50·2	11 16·0	1·3 1·0	7·3 5·8	13·3 10·5
14	11 33·5	11 35·4	11 01·9	1·4 1·1	7·4 5·7	13·4 10·4	14	11 48·5	11 50·4	11 16·2	1·4 1·1	7·4 5·9	13·4 10·6
15	11 33·8	11 35·6	11 02·1	1·5 1·2	7·5 5·8	13·5 10·5	15	11 48·8	11 50·7	11 16·5	1·5 1·2	7·5 5·9	13·5 10·7
16	11 34·0	11 35·9	11 02·4	1·6 1·2	7·6 5·9	13·6 10·5	16	11 49·0	11 50·9	11 16·7	1·6 1·3	7·6 6·0	13·6 10·8
17	11 34·3	11 36·2	11 02·6	1·7 1·3	7·7 6·0	13·7 10·6	17	11 49·3	11 51·2	11 16·9	1·7 1·3	7·7 6·1	13·7 10·8
18	11 34·5	11 36·4	11 02·9	1·8 1·4	7·8 6·0	13·8 10·7	18	11 49·5	11 51·4	11 17·2	1·8 1·4	7·8 6·2	13·8 10·9
19	11 34·8	11 36·7	11 03·1	1·9 1·5	7·9 6·1	13·9 10·8	19	11 49·8	11 51·7	11 17·4	1·9 1·5	7·9 6·3	13·9 11·0
20	11 35·0	11 36·9	11 03·3	2·0 1·6	8·0 6·2	14·0 10·9	20	11 50·0	11 51·9	11 17·7	2·0 1·6	8·0 6·3	14·0 11·1
21	11 35·3	11 37·2	11 03·6	2·1 1·6	8·1 6·3	14·1 10·9	21	11 50·3	11 52·2	11 17·9	2·1 1·7	8·1 6·4	14·1 11·2
22	11 35·5	11 37·4	11 03·8	2·2 1·7	8·2 6·4	14·2 11·0	22	11 50·5	11 52·4	11 18·1	2·2 1·7	8·2 6·5	14·2 11·2
23	11 35·8	11 37·7	11 04·1	2·3 1·8	8·3 6·4	14·3 11·1	23	11 50·8	11 52·7	11 18·4	2·3 1·8	8·3 6·6	14·3 11·3
24	11 36·0	11 37·9	11 04·3	2·4 1·9	8·4 6·5	14·4 11·2	24	11 51·0	11 52·9	11 18·6	2·4 1·9	8·4 6·7	14·4 11·4
25	11 36·3	11 38·2	11 04·5	2·5 1·9	8·5 6·6	14·5 11·2	25	11 51·3	11 53·2	11 18·8	2·5 2·0	8·5 6·7	14·5 11·5
26	11 36·5	11 38·4	11 04·8	2·6 2·0	8·6 6·7	14·6 11·3	26	11 51·5	11 53·4	11 19·1	2·6 2·1	8·6 6·8	14·6 11·6
27	11 36·8	11 38·7	11 05·0	2·7 2·1	8·7 6·7	14·7 11·4	27	11 51·8	11 53·7	11 19·3	2·7 2·1	8·7 6·9	14·7 11·6
28	11 37·0	11 38·9	11 05·2	2·8 2·2	8·8 6·8	14·8 11·5	28	11 52·0	11 53·9	11 19·6	2·8 2·2	8·8 7·0	14·8 11·7
29	11 37·3	11 39·2	11 05·5	2·9 2·2	8·9 6·9	14·9 11·5	29	11 52·3	11 54·2	11 19·8	2·9 2·3	8·9 7·0	14·9 11·8
30	11 37·5	11 39·4	11 05·7	3·0 2·3	9·0 7·0	15·0 11·6	30	11 52·5	11 54·5	11 20·0	3·0 2·4	9·0 7·1	15·0 11·9
31	11 37·8	11 39·7	11 06·0	3·1 2·4	9·1 7·1	15·1 11·7	31	11 52·8	11 54·7	11 20·3	3·1 2·5	9·1 7·2	15·1 12·0
32	11 38·0	11 39·9	11 06·2	3·2 2·5	9·2 7·1	15·2 11·8	32	11 53·0	11 55·0	11 20·5	3·2 2·5	9·2 7·3	15·2 12·0
33	11 38·3	11 40·2	11 06·4	3·3 2·6	9·3 7·2	15·3 11·9	33	11 53·3	11 55·2	11 20·8	3·3 2·6	9·3 7·4	15·3 12·1
34	11 38·5	11 40·4	11 06·7	3·4 2·6	9·4 7·3	15·4 11·9	34	11 53·5	11 55·5	11 21·0	3·4 2·7	9·4 7·4	15·4 12·2
35	11 38·8	11 40·7	11 06·9	3·5 2·7	9·5 7·4	15·5 12·0	35	11 53·8	11 55·7	11 21·2	3·5 2·8	9·5 7·5	15·5 12·3
36	11 39·0	11 40·9	11 07·2	3·6 2·8	9·6 7·4	15·6 12·1	36	11 54·0	11 56·0	11 21·5	3·6 2·9	9·6 7·6	15·6 12·4
37	11 39·3	11 41·2	11 07·4	3·7 2·9	9·7 7·5	15·7 12·2	37	11 54·3	11 56·2	11 21·7	3·7 2·9	9·7 7·7	15·7 12·4
38	11 39·5	11 41·4	11 07·6	3·8 2·9	9·8 7·6	15·8 12·2	38	11 54·5	11 56·5	11 22·0	3·8 3·0	9·8 7·8	15·8 12·5
39	11 39·8	11 41·7	11 07·9	3·9 3·0	9·9 7·7	15·9 12·3	39	11 54·8	11 56·7	11 22·2	3·9 3·1	9·9 7·8	15·9 12·6
40	11 40·0	11 41·9	11 08·1	4·0 3·1	10·0 7·8	16·0 12·4	40	11 55·0	11 57·0	11 22·4	4·0 3·2	10·0 7·9	16·0 12·7
41	11 40·3	11 42·2	11 08·3	4·1 3·2	10·1 7·8	16·1 12·5	41	11 55·3	11 57·2	11 22·7	4·1 3·2	10·1 8·0	16·1 12·7
42	11 40·5	11 42·4	11 08·6	4·2 3·3	10·2 7·9	16·2 12·6	42	11 55·5	11 57·5	11 22·9	4·2 3·3	10·2 8·1	16·2 12·8
43	11 40·8	11 42·7	11 08·8	4·3 3·3	10·3 8·0	16·3 12·6	43	11 55·8	11 57·7	11 23·1	4·3 3·4	10·3 8·2	16·3 12·9
44	11 41·0	11 42·9	11 09·1	4·4 3·4	10·4 8·1	16·4 12·7	44	11 56·0	11 58·0	11 23·4	4·4 3·5	10·4 8·2	16·4 13·0
45	11 41·3	11 43·2	11 09·3	4·5 3·5	10·5 8·1	16·5 12·8	45	11 56·3	11 58·2	11 23·6	4·5 3·6	10·5 8·3	16·5 13·1
46	11 41·5	11 43·4	11 09·5	4·6 3·6	10·6 8·2	16·6 12·9	46	11 56·5	11 58·5	11 23·9	4·6 3·6	10·6 8·4	16·6 13·1
47	11 41·8	11 43·7	11 09·8	4·7 3·6	10·7 8·3	16·7 12·9	47	11 56·8	11 58·7	11 24·1	4·7 3·7	10·7 8·5	16·7 13·2
48	11 42·0	11 43·9	11 10·0	4·8 3·7	10·8 8·4	16·8 13·0	48	11 57·0	11 59·0	11 24·3	4·8 3·8	10·8 8·6	16·8 13·3
49	11 42·3	11 44·2	11 10·3	4·9 3·8	10·9 8·4	16·9 13·1	49	11 57·3	11 59·2	11 24·6	4·9 3·9	10·9 8·6	16·9 13·4
50	11 42·5	11 44·4	11 10·5	5·0 3·9	11·0 8·5	17·0 13·2	50	11 57·5	11 59·5	11 24·8	5·0 4·0	11·0 8·7	17·0 13·5
51	11 42·8	11 44·7	11 10·7	5·1 4·0	11·1 8·6	17·1 13·3	51	11 57·8	11 59·7	11 25·1	5·1 4·0	11·1 8·8	17·1 13·5
52	11 43·0	11 44·9	11 11·0	5·2 4·0	11·2 8·7	17·2 13·3	52	11 58·0	12 00·0	11 25·3	5·2 4·1	11·2 8·9	17·2 13·6
53	11 43·3	11 45·2	11 11·2	5·3 4·1	11·3 8·8	17·3 13·4	53	11 58·3	12 00·2	11 25·5	5·3 4·2	11·3 8·9	17·3 13·7
54	11 43·5	11 45·4	11 11·5	5·4 4·2	11·4 8·8	17·4 13·5	54	11 58·5	12 00·5	11 25·8	5·4 4·3	11·4 9·0	17·4 13·8
55	11 43·8	11 45·7	11 11·7	5·5 4·3	11·5 8·9	17·5 13·6	55	11 58·8	12 00·7	11 26·0	5·5 4·4	11·5 9·1	17·5 13·9
56	11 44·0	11 45·9	11 11·9	5·6 4·3	11·6 9·0	17·6 13·6	56	11 59·0	12 01·0	11 26·2	5·6 4·4	11·6 9·2	17·6 13·9
57	11 44·3	11 46·2	11 12·2	5·7 4·4	11·7 9·1	17·7 13·7	57	11 59·3	12 01·2	11 26·5	5·7 4·5	11·7 9·3	17·7 14·0
58	11 44·5	11 46·4	11 12·4	5·8 4·5	11·8 9·1	17·8 13·8	58	11 59·5	12 01·5	11 26·7	5·8 4·6	11·8 9·3	17·8 14·1
59	11 44·8	11 46·7	11 12·6	5·9 4·6	11·9 9·2	17·9 13·9	59	11 59·8	12 01·7	11 27·0	5·9 4·7	11·9 9·4	17·9 14·2
60	11 45·0	11 46·9	11 12·9	6·0 4·7	12·0 9·3	18·0 14·0	60	12 00·0	12 02·0	11 27·2	6·0 4·8	12·0 9·5	18·0 14·3

xxv

this figures into our computing altitude, it is not a factor in determining GHA and declination.)

v and d Corrections

As compared with the direct determination of GHA and Dec. for the sun, the v and d corrections for the moon and planets have the appearance of nuisance factors. The value d in the main tabular entries for the moon is simply the hourly increment of increase or decrease in declination for the particular entry. These hourly d values vary considerably since they are contingent upon the orbital positions of both moon and earth. The v values are less apparent. The table for increments and corrections is constructed on the assumption that the moon's GHA changes 14°19' in the period of 60 minutes. However, during the year we will find that the actual change may be as much as 14°32'. The v factor is thus the amount in arc by which the actual hourly change in GHA exceeds 14°19'. For example, the first entry for the moon, May 16, gives a GHA of 267°36.4'. The entry for the succeeding hour is 282°07.7' and the value of v is given as 12.3. This means that the difference between the two entries exceeds the standard 14°19' by 12.3' of arc. A correction for v (Corr^n) is thus an interpolation involving the odd minutes and the supplemental increment v. For the moon v correction is invariably added; d correction is added or subtracted contingent upon whether declination is increasing or decreasing at the time.

Example: Determine the moon's GHA and Dec. for May 16, 1982, 15 46 30 GMT.

GMT 1500	GHA 125°27'; v, 12.4'	Dec. 14° 52.7' S; d, 9.4'
corr. (46'30")	11°05.7'	
v/d corr.	+9.6'	−7.3'
GMT 15 14 30 GHA	136°42.3'	Dec. 14° 45.4'S

For the planets, v and d factors are given at the bottom of the page. The corrections are generally negligible but may amount to a minute or more of arc when applied to increments of 30 minutes or more.

Example: Determine the GHA and Dec. for the planet Jupiter and the star Vega May 17, 1982, GMT 08 47 23.

Jupiter

	GHA	$(v = 2.7)$	Dec. $(d = 0.1)$
0800	143°32.4'		11°08.6'S
corr.	11°50.8'		
v/d corr.	+2.1'		
	155°25.3'		

Vega

	GHA		Dec.
GHA♈	354°41.6'	0800	38°45.8'N
corr.	11°52.7'		
GHA♈	6°34.3'	(08 47 23 GMT)	
SHA	80°54.7'		
GHA	87°29.'		

Question: At the time of the above observation, a bright star is seen a few degrees due west of Jupiter. See if you can identify it by referring to the data for stars in the appropriate column of Figure 3.7. Answer: Since we know the star is to be due west of Jupiter it will have approximately the same declination. Also, to be west by a few degrees, its GHA must be greater than that of Jupiter by a few degrees. We know GHAΥ to be 6°34′. What star has the appropriate SHA and Dec. to fulfill the requirements? Spica! Indeed, a conspicuous navigational star. At the time identical to that for our observation of Jupiter, Spica has a GHA of 165°30.4′, a Dec. of 11°04.2′S. Thus, one of the techniques of star identification.

Aside from its main entries as exemplified in Figure 3.7, the *Nautical Almanac* provides other useful information: data for star identification, standard times for different world locations, altitude correction tables for refraction, dip, and parallax.

HOROLOGY

We are reminded that Captain Joshua Slocum is reported to have circumnavigated the world with only a dollar alarm clock to serve as chronometer (*cf.* Note 3.4). Compared to the earliest of navigators he was fortunate. The perfection of a reliable chronometer is fairly recent (by Harrison, circa 1735). Early clocks, if you can call them that, made use of hourglasses, sand, and water, and the gnomon or shadow stick was adapted to the sundial.* Before that, time, often only in terms of a calendar, was measured by periodic phenomena in the heavens: the solar day and year, the sidereal day, and the lunar month. Rotations of the Great Bear and the Lesser Bear about the polar star were utilized as sidereal "clocks." Any periodic phenomenon would do. In his study of the acceleration of free-falling bodies Galileo timed events by counting his own pulse.

Mechanical clocks date from the thirteenth century. The first were weight-driven (forerunners of the cuckoo). Later, coiled springs were used as the driving force. Much higher accuracy was reached in the eighteenth century with application of the pendulum. The first bona fide chronometer was constructed by John Harrison, circa 1735. And thereby hangs the tale of determining longitude by time (*cf.* Note 3.5).

Until recently chronometry was dominated by the mechanical escapement. By midnineteenth century chronometers became sufficiently less expensive that every large vessel plying the seas carried two or more. It was the responsibility of the navigation officer to wind, rate, and, above all, coddle the ship's timepieces. Until recently chronometers have been very expensive. Rare was the cruising sailor who could boast a reliable chronometer, gimballed and displayed, as it would be, in a brass-festooned, velvet-lined box.

With the production of cheap quartz clocks and watches, that has all changed. This writer's present chronometer is a twenty-dollar digital watch (Texas Instruments) which keeps better time (about 10 seconds slow per month) than mechanical chronometers costing twenty times as much.

Nowadays, timekeeping represents a very sophisticated technology making use of the rapid vibrations of crystals or atomic events. The astronomer continually frets after

---

*The best sand glasses utilized pulverized eggshell for uniformity of grain. It was learned that the sand flowed faster if heated, a bit of practical wisdom soon passing into the lore of watch-keeping. By warming the glass, time could be made to pass more quickly. The traditional bells as struck by the watch officer were determined by turning the glass.

greater and greater accuracy—milli-milliseconds of accuracy. The navigator can be less demanding. But he does need to remind himself that a 4-second error of time can translate into as much as a *one-mile error* in a position line (*cf*. Note 3.2). And without a chronometer or accurate time, he will be reduced to latitude observations and dead reckoning.

NOTES

Note 3.1

Equation of Time: The mean sun is the fictitious, ideal sun that sweeps out equal hour angles in equal units of time. It is the sun of uniform motion. The true sun, on the other hand, is a sun of nonuniform motion so that with rare exceptions the two suns, mean and true, do not coincide. At any time, the difference between the two is a matter of arc-angle, and that arc converted to time is known as the equation of time.

There are two factors influencing the apparent motion of the true sun which introduce nonuniformity into its motion. One is the fact that the orbital speed of the earth varies with respect to position in the orbit. According to Kepler's second law of planetary motion, the line adjoining the earth and sun sweeps out equal areas in equal time. Thus, as the earth nears perihelion (Figure 2.12) its orbital speed increases; as it approaches aphelion its orbital speed decreases. The second factor is due to the inclination of the earth's polar axis to the equatorial plane. It is this inclination which generates the ecliptic, the sun's apparent path through the stellar background. Now if the sun's apparent motion were uniform along the ecliptic (it is not, due to the first factor above), it would not be uniform in the equinoctial plane. If we consider the sun's path on the ecliptic (see Figure 3.9), we observe that at the solstices, summer and winter, the motion is consistently easterly translating into comparatively uniform motion along the equinoctial. However, when the sun approaches the equinoxes the motion is more northerly or southerly. Hence, easterly regression along the equinoctial varies from season to season.

The equation of time signifies the arc that separates the mean from the true sun. Due to nonuniform motion of the true sun the magnitude of the equation is itself variable. For extremes of range we can consult the *Nautical Almanac*. In the 1982 *Almanac*, for example, the equation of time varies from $-14m\ 17s$ in February (the true sun is 14m 17s behind the mean sun) to $+16m\ 24s$ in November when the true sun is ahead of the mean sun.

The equation of time is useful in determining the time of meridian passage of the true sun.

Example: On March 2, 1982, at a DR position 45N, 130W, I wish to determine the time of meridian transit for the true sun. (Observation of the sun's altitude at meridian transit affords me a quick determination of latitude.) An hour angle of 130°W is 8h 40m late on Greenwich,

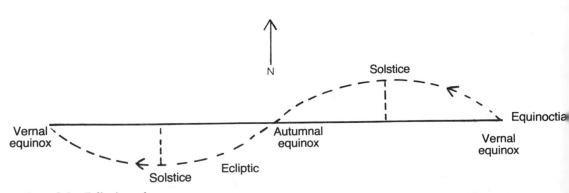

Figure 3.9 Ecliptic path

meaning local mean noon at 130°W is 20 40 00 GMT. From the *Almanac* I find the equation of time to be $-12m$ 14s, that is, apparent time is 12m 14s slow on mean time. Therefore, to determine the mean time for meridian transit I must *add* 12m 14s to my local noon; i.e., 20 52 14 GMT is the time of meridian passage.

Note 3.2

Time checks can be obtained worldwide on various national and international broadcasts. The most convenient and most familiar to cruising navigators are the continuous broadcasts from WWV, Fort Collins, and WWVH, Hawaii. These broadcasts offer continuous time checks and can be heard on the shortwave radio frequencies of 2.5, 5. 10, 15, and 20 MHz (and 25 MHz from Fort Collins).

There is a somewhat complicated tonal pattern to these broadcasts (see *Radio Navigational Aids,* published by DMAHTC, U. S. Government Printing Office) but the important feature is that correct time is given on every minute throughout the day. Furthermore, brief storm warnings covering the Atlantic and eastern Pacific are broadcast 8, 9, and 10 minutes after the hour from WWV. And from WWVH, storm warnings covering the central and western Pacific are broadcast 48, 49, and 50 minutes after the hour. For "unusually widespread weather conditions," the warning broadcasts may continue through the fifty-first minute after the hour.

In the writer's experience the latter broadcasts proved very useful on the "milk run" through the South Pacific. They frequently identified the geographic range for the active intertropical convergence zone where line squalls are likely to prevail. (So long as we are being confessional, let me add that whereas there was no particular comfort in learning, say, that squalls lay ahead on the passage to Rarotonga, there was at least some compensatory solace in knowing that at the distant and chill location of 50°N, 155°W winds of 50 knots were expected within a 500-mile radius.)

Note 3.3

One of the most poignant episodes in the history and philosophy of science revolves around the Copernican revolution. Both the geocentric view (Ptolemy) and the heliocentric view (Copernicus) made accurate predictions of solar and planetary motion. A crucial issue was that of retrograde motion of a planet whose orbit is superior to that of the earth (see Note 2.4). Mars, for example, marches across the stellar background of the sky, slows, reverses itself, and then again resumes its eastward march.

The earliest theories of astronomy had celestial bodies rotating in concentric spheres. The theory of Ptolemy (Claudius Ptolemaeus, circa 150 A.D.) was more mathematical. In simplest form, the earth was placed at the center of the universe in a stationary state. As seen from the earth the orbit of Mars was then generated by two orbital motions, a primary circular orbit of a point, the deferent, about the earth complicated by an epicyclical orbit of the body about a point moving along the deferent. Figure 3.10 presents the simplest of epicyclical models. E is the earth. The point C travels on its sidereal period about the deferent circle (the larger circle). The body itself revolves in the epicycle wherein the epicyclical motion augments that along the deferent. In the lower half, the epicyclical motion is a subtractive factor. Between a and b, however, the resultant motion beomes more complex. At a and b, the westerly motion in the epicycle just counterbalances the easterly motion in the deferent. Therefore, at these points M appears stationary against the uniform stellar background. Between that short interval a–b, however, the westerly motion in the epicycle exceeds that of easterly motion in the deferent and M appears to move in retrograde fashion. This is a Ptolemaic model at its simplest. In order to account for ever-increasing small discrepancies of motion, epicycles on epicycles were introduced, and the center of the deferent was displaced from the earth's position at E. All, we might say, for computational purposes.

The great work of Ptolemy, the *Almagest,* was a compendium of observations, computations, and theory. As such, it would qualify as the earliest of almanacs.

It is sometimes thought that Copernicus put an end to the computational gimmickry of Ptolemy. Actually this was not so. Although Copernicus did place the sun at the center of the universe, he retained epicyclical devices. Indeed, one historian of science has argued that contrary to an application of the principle of parsimony, the Copernican theory was actually one of greater

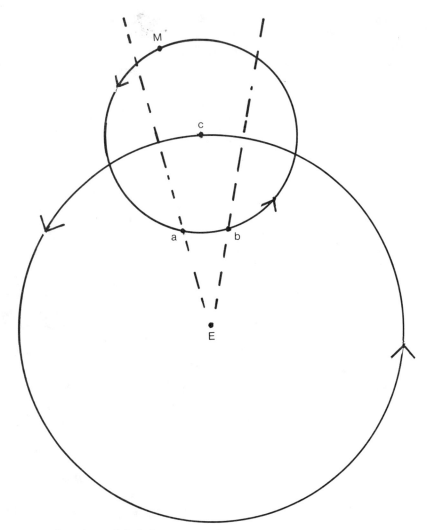

Figure 3.10   Ptolemaic model of planetary motion

complexity. Only when the Copernican heliocentric model was adapted to Kepler's laws of planetary motion did our modern conception of the solar system emerge.

What is interesting in all this is that great theoreticians and observers in astronomy did resort to computational devices. One philosopher embracing this kind of pragmatism called it the "philosophy of 'as if.'" Indeed, one might say that the modern navigator proceeds "as if" the earth is the center of the universe and all apparent motion is real.

Note 3.4

Amidst the bounteous folklore of navigation are those myths and facts of pigeon-homing, the salmon's lusting for the very pebbles of its birth, and Joshua Slocum's getting around the world on a dollar alarm clock that he periodically boiled to keep running. So it should come as no surprise that a navigator can do well, quite well, without a chronometer; but a sextant he must have. The old practice was to sail the latitudes. As local noon approaches, the navigator uses his sextant to follow the sun to culmination (i.e., its highest altitude) and from this reading he can easily determine his latitude. Once the latitude of his destination is reached, then he can sail down his latitude, west or east, to his destination. However, without an accurate timepiece to help in the precise determination of longitude, the estimated time of arrival will be a matter of conjecture based as it will be on protracted dead reckoning.

Of the lore of the dollar clock, Captain Slocum wrote:

> Looking over the journals of all the old voyagers I see none, working the old fashioned methods, so nearly correct as the *Spray* has been in making her landfalls. . . . I never did better when I had even the best of chronometers and officers to assist—now will you tell me where it comes in? my "chro" is a one-dollar tin clock! And of course, is almost no time piece at all—I have to boil her often to keep her at it, from noon to noon, through the months.
>
> Some thinking man will help me out on this else I will never be able to explain how it is done—The one thing most certain about my sea reckonings: They are not kept with any slavish application at all and I have been right every time and seemed *to know* that I was right. (Slocum, *Sailing Alone Around the World,* pp. 56-57)

I am unaware as to whether any "thinking man" ever came to Captain Slocum's rescue in the matter, but since he had many years' experience as a licensed captain, we may conjecture that he relied on more than casual intuition. Although for his longest oceanic passage he claimed to rely upon intuition rather than "slavish calculations," there is "intuition" and there is intuition.

Slocum did run down his latitude (or, as he called it, "running down his longitude"); he kept a DR track, and on his forty-third day out, he took observations to determine longitude by "lunar distance," a method usually requiring two assistants as well as very tedious calculation (*cf.* Note 8.5). Slocum was justifiably proud in finding that his DR position checked within 5 miles of his longitude as determined by the method of "the lunarian."

Note 3.5

Efforts to map the world onto a grid of latitude and longtitude go back at least to Hipparchus (circa 160 B.C.). Although determining latitude was a relatively simple problem for the early navigator (see Chapter 8) that of determining longitude proved very difficult. Determining longitude reduces to a problem of timing distinctive celestial events at different locales. And since the modern chronometer was not perfected until 1735 (and only came into general use some 100 years later) the accurate determination of longitude is of fairly recent vintage.

The principle of finding longitude by timing is straightforward. Consider a predictable celestial event such as a lunar eclipse. All observers in positions to witness the eclipse will see it occur simultaneously although their local timing of the event will differ according to longitude. Thus if two observers in different locales could compare local times of the eclipse, that difference in local time could be translated into a difference of longitude. For example, suppose the difference in timing of a lunar eclipse between, say, Leipzig and Moscow is 1h 45m (local apparent times), then the two locales will differ in longitude by 26°15′.

This method goes back at least to Hipparchus, and Galileo revived an interest in the method with his telescopic discovery of four of Jupiter's moons. Galileo proposed that if reliable tables could be developed for predicting the frequent eclipses and occultations of Jupiter's moons then accurate local timing of the events would yield information as to longitude. In principle the method is sound. However, early attempts to apply it were unsuccessful. One, there were observational difficulties, and two, and more important, means for the accurate local timing of eclipses did not then exist.

Other methods for finding longitude involved observing occultation of stars (i.e., hiding of stars) by the moon's retrograde motion across the sky and time of lunar transit. In both cases time differentials between places of observation were converted to differences in longitude. In principle all such methods should work but the computations can be complex and the observations awkward. None offered the navigator a feasible solution to the problem of finding longitude at sea. And most suffered or were impracticable simply because the navigator did not have an accurate timepiece available.

As early as 1498 substantial rewards were being offered for a solution to the problem of finding longitude at sea. The most famous of these was the prize offered by the British Parliament in 1715. The prize was attractive, ranging from 10,000 pounds for 60' accuracy to as much as 20,000 pounds for 30' accuracy at the end of a transatlantic voyage. At that time such a prize would have provided the recipient a handsome income for life.

The Flemish astronomer Reiner Gemma Frisius (1510–1555) was the first to suggest that, as a theoretical possibility, time differences between a standard meridian and an observer's meridian could be utilized to determine longitude. However, the appropriate timepieces did not exist. Obviously not any timepiece would do. It had to have an accuracy within the limits of the modern chronometer. The prize offered by Parliament went to John Harrison for his invention of a chronometer, but only after he had constructed four different models and persevered over a Parliamentary Board that begrudged every portion of the prize he eventually secured. Harrison's last chronometer to be tested showed an error of only 54 seconds after a 4-month voyage—a remarkable result in that day but easily surpassed nowadays by a quartz watch costing no more than 25 dollars. With the invention of the chronometer, essentially two methods evolved for determining longitude: one, the method of measuring lunar distance, preceded the general availability of reliable chronometers but depended on tabular data accurately specifying coordinates of sun, moon, and selected stars.

The rationale for the method of lunar distance is this. The moon's motion relative to the sun and fixed background stars is fairly rapid (about 30' per hour). Therefore, if we can tabulate lunar distances as should be observed at Greenwich meridian, then a measure of lunar distance from some other vantage point on earth will enable the observer to infer GMT. This, coupled with knowledge of local mean time, as obtained, say, from meridian transit observations, will enable the observer to compute his longitude.

Knowledge of the method goes back to Johannes Werner, 1514, but tabular data of lunar distances were not available until late in the eighteenth century. Furthermore the computational difficulties of "clearing the distance" of the effects of refraction and parallax (i.e., of reducing the observed arc-distance to what it would be at the center of the earth) all but put the method beyond the reach of the practical navigator. (The computations of clearing the distance are indeed tedious. But the method still has use today if the navigator is deprived of all conventional means for checking his time. The essential computations as detailed for the hand calculator can be found in Shufeldt, H. H., and Newcomer, K. E., *The Calculator Afloat.*)

The second method devolves more nearly on modern celestial practice. Solving for the missing elements in the fundamental celestial triangle (see Chapter 4), we determine the HA as being between our meridian and that of, say, the sun. This gives us local apparent time, which with GMT and the application of the equation of time yields longitude. The trigonometric solution (or that from sight reduction tables) requires our knowing our latitude and the altitude and declination of the sun at a precise time, GMT.

CHAPTER FOUR

Navigational Astronomy: The Celestial Triangle

In Chapters 2 and 3 we have established systems of coordinates such that positions and time relationships on the celestial sphere are isomorphic to those of the terrestrial sphere. By *isomorphic* we mean the two systems are geometrically congruent. For every point and configuration on the celestial sphere there is a corresponding point and configuration on the earth's surface, and vice versa. Thus the terrestrial poles and the equator are projected to the celestial sphere, giving us the celestial poles and the equinoctial. Our geographic position on earth corresponds to a zenith position in the heavens. On the other hand, the positional coordinates of a celestial body have a corresponding set of coordinates on the earth's surface. Knowing the interchangeable coordinates of the pole (north or south according to the observer's hemisphere), the observer's position, and the location of a celestial body, we can set up the vertices of a triangle on two different spheres, one, the terrestrial sphere, the other, the celestial sphere.

For the terrestrial sphere the vertices are the nearest geographic pole, P, the assumed position of the observer, AP, and the substellar or geographical position of the celestial object, GP. Great circles intersecting these vertices give us the terrestrial triangle as in Figure 4.1a.

For the celestial sphere the corresponding vertices are the elevated pole, P, the zenith position of the observer, Z, and the position of the celestial object, M. Great circles intersecting these vertices give us the celestial triangle as in Figure 4.1b.

Although the coordinates of the vertices of the two triangles are interchangeable, we concentrate on the terrestrial triangle for purposes of measuring distance. The arc segments of great circles on the earth's surface are convertible to distance, one minute of arc being equal to one nautical mile. Those on the boundless celestial sphere are not convertible.

To construct the terrestrial triangle we select the pole P, north or south according to our latitude, establish the latitude and longitude of our assumed position AP, and plot the geographic position GP of the body according to the Greenwich hour angle GHA and declination d.

REVIEW OF DEFINITIONS

It is not readily apparent from Figures 4.1a and 4.1b how to obtain the measures of arc-distance in the navigational triangle. Before proceeding to a discussion of the role of altitude and sextant observation in this matter, let us first review the pertinent definitions of concepts introduced in the foregoing chapters.

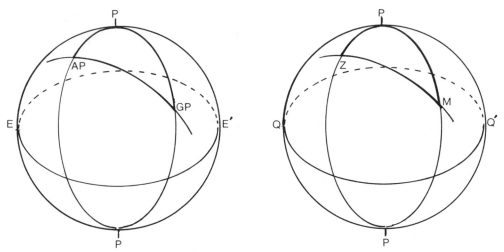

Figure 4.1a   Terrestrial triangle   *Figure 4.1b*   Celestial triangle

Terrestrial Concepts

Great Circle: A line on the surface of a sphere made by passing a plane through the center of the sphere. Being the geodesics of the sphere, such lines constitute shortest distances on the earth's surface.

Equator (Q):   The great circle on the earth's surface generated by a plane perpendicular to the polar axis and passing through the earth's center. The equator divides the earth into its northern and southern hemispheres.

Small Circle: A circle on the surface of a sphere made by a plane passing through the sphere at points other than the center of the sphere.

Latitude (L):   An angle at the earth's center between the equatorial plane and a point on the earth's surface, also measured as the arc subtended by that angle. Parallels of latitude are small circles parallel to the equatorial plane.

Meridians of Longitude: Great circles generated by planes passing through the terrestrial poles and necessarily perpendicular to the equator.

Prime Meridian (G):   The upper branch of the meridian passing through Greenwich, England. The standard meridian for measuring both time and longitude.

International Date Line: The lower branch of the meridian passing through Greenwich. The new day at Greenwich begins the moment the mean sun crosses this line.

Longitude (λ):   Meridians of longitude as measured through 180° east or west of Greenwich.

Nautical Mile: One minute of arc of a great circle inscribed on the earth's surface. One degree is equal to 60 nautical miles.

Celestial Concepts

Hour Circle: Any celestial meridian made by projecting meridians of longitude to the celestial sphere.

Declination (d): The isomorphic counterpart of latitude; i.e., an angle at the geocentric center of the celestial sphere, between the equinoctial plane and a celestial object.

Hour Angle (HA): An angle between any two hour circles, or between a meridian of longitude and an hour circle in the celestial sphere, measured east or west through 180°.

Meridian Angle (t): The hour angle between the observer's meridian and the hour circle through an observed body.

Local Hour Angle (LHA): The hour angle between the observer's meridian and an hour circle through a celestial object, measured westerly through 360°.

Greenwich Hour Angle (GHA): The hour angle between the prime meridian of Greenwich and an hour circle through a celestial object, always measured westerly through 360°.

Equinoctial (QQ'): The celestial equator as projected by the earth's equatorial plane.

Ecliptic: The apparent path of the sun through the stellar sphere as generated by the earth's axial orientation and orbit of revolution; also, a great circle generated by a plane cutting the equatorial plane at an angle of 23½°, the points of intersection being the spring and autumnal equinoxes.

Aries, or the *First Point of Aries (♈):* The point on the equinoctial that is reference for all hour circles identifying the position of stellar objects; also, the vernal or spring equinox, the point at which the sun passes from south declination to north declination in its apparent annual track along the ecliptic.

Sidereal Hour Angle (SHA): The hour angle measured westerly between the meridian of Aries and that through a particular star; SHA added to GHA of ♈ gives GHA of the body.

NAVIGATIONAL TRIANGLE

The so-called navigational triangle makes use of both the terrestrial and celestial systems of references. For the most part, it focuses upon the celestial triangle, but in matters of distance the reference is in terms of terrestrial coordinates. In order to bring distance into the picture we need to introduce the horizon as the basis of observation. For this we introduce two systems of reference, one the polar-equatorial system, the other, the zenith-horizon system.

Polar-Equatorial System

Projecting the earth's polar axis and equator onto the celestial sphere gives us a reference system as pictured in Figure 4.2a. Here Pn–Ps designates the polar axis and Q–Q' the equinoctial. The meridian through M is the hour circle through the celestial object M, d is the declination of M. The GHA of M, not shown, would be the hour angle between the hour circle through Greenwich and that through M measured in a westerly direction. The arc MQ represents the declination of M (also indicated as angle at the center of the sphere). The arc MPn is the complement of d (i.e., 90° − d) and is known as the *polar distance* of the body M.

Figure 4.2b gives the same frame of reference but as visualized looking down from the pole. Here the radial lines from Pn to G, ♈, and M are the hour circles through Greenwich, Aries, and the body M. The GHA of M is the GHA♈ plus the SHA of M.

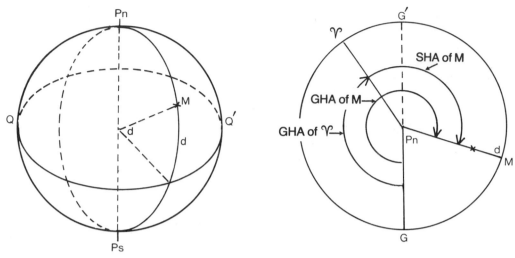

Figure 4.2a   Polar system   *Figure 4.2b*   Polar system

Zenith System

In the zenith system we are oriented on the zenith-nadir axis. In Figure 4.3a, HH' is a great circle inscribing the horizon. All great circles passing through the zenith and the nadir are perpendicular to the horizon and are known as *vertical circles*. Hence the altitude h of the body M above the horizon HH' is measured along the vertical circle through M. The complement of the altitude of M is the *coaltitude* of M. As presented in Figure 4.3a the perimeter of the circle through PnZHH' is the great circle through the poles, zenith, and the east and west horizon points. That being the case, the arc ZQ' is the latitude of Z. This is simply the altitude of the zenith above the equatorial plane QQ'. The complement of this latitude is the zenith distance, i.e., the distance of the zenith from the pole.

Figure 4.3b shows the view from the zenith. Pn is the north pole. The angle between the meridian through Pn and the vertical circle through M is the *true azimuth* of M (i.e., the true bearing of M at Z).

FUNDAMENTAL NAVIGATIONAL TRIANGLE

Combining the polar frame with its equinoctial plane and the zenith frame with the horizontal plane now gives us the fundamental navigational triangle. Figure 4.4 shows how the triangle is constructed. The hour circle through the pole Pn, the zenith Z, and the pole Ps is the observer's meridian or hour circle. The arc from Z to the equinoctial Q–Q' is the latitude of the observer. The great circle from zenith Z through the body M is the vertical circle of the body. The arc MH from the horizon to the body is the altitude of M. The arc MZ is the complement of MH, and is known as the coaltitude of M (also known as the *zenith distance* of M). It is along this arc MZ that the true bearing of M from Z is measured. Finally, the vertical meridian through M and the celestial poles is the hour circle through the body. The arc from the equinoctial to M is the declination of M and the arc MPn is the polar distance of M, or its codeclination. Figure 4.5 shows the same triangle without the details of the reference systems. We now have a spherical triangle with three sides and three interior angles:

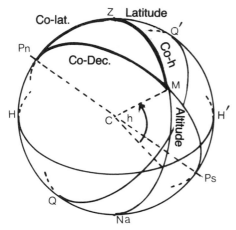

Figure 4.3a   Zenith system

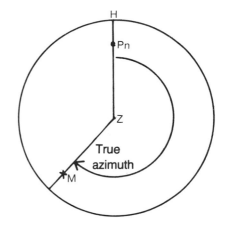

Figure 4.3b   Zenith system

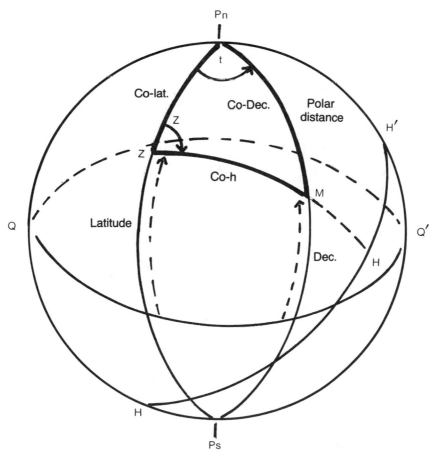

Figure 4.4   Navigational triangle

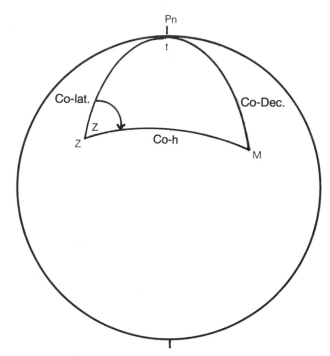

Figure 4.5   Navigational triangle

Sides: (1) PnZ = colatitude, or zenith distance
              (2) ZM = coaltitude, or 90° − altitude
              (3) PnM = codeclination, or polar distance

Angles:
              (1) ZPnM (t):   meridian angle, the hour angle between the observer at Z and the body M
              (2) PnZM (Z):   azimuth angle between M and Z
              (3) PnMZ: parallactic angle, hour angle between Z and P as seen from M (of no navigational interest)

The spherical triangle in Figure 4.5 differs from a plane Euclidean triangle in that, for the sides, arc now replaces simple linear measure. Where it is relevant to convert arc to distance it is possible to do so by taking one minute of arc as equal to one nautical mile upon the earth's surface.

We know from the laws of trigonometry (the law of cosines and the law of sines) that if any two sides and their included angle are known then we can solve for the remaining side and two angles. This applies both to plane and spherical triangles.

Consider, now, the case where we can specify the coordinates for Z and M in Figure 4.4. From the given coordinates of our zenith position Z we know the value of the colatitude. And from the given coordinates from the body M, we know the value of the codeclination, or the polar distance, of M. The difference in longitudinal measures of Z and M respectively gives us the hour angle between the two, or, as it is usually called, the meridian angle t. By virtue of the laws of trigonometry it is now possible to solve for the remaining side, coaltitude, and for the zenith angle z of M from Z. In the mathematical argument,

$$\cos(\text{co-h}) = \cos(\text{co-L}) \times \cos(\text{co-Dec.}) + \sin(\text{co-L}) \times$$
$$\sin(\text{co-Dec.}) \times \cos t \qquad\qquad \text{(Formula 4.1)}$$

and

$$\sin z = \frac{\sin(\text{co-Dec.})}{\sin(\text{co-h})} \times \sin t \qquad\qquad \text{(Formula 4.2)}$$

For actual computations these formulae shall be transposed into more manageable form(see Chapter 5). However, it is clear that the coaltitude of M at Z (and hence the altitude) and also the azimuth angle of M from Z can be determined once we specify the positional coordinates of our zenith Z and the body M. The positional coordinates for Z are determined by our specifying the latitude and longitude of an assumed position of observation, namely some point close to our DR position. The positional coordinates of M are simply the GHA and declination of that body as determined from the *Nautical Almanac* for the time of observation.

However, we do run into a bit of a puzzle here. Our purpose in utilizing celestial navigation is to make a precise determination of our position, *not* to assume it. We would like an accurate determination of the coordinates of our zenith position Z, yet we begin by assuming what those coordinates are. How do we get from an assumed to a corrected actual position?

INFERRING POSITION FROM SEXTANT OBSERVATION

Before proceeding, we should again be reminded of the congruence of our celestial and terrestrial coordinate systems. As we have seen, for angles, arcs, and vertices on the celestial triangle there are congruent angles and vertices on the terrestrial sphere. Strict congruence breaks down only when we compare arc on the earth's surface with that on the celestial sphere. The earth has a finite radius and circumference, one minute of arc (1/21,600th of the circumference of the earth) is one nautical mile by definition (i.e., 6,076.1 feet). For all practical purposes the radius and circumference of the celestial sphere are infinite and a minute of arc on the celestial sphere would itself expand to an infinite distance.

Table 4.1 summarizes the congruence of the terrestrial and celestial spheres.

Table 4.1
Congruence of Triangles

	Terrestrial	*Celestial*
Vertices	Poles, Pn, Ps	Elevated poles, Pn, Ps
	Assumed position, AP	Zenith position, Z
	Geographical position, GP	Celestial position, M
Angles	Hour angle, *HA*	Meridian angle, t
	Azimuth angle, Z	Azimuth angle, Z
	(not significant)	Parallactic angle
Arcs	Declination of M	Declination, d
	Latitude of observer	Latitude of Z
	Altitude of body	Altitude
	Codeclination	Codeclination
	Colatitude	Colatitude
	Coaltitude	Coaltitude

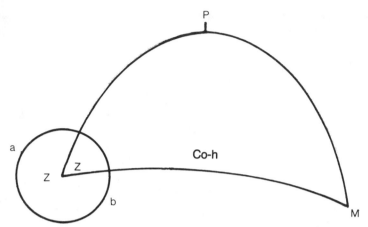

Figure 4.6   Circle of uncertainty about Z or AP

So far as arcs are concerned, the sets of terms for the two systems are interchangeable. There is, however, an important difference between the two. All arcs in the terrestrial system are convertible to distance on the earth's surface, one minute of arc being equal to one nautical mile. Thus, if we know the altitude of a body at a position corresponding to Z, and, therefore, the coaltitude, we would then know the distance between AP and GP.

The actual procedure for plotting a position line does not, however, rely upon a simple interpretation of coaltitude. Rather, we begin by assuming a position near or about our DR position at the time of observing a celestial body. Since this assumed position is merely an approximation we will want to correct or adjust it for accuracy. We might say that our assumed position is surrounded by an aura of uncertainty as in Figure 4.6. This figure duplicates Figure 4.5 except that a circle of uncertainty is inscribed about the assumed position of Z. We have acknowledged our uncertainty, but by specifying a definite set of coordinates for assumed position we obtain provisional values for colatitude and meridian angle t. These two values coupled with knowledge of declination of the observed body enable us to compute the coaltitude, hence altitude and azimuth angle, of that body as it would be observed at the assumed position. Now if our actual sextant observation is not identical with our computed altitude we are at least assured of one thing: we are not, then, precisely at our assumed position. The observed altitude may be greater, or it may be less, than our computed altitude. By how much is a matter of arc, and this arc can be translated into terrestrial distance. Knowledge of this difference in arc between a computed and an observed altitude coupled with knowledge of the bearing of the body enables us to strike an improved position, a corrected one, with reference to our assumed position.

The procedure for computing altitude and azimuth of a body at an assumed position is known as *sight reduction*. The various procedures of sight reduction we leave to the following chapter. For the present, let us assume that we know how to compute the altitude of a body for an assumed position at a specified moment of time. Then in taking a celestial observation we would have the following:

1. the computed altitude Hc of an observed body, at an assumed position;
2. a computed azimuth angle Z, hence a true azimuth, of the body at the assumed position; and

3. the observed altitude Ho of the body at the time that figures into the computation of 1. and 2. (Ho being the sextant altitude, hs, adjusted for essential corrections).

With this information we now may move from uncertainty of position to a degree of certainty. How this is done represents one of the more ingenious innovations in all of navigation.

LINE OF POSITION: METHOD OF MARCQ ST. HILAIRE

The altitude-intercept method for plotting a line of position was introduced in 1875 by the French navigator Marcq St. Hilaire and has come to dominate all other means for plotting celestial lines of position. In brief, if we know what the altitude and true azimuth of a given body are at our assumed position then our actual observation tells us where we are with respect to that assumed position.

First we need the notion of the intercept. And from that we proceed to circles of equal altitude and the line of position as such.

Intercept

Consider again the circle of uncertainty about Z as presented in Figure 4.6. Keeping position by dead reckoning leads us to specify coordinates for Z. However, we are uncertain of our DR position; so, let us make a generous allowance for error. We can be anywhere within the circle of uncertainty (a circle of 1° might be ample allowance). For example, we might be at a point corresponding to a in Figure 4.6, or at one corresponding to b. We don't know. However, by taking an assumed position Z we can calculate an altitude Hc for the observed body and its true azimuth. Now, if we are at point a or if we are at point b or if we are at any other point, that fact will be revealed by our actual sextant observation. Suppose we are actually at position a. Then our actual coaltitude would be greater than our computed one. This in turn means the altitude Ho of M as observed at a will be less than the altitude Hc as computed for the assumed position at Z. By a similar rationale, if we were actually at b, our coaltitude would be shortened and our observed altitude Ho would be greater than the computed Hc.

Figure 4.7 shows this relationship of altitude to distance from GP, the substellar point of the observed body. As in other great-circle segments in the earth's surface, arc-angle converts to distance on the basis of one minute of arc equalling one nautical mile. Hence, the difference between the computed Hc and the observed Ho translates into distance: a difference in altitude of one minute means a difference in distance of one nautical mile as measured along the true azimuth of the body (*cf*. Note 4.1).

The difference *a* between the observed altitude Ho and the computed altitude Hc is known as the *intercept* of the body. If Ho is greater than Hc (altitude ht) the observer is closer to the GP of the observed body M than is the assumed position. The intercept is toward (T) the body M and is so indicated for plotting. On the other hand, if Ho is less than Hc (altitude ha) the observer is farther away: the intercept is away (A) and is so indicated for plotting, all plotting being done along the true azimuth.

In summary, then, our procedure is clear:

1. Assume a position (corresponding to Z in the celestial triangle) on the basis of our DR position.

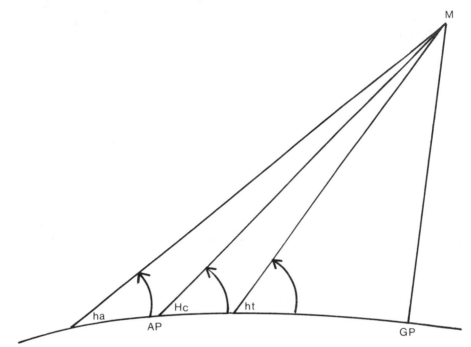

Figure 4.7   Altitude away or toward the body

2. Compute the altitude Hc and the true azimuth Zn of the observed celestial body.
3. Compare Hc (computed altitude) and Ho (observed altitude) to determine the intercept:
   a. if Ho > Hc, the intercept is *toward, a*T,
   b. if Ho < Hc, the intercept is *away, a*A.
4. The magnitude of the intercept indicates distance, one minute of altitude being equal to one mile of distance.
5. The actual plot is to be made from the assumed position with the intercept being struck along the axis of the true azimuth of the body.

The translation of intercept into position, however, is not quite so simple as we have laid it out. We cannot pinpoint our position with a single intercept. For any given intercept there is a host of positions compatible with that intercept.

Our situation is complicated by the fact that whereas we are sure of the position of the celestial body M at the time of our observation, we cannot be sure of the true zenith position Z. Hence, we cannot be sure that the computed true azimuth is indeed the true azimuth of M from our actual position. The intercept orients us with respect to an assumed position, but there are many other points, i.e., other positions, compatible with our computed Hc. And there are many points on the earth's surface compatible with the actual observation Ho. Thus the intercept, Ho − Hc, does not specify a single point. Rather it indicates a set of points which generate a line of position.

Circles of Equal Altitude
The computation of Hc and Zn is associated with the unique specification of our zenith

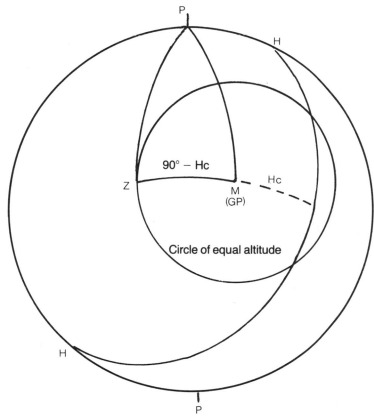

Figure 4.8 Circle of equal altitude

Z. If the true azimuth Zn were unknown or doubtful then we would find a whole set of locations on the earth's surface where the altitude of M at the time of observation would be identical. These locations, the locus of all positions observing the same altitude, are known as a circle of equal altitude.

We can illustrate the circle of equal altitude in one of two ways. In Figure 4.8, a circle of equal altitude has the GP below M as its center with the coaltitude as its radius. The circle passes through Z, but any other position on the circle will yield an altitude of M equal to Hc. (Note that the radius of the circle of equal altitude is 90 − Hc, the coaltitude, and not Hc itself. The greater the altitude, the closer the observer is to the geographic point directly beneath the body.) In Figure 4.9, we visualize the locus of all points yielding an altitude of M equal to Hc. For each point in the series of all points yielding the altitude Hc there is a horizon line associated with it. The set of all such horizon lines then forms a cone that is tangent to the earth at the circle of equal altitude. Thus we visualize two surfaces: one, the cylinder of parallel rays all of which strike the earth at an equal angle, and two, the cone of horizon lines. The intersection of these two surfaces occurs with the angle Hc and defines our circle of equal altitude.

Up to this point we have discussed circles of equal altitude only with respect to computed altitudes. It may occur to the reader that if we locate GP at the time of an observation then we can draw a circle of equal altitude utilizing our observed altitude to

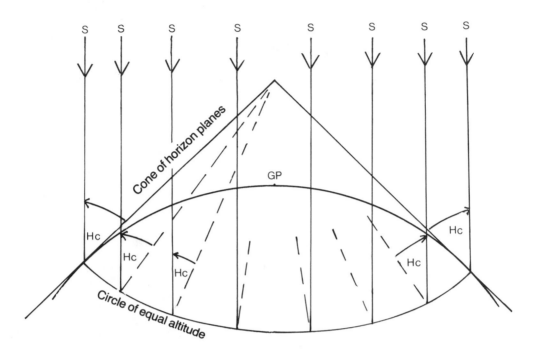

Figure 4.9 Circle of equal altitude

determine its radius (radius = coaltitude). We could then locate our position somewhere on that circle. This would indeed be a simple and valid procedure, but the small scale necessitated by the great distances involved would make that procedure imprecise.

Lines of Position

In celestial navigation an LOP is generally a segment of a circle of equal altitude. Since the radius of such a circle under most conditions of observation is of considerable magnitude any segment of the circle can be represented accurately by a straight line tangent to the circle. Thus, if we know the true azimuth of the GP of our body, we may plot that true azimuth as a segment of the radius intersecting our assumed position. A segment of a circle of equal altitude, an LOP, can then be presented by constructing a line perpendicular to the true azimuth at a point compatible with our assumed position AP and the intercept as obtained by comparing Ho and Hc.

The procedure for plotting an LOP is shown in Figure 4.10. At the assumed position AP in the terrestrial coordinates the true azimuth line is struck in the direction of GP. A line perpendicular to the true azimuth can be constructed at AP (in this case the broken line Hc). This, however, is unnecessary and is presented here only as a reference line. The actual LOP is constructed at a point determined by the intercept.

For purposes of exemplification, two LOP's are shown in Figure 4.10, one with an intercept aT, where Ho > Hc, and the other with an intercept aA, where Ho < Hc. The broken line is the segment of the circle of equal altitude for Hc as computed. In practice, the line for Hc is never plotted. It serves only as the reference point for striking the intercept along the true azimuth Zn.

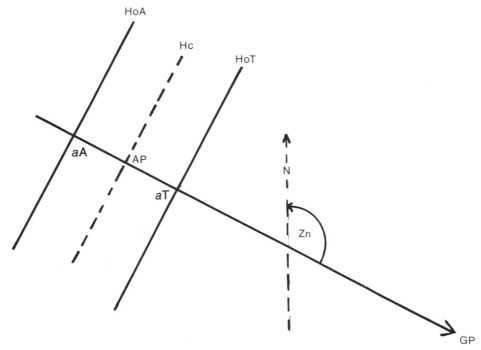

Figure 4.10 LOP's and intercepts

The actual plot of our LOP is done in the following manner. Through the assumed position corresponding to our zenith Z we plot a segment of the true azimuth Zn, of M from Z. At the point Z (our AP) on Zn we locate the intersection of the circle of equal altitude, Hc (the broken line in Figure 4.10). From that point we strike the distance of the intercept, away or toward, as the case may be, along the true azimuth line. At the extremity of the intercept, we construct a line perpendicular to the true azimuth of the body. This is our line of position, a segment of the circle of equal altitude corresponding to Ho.

In summary, then, a sextant observation yields an observed altitude Ho. For the time of the observation we determine an assumed position compatible with our DR. With knowledge of time, AP, and GP, we can compute the altitude Hc and the true azimuth Zn (Chapter 5). Comparing Ho and Hc gives us the intercept *a*. At the extremity of the intercept we construct an LOP perpendicular to Zn. If Ho > Hc the LOP is plotted in the direction toward the GP, as in the case of HoT in Figure 4.10. If Ho < Hc, the LOP is plotted away from the GP as in the case of HoA in Figure 4.10 (*cf.* Note 4.2).

Before turning to the actual computations of Hc and Zn, there are two matters that call for qualification. In the one matter, recall that Z designates the zenith (or AP) and/or the azimuth angle, and Zn designates true azimuth. They should not be confused. Moreover, Z, azimuth angle, is not always identical with true azimuth, Zn, as in fact they are in Figures 4.4 and 4.5. Azimuth angle is always measured within the navigation triangle and may or may not be identical to true azimuth, which is always measured as a true bearing from true north. The conversion of Z to Zn will be fully covered in Chapter 5.

In the second matter, that of comparing Ho and Hc to obtain the intercept, we have Ho as our observed altitude, the observation being taken with a sextant. As we shall see, one needs to apply several corrections to the sextant altitude hs in order to obtain the legitimate Ho. That is to say, Ho is sextant altitude hs, corrected for error. Sextant error may include instrument error, personal error, and systematic error, all of which are discussed in Chapter 6.

The Celestial Fix
One further note—a single LOP will not give us a fix. All it tells us is that our position is to be located somewhere on the LOP. It might be reasonable to assume that we are somewhere along that line within some brackets of uncertainty. However, we may "fix" our position, as it were, by taking an observation on another body, determining a line of position for it, and then locating our position at the intersection of the two LOP's.

Such an intersection of LOP's does not result in a unique determination of position. As we see in Figure 4.11, two circles of equal altitude intersect at two nodal points, AB1 and AB2. However, the distances between the two points are so great that our DR position would definitely favor one over the other. The routine for plotting such fixes is described in Chapter 10.

Summary for Plotting the LOP
The steps in plotting an LOP are as follows:

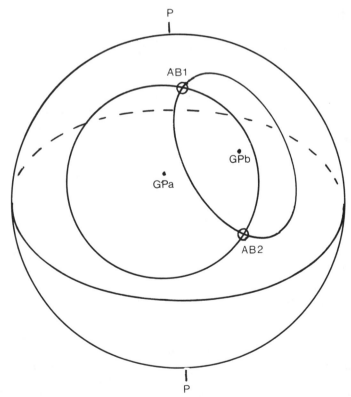

Figure 4.11   Celestial fix, the intersection of two LOP's

1. A sextant observation yielding an observed altitude Ho is made at a precise moment GMT.
2. For that time, a best estimate of position, DR, is made (i.e., our assumed position). This is taken as the assumed position corresponding to Z in the celestial triangle and yields an assumed longitude $a\lambda$ and an assumed latitude aL.
3. For the appropriate GMT, the GHA of the body and its declination are found in the *Nautical Almanac*.
4. Meridian angle t is found by comparing our assumed longitude $a\lambda$ and the GHA of the body.
5. From the above we obtain the following: colatitude ($90° - a$L), declination, and meridian angle t. These constitute two sides and the included angle of our navigational triangle.
6. From knowledge of 5. above we calculate Hc and Z.
7. With a knowledge of Ho, Hc, and Zn, we plot a line of position (LOP) with respect to our assumed position at Z.

Note that under point 5., we have simply indicated that the computation on Hc and Z follows from the prerequisite information. There are a number of ways that the computation can be made. One is by solving the fundamental trigonometric formulae, the method preferred throughout this work; most others are by recourse to various sight reduction tables. In recent times, the use of sight reduction tables has dominated nearly all of celestial navigation. However, with the advent of inexpensive calculators, solution by direct computation reasserts itself as the most accurate and most convenient method for deriving Hc and Zn. It is to direct computation we now turn, leaving the discussion of sight reduction tables as an addendum.

NOTES

Note 4.1

One nautical mile (1,852 meters or 6,076.1 feet) is defined as being equal to one minute of arc on a great circle of the earth's surface. Since there are 60' in 1°, the earth's circumference would be 60' × 360° or 21,600'. (Actually the earth is something of an oblate spheroid, its equatorial diameter being approximately 23 miles longer than its polar diameter. The circumference of the earth in the equatorial plane is actually 21,639 nautical miles.)

Since Z and M in Figure 4.4 readily convert to AP and GP on the earth's surface it should be apparent that the arc-angle measure of altitude translates into a measure of distance, a minute of arc being equal to one nautical mile.

This relation of arc-angle to distance can be made more explicit by referring to Figures 4.12 and 4.13. First, we note that the altitude and coaltitude measures in the navigational triangle, Figure 4.4, have the center of the earth as their origin (also in Figure 4.3a). As obtained from a sextant observation, altitude is measured at the surface of the earth beneath the zenith position. In Figure 4.12 we show that for a stellar source the light rays can be considered parallel between the center and the periphery of the earth. This is because of the very great distances of stellar objects. Ha represents the observer's apparent horizon beneath his zenith, and He the actual horizon plane at the center of the earth. Because the light rays from the source S are considered parallel, then the altitude Ha as measured on the surface of the earth is identical to the altitude He as measured at the center of the earth. (For relatively nearby objects, such as the moon, the two altitudes will not be identical. The difference between Ha and He in such a case is known as parallax.)

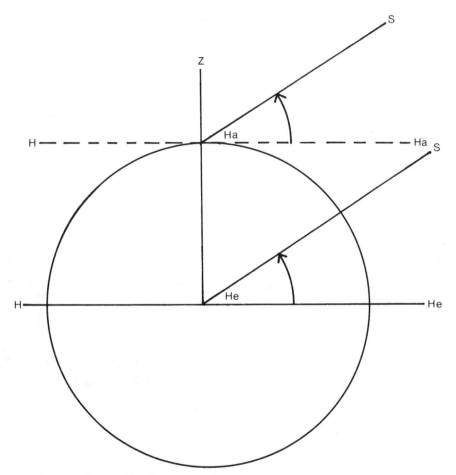

Figure 4.12   Equality of altitude: zero parallax

The relation of angle measured at the center of the earth to altitude measured at the surface of the earth is shown in Figure 4.13. Since the rays from the stellar source are considered parallel, angles a, a + b, etc., are equal as between the center and the surface of the earth. For convenience we show the star as one with zero declination. If we were located at the equator the altitude of S at transit of our meridian would be 90°. Should we move our location to a latitude of a° the measured altitude would be 90° − a° and our coaltitude would be a°. If our latitude is (a + b)°, the altitude will be 90° − (a + b)° and our coaltitude will be (a + b)°, and so on. Note, however, that the identity of latitude and coaltitude exists only because we have taken the liberty of selecting S at zero declination. Generally, we are observing bodies with non-zero declination and we cannot infer latitude directly from an altitude observation.

Note 4.2
Another way, graphically, to conceive of the intercept and line of position is presented in Figure 4.14.

Here the circle of equal altitude for Hc intersects the circle of our uncertainty that circumscribes Z. Our uncertainty as to position means, of course, we can be anywhere within our circle of uncertainty. Suppose now Ho − Hc = +a. Within the circle of uncertainty we could be at a1 or a2 or anywhere along the set of intervening points. If our intercept is +a then the line through a1 and

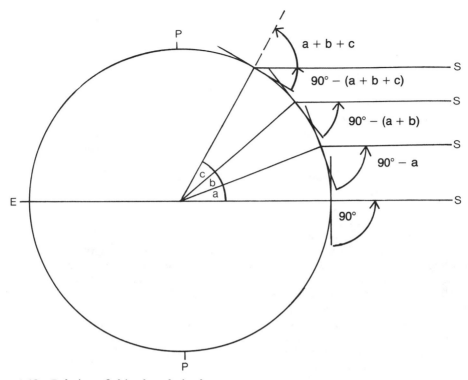

Figure 4.13 Relation of altitude to latitude

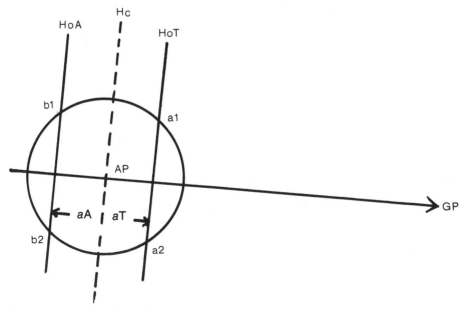

Figure 4.14 Intercept and the circle of uncertainty

a2 represents a line of position, i.e., a segment of the adjusted circle of equal latitude. And, *mutatis mutandis,* the line through b1 and b2 is the line of position for an intercept Ho − Hc = −b. There is nothing particularly objectionable about this way of combining uncertainty with certainty but the standard procedure of crossing different LOP's eliminates the factor of uncertainty as to where the observer is on a single LOP.

The line of position is said to have been discovered by Captain Thomas H. Sumner in 1837, hence the term *Sumner line* for LOP. At that time it was customary to compute longitude on the basis of an accurate timing of an observation. That computation depended on accurate knowledge of latitude. As Captain Sumner reports the discovery, he was approaching the English coast, his position uncertain and the sky overcast. As the sun broke through momentarily, he took an observation. With an assumed latitude he computed his longitude. Since he was uncertain of his latitude, he tried two other latitudes, much as if he were operating within his own circle of uncertainty. For each of the three latitudes he was able to compute a longitude. When he plotted these three geographic points, each with an assumed latitude and a computed longitude, lo! he found them to lie on a straight line. And sailing down this line to intercept the coast he was able to make a nicely foreseeable landfall.

As it happened, the three points that Captain Sumner plotted lay in a straight line toward his landfall-destination. That was a bit of luck. Assuming three different latitudes and computing the longitudes, from time and altitude, he obtained three positions each of which yielded the same true course to his destination. There was a bit of serendipity involved. The three points need not have aligned themselves on the track toward destination. What Sumner discovered in his good fortune was the line of equal altitude. By creating the situation in which assumed latitudes and their respective computed longitudes had to be compatible with an observed altitude, he did, in fact, construct a segment of a line of equal altitude, that is to say, an LOP.

CHAPTER FIVE

Sight Reduction

In general sight reduction is the procedure by which we compare an observed altitude of a celestial body with a computed altitude of that body for an assumed position; the difference between the two altitudes will be the basis for plotting a line of position. Plotting a celestial line of position always involves a sextant observation, but the core of sight reduction is the method for computing an altitude of a celestial body for a given time at a given position.

Were we to consult a reference work such as *Bowditch* we would find a great number of methods of sight reduction, many of which would be only of historical interest. By and large, however, these methods can be divided into two classes: one, those involving tables of precomputed solutions of altitude and azimuth, and two, those involving direct computation of the basic trigonometric formulae. Until fairly recently, the use of sight reduction tables such as *H. O. 229* and *H. O. 249* had dominated all other methods. However, the perfection of the modern hand calculator, the more inexpensive ones being a fraction of the cost of a set of *H. O. 229* tables, has rendered the direct computation of basic trigonometric formulae both feasible and advantageous.

The reader familiar with logarithms knows that their manipulation can be cumbersome if both multiplication-division and addition-subtraction are involved. In the past, methods such as that of haversines (*cf.* Note 5.1) were improvised to circumvent some of the computational difficulties. However, the modern calculator handles all computations according to an easy routine of sequential operations. The present-day navigator equipped with an inexpensive calculator can now carry out his sight reduction computations with a speed, economy, and generality surpassing those implicit in any of the traditional tabular routines (*cf.* Note 5.2).

In this book, direct computation of trigonometric formulae will be emphasized throughout, and the computations will require nothing more than a hand calculator that can perform trigonometric functions. A brief discussion of sight reduction by means of *H. O. 249* tables is included as an addendum.

SOLVING FOR Hc AND Z

The two quantities solved for by either direct computation or tabular sight reduction are the computed altitude Hc and the azimuth angle Z. The basic formulae for direct computation are:

$$\sin Hc = \sin L \sin d + \cos L \cos d \cos t \qquad \text{(Formula 5.1)}$$

and

$$\cos Z = \frac{\sin d - \sin L \sin Hc}{\cos L \cos Hc} \qquad \text{(Formula 5.2)}$$

where L, d, and t are latitude, declination, and meridian angle, respectively (for basic concepts in trigonometry see Note 5.3).

Note that these two formulae differ from Formulae 4.1 and 4.2 given in the previous chapter. In the first place, the latter formulae involve colatitude, codeclination, and coaltitude as directly incorporated into the nautical triangle, Figure 5.1. On the other hand Formula 5.1 involves latitude and declination directly. It is derived from Formula 4.1 by virtue of the basic trigonometric relationships:

$$\sin \alpha = \cos (90° - \alpha)$$
$$\cos \alpha = \sin (90° - \alpha)$$

In other words the sine of a function is identical with the cosine of its complementary or cofunction, and vice versa (see Note 5.4 for some details on derivations).

In the second place, Formula 5.2 represents a different derivation than Formula 4.2 of the preceding chapter. Mathematically, Formula 5.2 represents an application of the law of cosines whereas Formula 4.2 is an application of the law of sines. Utilizing the law of sines, an alternative solution for Z is:

$$\sin Z = \frac{\sin t \cos d}{\cos Hc} \qquad \text{(Formula 5.3)}$$

and if that is not enough there is still another alternative:

$$\tan Z = \frac{\sin LHA}{\cos L \tan d - \sin L \cos LHA} \qquad \text{(Formula 5.4)}$$

At first glance Formula 5.3 might be preferred to Formula 5.2 for computing Z—fewer terms, fewer operations. However, Formula 5.2 has an important advantage and should be the preferred one. The sine of the angle α is identical with the sine of the angle $180° - \alpha$! Hence in solving for sine Z in Formula 5.3 we obtain a value that holds for Z and for $180° - Z$. Thus there is a possible ambiguity.* That is not the case for cosines. The cosine of the angle $180° - \alpha$ will be opposite in sign to the cosine of the angle α.

Note that your calculator will give you the smallest angle for which a function holds; i.e., the angle α, not $180° - \alpha$ in the case of sines.

There is one case where Formula 5.4 is the preferred one. That is when the navigator wishes to determine an azimuth when only time (for HA), latitude, and declination are considered. Such is the case, for example, when he wishes to plot a curve of true azimuths against time to be used in determining compass error by virtue of bearings on the sun (see Chapter 9, Note 9.1).

As in the case of sines, the tangent of the angle α is equal numerically to the tangent of angle $180° - \alpha$; but unlike the case of sines, it will be opposite in value; i.e., $\tan \alpha = - \tan (180° - \alpha)$. In using Formula 5.4, if Z as computed on your calculator is negative, simply subtract the value from 180°. For example, if the computed Z is $-50°$, the actual Z in the nautical triangle is 130°.

---

*The angles α and $180° - \alpha$ are known as supplementary angles. The ambiguity of supplements is avoided in the case of Formula 5.2. It is also avoided in Formula 5.4. But note that LHA is not always identical with the meridian angle t. LHA is always measured westerly and therefore can exceed 180°. The angle t like LHA is also measured between meridians passing through Z and M, but measured east or west to 180°.

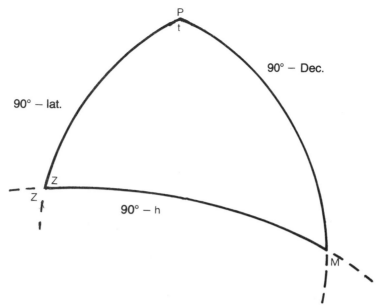

Figure 5.1 Navigational triangle

Computational Procedures
The navigator can proceed by directly computing Hc and Z from Formulae 5.1 and 5.2. Without the aid of a calculator he could do this with the help of tables of the logarithms of trigonometric functions. Indeed, this was the basic method prior to the development of comprehensive sight reduction tables. However, the pencil-and-paper computations are cumbersome: the arithmetic manipulations themselves are detailed and subject to error; but more important, although logarithms facilitate the operations of multiplication, division, and exponentials, they are of no help in addition and subtraction. Therefore, solving for Hc (Formula 5.1) would involve two separate operations: first, those involving multiplication and division in which logarithms could be used, and second, those involving addition and subtraction carried out solely by basic arithmetic. One need only try his hand at the traditional method to show how time-consuming the computations are.

Computation by Basic Calculator
As we have indicated, modern calculator technology has rendered both direct computation (as above) and the use of sight reduction tables nearly obsolete. Some calculators, the relatively expensive ones, have internal programs such that a few basic entries are made and presto! Hc or Z spills out. But the advantages are minimal and the navigator can get by very well with a basic math and science calculator costing a fraction of the price of the more exotic item.

At the outset, note that all angular computations are carried out in decimal notation. Thus all odd minutes of arc must be converted to decimals by dividing those odd minutes by 60. This can easily be done on the calculator, and, with practice, the conversions are often done mentally. Conversion to decimals and reconversion of decimals to odd minutes of arc therefore become routine.

We should also take note of the bracketing operation of the calculator. All computations are carried out sequentially. But those involving separate multiplication or division operations are bracketed off from those involving addition or subtraction. The simplest of examples follows. As written here, the simple formula:

$a + b \times c$

is ambiguous. For clearly,

$(a + b) \times c$

is not the same as

$a + (b \times c)$

The parentheses eliminate the ambiguity.

The calculator includes keys for parentheses within its set of operator keys. Therefore, it is always helpful to visualize the computational formula with appropriate sets of parenthetical or bracket operations. Hence Formula 5.1 is rendered explicit for the calculator:

$$Hc = \sin^{-1} [(\sin L \sin d) + (\cos L \cos d \cos t)] \qquad \text{(Formula 5.1′)}$$

The overall brackets inform the calculator that it is to add the results from the separate calculations specified within the inner brackets. Note also that $\sin^{-1}$ is the notation for the inverse of the sine. This notation indicates that the quantity that follows $\sin^{-1}$ is equal to the sine of Hc.

In a similar vein, we have

$$Z = \cos^{-1} \frac{[(\sin d) - (\sin L \sin Hc)]}{(\cos L \cos Hc)} \qquad \text{(Formula 5.2′)}$$

in which brackets again eliminate any ambiguities involving the conjunction of multiplication-division with addition-subtraction.

We do not intend in this discussion to provide a manual for the use of the calculator. Many readers will already be familiar with the use of basic calculators, and the manuals accompanying the purchase of any of the suitable calculators (Texas Instruments, Casio, Sharp, Hewlett-Packard, etc.) will prove sufficient to indoctrinate the beginner in their use. However, as a preview to actual computational exercises, we draw attention to some features of our basic calculators. The display in Figure 5.2 is much like that of any of the inexpensive calculators that include trigonometric functions. One set of keys provides for numerical data entries; another, for trig functions such as sin, cos, tan; and yet another set, for operations such as add $(+)$, subtract $(-)$, multiply $(\times)$, and divide $(\div)$. Still another set can be said to deal with logical operations such as bracketing and memory instructions, STO, RCL, and getting the inverse of a function INV. In our navigation problems we shall utilize but a small part of our calculator's total capability. We shall make data entries, transform them according to trigonometric functions, and multiply-divide and add-subtract according to the sequences and enclosures provided for by bracketing. Our answers are usually obtained by finding the angle which is the inverse of a trigonometric function.

Computational Example: Utilizing a DR position, the time of observation, and the *Nautical Almanac*, we start with the following information:

Figure 5.2   Typical calculator keyboard

	Given	*Decimal Conversion*
t	= 40°30′	40.5°
d	= 10°36′N	10.6°N
L	= 20°40′N	20.67°N

Wanted: the computed altitude Hc and the azimuth angle Z. Applying Formula 5.1′ our procedure is as follows:

Step	Entry	Remarks	Step	Entry	Remarks
1	(	overall bracket	11	20.67	for L
2	(	first operation starts	12	cos	
3	20.67	for latitude L	13	×	multiply
4	sin		14	10.6	for d
5	×	multiply	15	cos	
6	10.6	for declination d	16	×	multiply
7	sin		17	40.5	for t
8	)	first operation closed	18	cos	
9	+	add second operation	19	)	second operation closed
10	(	second operation starts	20	)	overall bracket

By closing the double brackets, Step 20, we obtain the solution as expressed in the quantity on the right-hand side of Formula 5.1′. This result gives us the sine of the altitude Hc. To get Hc as such, we continue:

21	INV
22	sin

The display now reads 49.84°, or, converting to the odd minutes, we obtain 49°50.4′.
And solving for Z by virtue of Formula 5.2′ we have the following:

Step	Entry	Remarks	Step	Entry	Remarks
1	(		14	)	completes the numerator
2	(		15	÷	dividing by what follows
3	10.6	for d	16	(	
4	sin		17	20.67	for L
5	)		18	cos	
6	−	subtract	19	×	multiply
7	(		20	49.84	for Hc
8	20.67	for L	21	cos	
9	sin		22	)	completes the denominator
10	×	multiply	23	=	completes the division
11	49.84	for Hc	24	INV	
12	sin		25	cos	
13	)				

The display now gives the value of Z, namely, 98.18°.

TRUE AZIMUTH Zn FROM AZIMUTH ANGLE Z

Azimuth angle Z as computed via Formula 5.2 is the angle at the zenith between the observer's meridian and the vertical circle through the observed body. Only in special circumstances (as in Figure 5.1) will Z be identical with the true azimuth, i.e., the true bearing of the body M from the observer at Z. And keep in mind that it is the true azimuth Zn that we need in plotting our line of position.

---

*Meridian angle at the pole has been treated in three ways: (1) as angle t undifferentiated as to direction, (2) as hour angle *HA* which is differentiated as to east or west from the observer's meridian, and (3) as local hour angle LHA measured west through 360°. Meridian angle t is invariably utilized in computational formulae but *HA* or LHA have been used for various sight reduction tables.

Figure 5.3 presents the four possible spherical triangles that relate to celestial observations. In each case the pole which serves as the polar vertex is determined by the observer's latitude. The other factor which differentiates among the cases is the hour angle: east, if the body is rising, west, if it is past culmination and setting.* From the four cases in Figure 5.3, we can readily see:

$$\text{Case 1} \quad Zn = Z$$
$$\text{Case 2} \quad Zn = 180° - Z$$
$$\text{Case 3} \quad Zn = 180° + Z$$
$$\text{Case 4} \quad Zn = 360° - Z$$

These four cases can be codified into a set of rules to be found in all sight reduction tables.

For north latitude:

If HA is E (i.e., LHA > 180°) then Zn = Z
If HA is W (i.e., LHA < 180°) then Zn = 360° - Z

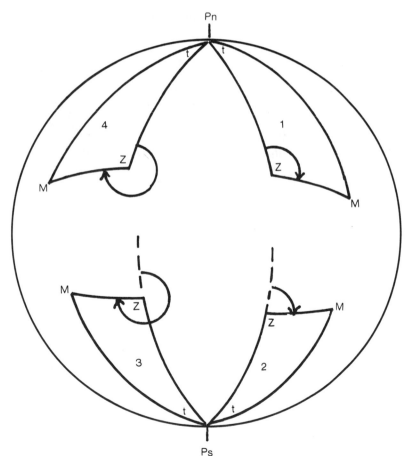

Figure 5.3 Four navigational triangles and true azimuths

For south latitude:

If HA is E (i.e., LHA $> 180°$) then Zn $= 180° - Z$
If HA is W (i.e., LHA $< 180°$) then Zn $= 180° + Z$

Again, Formulae 5.2, 5.3, and 5.4 all give us the azimuth angle Z. For plotting we must always use true azimuth Zn.

General Rules for Computation

In the foregoing example the observer's latitude and the body's declination were the same name (both north) and the entries for L and d were both positive. In the event declination differs in name from latitude then that d entry is negative in value. Making the entry negative is done by pressing the change-of-value key, $\boxed{+/-}$, *not by pressing the negative operator* $\boxed{-}$, which is an instruction to subtract.

In summary, the following rules are to be observed:

1. Latitude L, whose name establishes the polar vertex, and meridian angle t are always entered as positive values.
2. Declination d, if the *same* name as latitude L, is entered as a positive value; if *contrary* in name to L, it is entered as a negative value by means of the change-of-sign key, $\boxed{+/-}$.
3. True azimuth Zn is derived from azimuth angle Z by virtue of the rules given above.

In the following computational examples sight reduction requires our determining Hc and Zn. In each case we need L, d, and t to carry out the calculations. To get the intercept we compare Ho and Hc. For Ho, however, we need to correct sextant altitude hs for various sextant errors. Such corrections are included in the examples, although their explanation follows in Chapter 6.

Example 1: On May 17, 1982, at 22 47 15 GMT we observe the lower limb of the sun. Our DR position at that time is 28°42′N, 118°23′W. Find the computed altitude and true azimuth for plotting an LOP.

From the *Nautical Almanac* (see Figures 3.7 and 3.8):

GHA☉ 22 00	150°55′	
47′15″	11°48.8′	
GHA☉	162°43.8′,	Dec. 19°25′N

Applying our DR position, we obtain the following in decimal notation:

$$t = 162°43.8' - 118°23' = 44°20.8'$$
$$= 44.35°$$
$$d = 19.42°N$$
$$L = 28.70°N$$

Solving for Hc by Formula 5.1, we have:

$$\sin Hc = (\sin 28.7 \sin 19.42) + (\cos 28.7 \cos 19.42 \cos 44.35)$$
$$\sin Hc = 0.751216$$
$$Hc = \sin^{-1} 0.751216$$
$$Hc = 48.70° = 48°42'$$

Solving for Z by Formula 5.2, we have:

$$\cos Z = \frac{(\sin 19.42) - (\sin 28.7 \sin 48.7)}{(\cos 28.7 \cos 48.7)}$$

$$\cos Z = -0.048857$$

$$Z = 92.8°$$

To find the true azimuth Zn, latitude is north and HA is west, hence:

$$Zn = 360° - Z$$
$$= 360° - 92.8° = 267.2°$$

To find our intercept we would first correct the sextant observation hs for dip, index error, limb and refraction errors (see Chapter 6) to obtain the observed altitude Ho. Then we would compare Ho and Hc to arrive at the intercept. (Data for hs and the errors are not included.)

Example 2:   On May 16, 1982, an observation of the moon is taken at 06 46 15 GMT. At the time of the observation the DR position is 46°17′N, 41°15′W. Find Hc and Zn to use in plotting LOP.

From the *Nautical Almanac* (see Figures 3.7 and 3.8):

GHA☾06 00	354°44.3′, Dec.	16°13.4′S
46′15″	11°02.1′	
v/d corr.	+ 09.5′	− 06.7′
	5°56′	16°06.7′S

(v/d corrections for moon are explained in Chapter 3.)

Applying our DR position and converting to decimals:
t = 41°15′ − 5°56′ = 35.32°
d = 16.11°S
L = 46.28°N

Solving for Hc by Formula 5.1:

$$\sin Hc = (\sin 46.28 \sin -16.11) + (\cos 46.28 \cos -16.11 \cos 35.32)$$
$$Hc = \sin^{-1} (0.34123)$$
$$= 19.95°$$
$$= 19°57′$$

Solving for Z by Formula 5.2:

$$\cos Z = \frac{(\sin -16.11) - (\sin 46.28 \sin 19.95)}{(\cos 46.28 \cos 19.95)}$$
$$Z = \cos^{-1} (-0.80669)$$
$$= 143.8°$$

Since we are in north latitude and HA is east, Zn = Z. Hence true azimuth is also 143.8°.

As with the sun, the sextant altitude must be corrected for dip, index error, limb, and refraction. With the moon there is also a correction for parallax. Again, comparing Ho with Hc gives the intercept.

Example 3:   On May 17, 1982, an observation of the star Procyon is made at 20 46 45 GMT. At the time of observation, the DR position is 30°22'N, 19°37'W. Find Hc and Zn.

From the *Nautical Almanac:*

$GHA\Upsilon$ 20 00   175°11.2'
      46'45"   11°43.2'
               186°54.4'
SHA Procyon   245°24.8'
GHA Procyon   72°19.2', Dec. Procyon, 5°16.2'N

Applying our DR position, 30°22'N, 19°37'W:

t = 52°42.2' = 52.70°
d = 5°16.2'N = 5.27°N
L = 30.37°N

Solving for Hc:

sin Hc = (sin 30.37 sin 5.27) + (cos 30.37 cos 5.27 cos 52.70)
   Hc = $\sin^{-1}$ (0.56706)
      = 34.55°
      = 34°33'

Solving for Z:

$$\cos Z = \frac{(\sin 5.27) - (\sin 30.37 \sin 34.55)}{(\cos 30.37 \cos 34.55)}$$

   Z = $\cos^{-1}$ (−0.27424)
     = 105.92'

Since latitude is north and *HA* is west, Zn = 360 − Z, or Zn = 254.08°.

Star observations are corrected for index error, dip, and refraction. Comparing the Ho with the Hc gives the intercept.

Example 4:   On May 18, 1982, at 13 47 30 GMT, we observe the planet Venus prior to local sunrise. Our DR position at that time is 5°33'S, 122°04'W. Find Hc and Zn.

Solution:

GHA Venus 13 00   55°35.2'   Dec. 4°29.7'N
          47' 30"   11°52.5'   (d = 1.0)
v/d corr.   47   −   +0.8'
               67°27.7'   4°30.5'N

Applying our DR position 5°33'S, 122°04'W, we obtain:

  t = 54°36' = 54.6°
  d = 4°30.5'N = 4.51°N
  L = 5°33' = 5.55°S

Solving for Hc by Formula 5.1,

   sin Hc = (sin 5.55 sin −4.51) + (cos 5.55 cos −4.51 cos 54.6)
      Hc = $\sin^{-1}$ (0.56718)
         = 34.55° = 34°33'

Solving for Z by Formula 5.2,

$$\text{Cos } Z = \frac{(\sin -4.51) - (\sin 5.55 \sin 34.55)}{(\cos 5.55 \cos 34.55)}$$
$$Z = \cos^{-1}(-0.16283)$$
$$= 99.37°$$

Our latitude is south and our HA is east; therefore, $Zn = 180 - Z$, or 80.63°. Observations of Venus are corrected for index error, dip, and refraction plus an additional incremental error to be found in the *Nautical Almanac* (see Figure 6.7).

In the writer's opinion the sight reduction methods outlined here are preferred to any others. The reason is that they deal with the uncluttered nautical triangle without recourse to artificial constructions that serve as mathematical conveniences. There is, however, one construction that may indeed simplify computations. Whether it does or not is up to the individual.

Our alternative method of sight reduction involves both partition and construction, which enable us to break the familiar navigational triangle into two right triangles. We thereby will have recourse to Napier's simplifying rules for solving the right spherical triangle when a limited number of parts are known. The procedures are fully discussed in Note 5.5, Alternatives to the Conventional Methods of Computing H and Z. The reader is encouraged to try both methods to see which proves the more convenient.

Addendum on Sight Reduction by *H. O. 249*

Sight reduction by hand calculator has several advantages over that by any of the published tables: one, with practice the use of the hand calculator can be faster; two, it is more economical; three, the calculator is less bulky (e.g., what easily slips into your pocket replaces three volumes of *H. O. 249* or six volumes of *H. O. 229*); and four, and most important, its computational utility permits its use in a variety of navigational problems not covered by a single set of tables.

But regardless of the advantages of the hand calculator, sight reduction tables are in general use. We include a brief description of one such set, *H. O. 249*, doubtless the most popular tables among cruising navigators. (Strangely, *H. O. 249* bears the title *Sight Reduction Tables for Air Navigation* and is preferred over *H. O. 229*, *Sight Reduction Tables for Marine Navigation*. Although the latter tables are carried to greater accuracy, the ritual for interpolation is somewhat more complex than for *H. O. 249*. Furthermore, there are six volumes of *H. O. 229* as against only three of *H. O. 249*.)

Specimen pages of *H. O. 249*, Vols. 1 and 2, are reproduced in Figures 5.4, 5.5, and 5.6. Figure 5.4 is taken from Vol. 2 which can be used for any body within the range 0°–40°. Entry into the tables is made according to latitude, declination, and LHA. Since the overall entries are in whole degrees and since accuracy is contingent upon treating the minutes within the degrees, the greater part of the work in using these tables is taken up in interpolation.

To use these tables, we proceed in the following way:

1. For the time of our observation, GMT, we determine by *Almanac* the GHA and declination of the body.
2. We then compose an assumed position as close as possible to our computed DR position at the time of observation, such that (a) our latitude is a whole degree

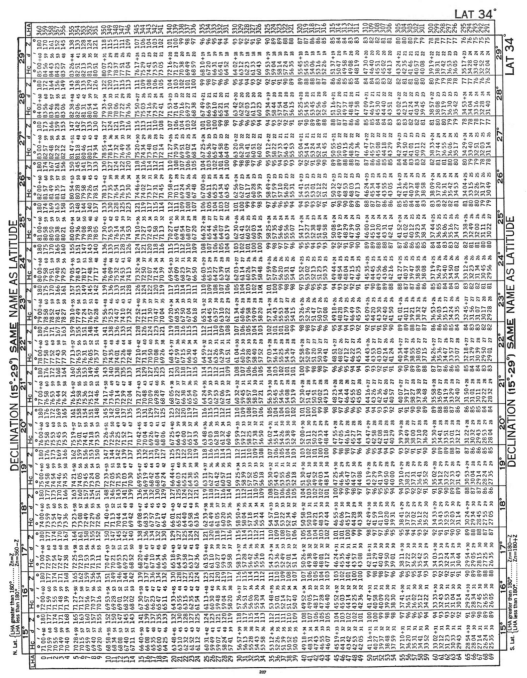

Figure 5.4   Specimen page from *H. O. 249*, Vol. II

and (b) LHA by virtue of LHA = GHA − λ will also be a whole degree. In other words, assume a position such that latitude L is a whole degree, and longitude λ when subtracted from the GHA of the body will yield an LHA which is also a whole degree.

3. Entry is now made into the tables according to (a) latitude, (b) declination whether *same* or *contrary* in name to latitude, and (c) LHA. These are all whole-degree entries.
4. For the appropriate entries in 3. above, withdraw the values for Hc, d, and Z.
5. Interpolate Hc for odd minutes of declination according to Table 5 as reproduced in our Figure 5.5. Note that value d is the increment of change in Hc for adjacent whole degrees of declination, and can be plus or minus according to whether Hc increases or decreases with an increase in declination. To interpolate, enter the horizontal column (') with odd minutes of declination and intersect that row with the vertical column for the appropriate d.
6. Correct the initial value of Hc, step 4., with the value taken from Table 5 (Figure 5.5). (Interpolation for Z, although appropriate, is ignored, since the fractional correction will not affect the position plot to an appreciable extent.)

Example: At the time of our observation of the sun, 19 46 30 GMT, May 17, 1982, our DR position is established as 34°13'N, 126°18'W. Determine altitude and azimuth, Hc and Z, for an appropriately selected assumed position.

From our specimen pages (Figure 3.7), we find:

GMT	GHA	Dec.
19 00	105°55.1'	
46'30"	11°37.5'	19°23'N
	117°32.6'	

Rounding off to nearest unit, and assuming L and λ to give whole-degree entries, we have:

$$L = 34°N$$
$$\lambda = 126°33'W, \text{ giving}$$
$$LHA = GHA - \lambda = 351°$$

Consulting Figure 5.4 with entries LHA = 351° and declination = 19° we obtain:

Hc = 73°00', d = +53, Z = 150°

For the odd minutes of the actual declination at the time of observation, we enter Table 5 (as in Figure 5.5) and for d = +53 and odd minutes of declination (') = 23, we would obtain the correction value of +20' to be added to Hc above. Thus:

$$Hc = 73°20'$$
$$Z = 150°$$
$$Zn = Z = 150°$$

However, an easy interpolation of Z for odd minutes of declination (between Dec. = 19° and Dec. = 20°) is in order. Thus a better determination is Z = 149°.

From the above tabular values, we proceed to plot an LOP by the intercept method comparing Hc and Ho, after correcting for observational errors.

Figure 5.6 presents a specimen page from *H. O. 249,* Vol. 1. This volume deals with selected stars for stellar observations. Again the navigator chooses a convenient assumed position close to his actual DR position, only this time he selects his assumed longitude $a\lambda$ such as to give a whole degree of LHA♈ where:

$$LHA♈ = GHA♈ - \lambda$$

Suppose, for example, the navigator at the time he wishes to observe assumes a

84   CELESTIAL FOR THE CRUISING NAVIGATOR

TABLE 5.—Correction to Tabulated Altitude for Minutes of Declination

338

Figure 5.5   Table of interpolation from *H. O. 249*

LAT 34°N   **LAT 34°N**

LHA ♈	Hc Zn	Hc Zn	Hc Zn	Hc Zn	Hc Zn	Hc Zn	Hc Zn
	*CAPELLA	ALDEBARAN	Diphda	*FOMALHAUT	ALTAIR	*DENEB	Kochab
0	31 03 053	26 41 088	36 54 167	24 27 195	27 29 262	50 38 302	21 55 349
1	31 43 053	27 31 088	37 04 169	24 14 196	26 40 262	49 56 302	21 45 349
2	32 22 053	28 21 089	37 13 170	23 59 197	25 51 263	49 13 302	21 35 349
3	33 02 053	29 10 089	37 22 171	23 44 198	25 01 264	48 31 302	21 26 349
4	33 42 054	30 00 090	37 29 172	23 29 199	24 12 264	47 49 302	21 17 350
5	34 22 054	30 50 090	37 35 173	23 12 200	23 22 265	47 07 302	21 08 350
6	35 03 054	31 40 091	37 40 175	22 55 201	22 33 265	46 25 302	20 59 350
7	35 43 054	32 29 091	37 44 176	22 37 202	21 43 266	45 42 302	20 51 350
8	36 23 055	33 19 092	37 48 177	22 18 202	20 54 267	45 00 302	20 42 351
9	37 04 055	34 09 093	37 50 178	21 59 203	20 04 267	44 18 302	20 34 351
10	37 45 055	34 58 093	37 51 179	21 39 204	19 14 268	43 36 303	20 26 351
11	38 25 055	35 48 094	37 51 181	21 18 205	18 25 268	42 55 303	20 19 351
12	39 06 055	36 38 094	37 51 182	20 57 206	17 35 269	42 13 303	20 11 352
13	39 47 055	37 27 095	37 48 183	20 35 207	16 45 269	41 31 303	20 04 352
14	40 28 056	38 17 096	37 45 184	20 12 208	15 55 270	40 49 303	19 57 352
	*CAPELLA	RIGEL	*Diphda	FOMALHAUT	Enif	*DENEB	Kochab
15	41 09 056	16 48 113	37 40 185	19 49 208	38 50 254	40 08 303	19 50 352
16	41 50 056	17 33 113	37 35 187	19 25 209	38 03 254	39 26 304	19 44 353
17	42 32 056	18 19 114	37 29 188	19 00 210	37 15 255	38 45 304	19 37 353
18	43 13 056	19 04 115	37 22 189	18 35 211	36 26 256	38 04 304	19 31 353
19	43 54 056	19 49 115	37 14 190	18 10 212	35 38 257	37 22 304	19 25 353
20	44 36 056	20 34 116	37 04 191	17 43 212	34 50 257	36 41 304	19 20 354
21	45 17 057	21 19 117	36 54 192	17 16 213	34 01 258	36 00 305	19 14 354
22	45 59 057	22 03 117	36 43 194	16 49 214	33 12 259	35 19 305	19 09 354
23	46 40 057	22 47 118	36 31 195	16 21 215	32 24 259	34 39 305	19 04 354
24	47 22 057	23 31 119	36 17 196	15 52 215	31 35 260	33 58 305	19 00 355
25	48 04 057	24 14 120	36 03 197	15 23 216	30 46 261	33 17 305	18 55 355
26	48 45 057	24 57 120	35 48 198	14 53 217	29 57 261	32 37 306	18 51 355
27	49 27 057	25 40 121	35 32 199	14 23 218	29 07 262	31 57 306	18 47 356
28	50 09 057	26 23 122	35 15 200	13 53 218	28 18 262	31 16 306	18 43 356
29	50 51 057	27 05 123	34 57 202	13 21 219	27 29 263	30 36 307	18 40 356
	CAPELLA	BETELGEUSE	*RIGEL	Diphda	*Alpheratz	DENEB	*Kochab
30	51 32 057	30 12 102	27 46 123	34 39 203	65 25 266	29 56 307	18 37 356
31	52 14 057	31 00 103	28 28 124	34 19 204	64 36 267	29 16 307	18 34 357
32	52 55 057	31 49 104	29 09 125	33 59 205	63 46 267	28 37 307	18 31 357
33	53 37 057	32 37 104	29 49 126	33 37 206	62 56 268	27 58 308	18 28 357
34	54 19 057	33 25 105	30 29 127	33 15 207	62 07 268	27 18 308	18 26 358
35	55 00 057	34 13 106	31 09 128	32 52 208	61 17 269	26 39 308	18 24 358
36	55 42 057	35 01 106	31 48 128	32 29 209	60 27 269	26 00 309	18 22 358
37	56 23 057	35 49 107	32 27 129	32 04 210	59 37 270	25 21 309	18 21 358
38	57 05 056	36 36 108	33 05 130	31 39 211	58 48 271	24 43 309	18 19 359
39	57 46 056	37 23 109	33 43 131	31 13 212	57 58 271	24 04 309	18 18 359
40	58 27 056	38 10 109	34 20 132	30 46 213	57 08 272	23 26 310	18 18 359
41	59 09 056	38 57 110	34 57 133	30 19 214	56 19 272	22 48 310	18 17 000
42	59 50 056	39 44 111	35 33 134	29 51 215	55 29 273	22 10 310	18 17 000
43	60 31 055	40 30 112	36 08 135	29 22 216	54 39 273	21 32 311	18 17 000
44	61 12 055	41 16 113	36 43 136	28 52 217	53 49 274	20 54 311	18 17 000
	*Dubhe	POLLUX	SIRIUS	*RIGEL	Diphda	*Alpheratz	Schedar
45	17 11 025	30 12 075	16 30 124	37 18 137	28 22 218	53 00 274	57 10 324
46	17 32 025	31 00 075	17 12 125	37 51 138	27 52 219	52 10 275	56 41 323
47	17 54 026	31 48 076	17 52 126	38 24 139	27 20 219	51 21 275	56 11 323
48	18 15 026	32 36 076	18 32 126	38 56 140	26 48 220	50 31 276	55 41 322
49	18 37 026	33 25 076	19 12 127	39 28 141	26 16 221	49 42 276	55 10 322
50	19 00 027	34 13 077	19 52 128	39 59 142	25 43 222	48 52 277	54 40 322
51	19 22 027	35 02 077	20 31 128	40 29 143	25 09 223	48 03 277	54 09 321
52	19 45 027	35 50 078	21 10 129	40 58 145	24 35 224	47 14 277	53 38 321
53	20 08 028	36 39 078	21 48 130	41 26 146	24 00 225	46 24 278	53 06 321
54	20 31 028	37 27 079	22 26 131	41 54 147	23 25 225	45 35 278	52 35 320
55	20 54 028	38 16 079	23 04 132	42 21 148	22 49 226	44 46 279	52 03 320
56	21 18 028	39 05 079	23 41 132	42 47 149	22 13 227	43 57 279	51 31 320
57	21 42 029	39 54 080	24 17 133	43 12 150	21 37 228	43 08 280	50 59 320
58	22 06 029	40 43 080	24 53 134	43 36 152	20 59 229	42 19 280	50 27 320
59	22 30 029	41 32 081	25 29 135	43 59 153	20 22 229	41 30 281	49 54 319
	*Dubhe	POLLUX	PROCYON	*SIRIUS	RIGEL	*Hamal	Schedar
60	22 54 030	42 21 081	32 08 107	26 04 136	44 21 154	62 49 254	49 22 319
61	23 19 030	43 10 082	32 55 108	26 38 137	44 42 156	62 01 255	48 49 319
62	23 44 030	44 00 082	33 43 108	27 12 137	45 02 157	61 13 256	48 17 319
63	24 09 030	44 49 082	34 30 109	27 46 138	45 20 159	60 25 257	47 44 319
64	24 34 030	45 38 083	35 17 110	28 18 139	45 39 160	59 36 258	47 11 319
65	24 59 031	46 28 083	36 03 111	28 51 140	45 56 161	58 47 259	46 38 318
66	25 25 031	47 17 084	36 50 111	29 22 141	46 11 162	57 58 260	46 05 318
67	25 50 031	48 07 084	37 36 112	29 53 142	46 26 164	57 09 261	45 32 318
68	26 16 031	48 56 085	38 22 113	30 24 143	46 39 165	56 20 261	44 59 318
69	26 42 032	49 46 085	39 07 114	30 53 144	46 52 167	55 31 262	44 26 318
70	27 08 032	50 35 086	39 53 115	31 22 145	47 03 168	54 42 263	43 52 318
71	27 34 032	51 25 086	40 38 116	31 51 146	47 12 169	53 52 263	43 19 318
72	28 01 032	52 14 087	41 22 116	32 18 147	47 21 171	53 03 264	42 46 318
73	28 27 032	53 04 087	42 07 117	32 45 148	47 28 172	52 13 265	42 13 318
74	28 54 033	53 54 088	42 51 118	33 12 149	47 34 174	51 24 265	41 40 318
	*Dubhe	POLLUX	PROCYON	*SIRIUS	RIGEL	*Hamal	Mirfak
75	29 21 033	54 44 088	43 34 119	33 37 150	47 39 175	50 34 266	66 07 319
76	29 48 033	55 33 089	44 18 120	34 02 151	47 43 177	49 45 267	65 34 318
77	30 15 033	56 23 089	45 00 121	34 25 152	47 45 178	48 55 267	65 00 317
78	30 42 033	57 13 090	45 43 122	34 49 153	47 46 180	48 05 268	64 26 316
79	31 09 033	58 02 090	46 25 123	35 11 154	47 46 181	47 16 268	63 52 316
80	31 37 033	58 52 091	47 06 124	35 32 155	47 44 183	46 26 269	63 17 315
81	32 04 034	59 42 092	47 47 125	35 53 156	47 41 184	45 36 270	62 41 314
82	32 32 034	60 32 092	48 27 126	36 12 157	47 37 185	44 46 270	62 06 314
83	32 59 034	61 21 093	49 07 128	36 31 158	47 32 187	43 57 271	61 30 313
84	33 27 034	62 11 093	49 46 129	36 49 160	47 25 188	43 07 271	60 53 313
85	33 55 034	63 01 094	50 25 130	37 06 161	47 17 190	42 17 272	60 17 312
86	34 23 034	63 50 095	51 02 131	37 22 162	47 08 191	41 27 272	59 40 312
87	34 51 034	64 40 096	51 40 132	37 37 163	46 58 193	40 38 273	59 03 312
88	35 19 034	65 29 096	52 16 134	37 51 164	46 46 194	39 48 273	58 26 311
89	35 47 034	66 19 097	52 52 135	38 04 165	46 33 196	38 58 274	57 48 311

LHA ♈	Hc Zn	Hc Zn	Hc Zn	Hc Zn	Hc Zn	Hc Zn	Hc Zn
	*Dubhe	REGULUS	PROCYON	*SIRIUS	RIGEL	ALDEBARAN	*Mirfak
90	36 15 034	30 07 096	53 26 136	38 16 167	46 20 197	63 57 233	57 11 311
91	36 43 034	30 56 096	54 00 138	38 27 168	46 04 198	63 17 235	56 33 310
92	37 11 035	31 46 097	54 33 139	38 37 169	45 48 200	62 36 236	55 55 310
93	37 39 035	32 35 098	55 06 141	38 46 170	45 31 201	61 54 237	55 17 310
94	38 07 035	33 24 098	55 37 142	38 54 171	45 13 202	61 12 239	54 39 310
95	38 36 035	34 14 099	56 07 144	39 01 173	44 53 204	60 29 240	54 01 310
96	39 04 035	35 03 099	56 36 145	39 06 174	44 33 205	59 46 241	53 22 309
97	39 32 035	35 52 100	57 04 147	39 11 175	44 11 206	59 02 243	52 44 309
98	40 00 035	36 41 101	57 30 148	39 15 176	43 48 208	58 17 244	52 05 309
99	40 29 035	37 29 101	57 56 150	39 18 178	43 25 209	57 33 245	51 27 309
100	40 57 035	38 18 102	58 20 152	39 19 179	43 01 210	56 47 246	50 48 309
101	41 25 035	39 07 103	58 43 154	39 20 180	42 35 211	56 02 247	50 10 309
102	41 53 034	39 55 104	59 04 155	39 19 181	42 09 212	55 16 248	49 31 309
103	42 21 034	40 43 104	59 24 157	39 17 183	41 42 214	54 29 249	48 52 309
104	42 49 034	41 32 105	59 43 159	39 15 184	41 14 215	53 43 250	48 13 309
	*Alkaid	REGULUS	Alphard	*SIRIUS	RIGEL	ALDEBARAN	*CAPELLA
105	18 28 042	42 19 106	35 10 134	39 11 185	40 45 216	52 56 251	66 40 309
106	19 01 043	43 07 107	35 45 135	39 06 186	40 15 217	52 09 252	66 01 308
107	19 35 043	43 55 107	36 20 136	39 00 187	39 45 218	51 21 253	65 23 308
108	20 09 043	44 42 108	36 54 137	38 53 189	39 14 219	50 34 254	64 42 307
109	20 43 044	45 29 109	37 28 138	38 45 190	38 42 220	49 46 254	64 03 307
110	21 18 044	46 16 110	38 01 139	38 36 191	38 09 221	48 58 255	63 23 306
111	21 52 044	47 03 111	38 33 140	38 26 192	37 36 222	48 10 256	62 42 306
112	22 27 045	47 49 112	39 05 141	38 15 194	37 02 224	47 21 257	62 02 305
113	23 02 045	48 35 112	39 36 142	38 03 195	36 28 225	46 33 258	61 21 305
114	23 37 045	49 21 113	40 06 143	37 49 196	35 52 225	45 44 258	60 40 305
115	24 12 045	50 07 114	40 35 144	37 35 197	35 17 226	44 55 259	59 59 304
116	24 48 046	50 52 115	41 04 146	37 20 198	34 40 227	44 07 260	59 18 304
117	25 24 046	51 37 116	41 32 147	37 04 199	34 03 228	43 18 260	58 37 304
118	25 59 046	52 21 117	41 58 148	36 47 201	33 26 229	42 28 261	57 56 304
119	26 36 047	53 05 118	42 24 149	36 29 202	32 48 230	41 39 262	57 15 304
	*Alkaid	REGULUS	*Alphard	SIRIUS	RIGEL	ALDEBARAN	*CAPELLA
120	27 12 047	53 49 120	42 49 150	36 11 203	32 10 231	40 50 262	56 33 304
121	27 48 047	54 32 121	43 14 152	35 51 204	31 31 232	40 01 263	55 52 303
122	28 25 047	55 14 122	43 37 153	35 30 205	30 51 233	39 11 264	55 10 303
123	29 01 048	55 56 123	43 59 154	35 09 206	30 11 234	38 22 264	54 28 303
124	29 38 048	56 37 124	44 20 155	34 47 207	29 31 235	37 32 265	53 47 303
125	30 15 048	57 18 126	44 40 157	34 23 208	28 50 235	36 43 266	53 05 303
126	30 52 048	57 58 127	45 00 158	34 00 209	28 09 236	35 53 266	52 23 303
127	31 29 049	58 38 128	45 18 159	33 35 210	27 28 237	35 03 267	51 42 303
128	32 07 049	59 16 130	45 35 161	33 09 211	26 46 238	34 14 267	51 00 303
129	32 44 049	59 54 131	45 51 162	32 43 212	26 04 239	33 24 268	50 18 303
130	33 22 049	60 31 133	46 05 163	32 16 213	25 21 239	32 34 269	49 37 303
131	33 59 049	61 07 134	46 19 165	31 48 214	24 38 240	31 45 269	48 55 303
132	34 37 050	61 42 136	46 31 166	31 20 215	23 55 241	30 55 270	48 13 303
133	35 15 050	62 16 138	46 43 168	30 51 216	23 11 242	30 05 270	47 32 303
134	35 53 050	62 49 139	46 53 169	30 21 217	22 27 242	29 15 271	46 50 303
	*Alkaid	ARCTURUS	SPICA	*Alphard	SIRIUS	BETELGEUSE	*CAPELLA
135	36 31 050	19 53 080	13 02 113	47 01 171	29 51 218	39 33 249	46 09 303
136	37 10 050	20 42 080	13 48 114	47 09 172	29 20 219	38 47 250	45 27 303
137	37 48 050	21 31 081	14 33 114	47 15 173	28 48 220	38 00 251	44 46 304
138	38 26 051	22 20 081	15 18 115	47 20 175	28 16 221	37 13 252	44 04 304
139	39 05 051	23 09 082	16 03 116	47 24 176	27 43 222	36 25 252	43 23 304
140	39 43 051	23 59 082	16 48 116	47 27 178	27 09 223	35 38 253	42 41 304
141	40 22 051	24 48 083	17 32 117	47 28 179	26 35 224	34 50 254	42 00 304
142	41 01 051	25 37 083	18 16 118	47 28 181	26 01 224	34 02 254	41 19 304
143	41 39 051	26 27 084	19 00 118	47 27 182	25 26 225	33 14 255	40 38 304
144	42 18 051	27 16 084	19 44 119	47 24 184	24 50 226	32 26 256	39 57 304
145	42 57 051	28 06 085	20 27 120	47 21 185	24 14 227	31 38 257	39 16 305
146	43 36 051	28 55 085	21 10 121	47 16 187	23 37 228	30 49 257	38 35 305
147	44 15 051	29 45 086	21 53 121	47 09 188	23 00 229	30 01 258	37 54 305
148	44 54 052	30 34 086	22 35 122	47 02 189	22 23 229	29 12 259	37 13 305
149	45 33 052	31 24 087	23 17 123	46 53 191	21 45 230	28 23 259	36 33 305
	Alkaid	*ARCTURUS	SPICA	*Alphard	PROCYON	BETELGEUSE	*CAPELLA
150	46 12 052	32 14 087	23 59 124	46 43 192	46 19 237	27 34 260	35 52 306
151	46 51 052	33 04 088	24 40 124	46 32 194	45 37 238	26 45 260	35 12 306
152	47 30 052	33 53 088	25 21 125	46 20 195	44 55 239	25 56 261	34 32 306
153	48 09 052	34 43 089	26 02 126	46 06 196	44 12 240	25 07 262	33 52 306
154	48 48 052	35 33 089	26 42 127	45 51 198	43 28 241	24 18 262	33 12 307
155	49 26 052	36 22 090	27 23 127	45 36 199	42 45 242	23 29 263	32 32 307
156	50 05 052	37 12 091	28 01 128	45 19 201	42 01 243	22 39 264	31 52 307
157	50 44 051	38 02 091	28 40 129	45 01 202	41 16 244	21 50 264	31 12 307
158	51 23 051	38 52 092	29 18 130	44 42 203	40 32 245	21 00 265	30 33 308
159	52 02 051	39 41 092	29 56 131	44 21 205	39 47 245	20 11 265	29 53 308
160	52 41 051	40 31 093	30 33 132	44 00 206	39 01 246	19 21 266	29 14 308
161	53 20 051	41 21 094	31 10 133	43 38 207	38 16 247	18 31 266	28 35 308
162	53 58 051	42 10 094	31 46 134	43 15 208	37 30 248	17 42 267	27 56 309
163	54 37 051	43 00 095	32 22 134	42 51 210	36 43 249	16 52 268	27 17 309
164	55 15 051	43 49 095	32 57 135	42 26 211	35 57 249	16 02 268	26 39 309
	*Dubhe	Alkaid	*ARCTURUS	SPICA	REGULUS	*PROCYON	CAPELLA
165	62 05 000	55 53 050	44 39 096	33 32 136	64 59 212	35 10 250	26 00 309
166	62 05 359	56 32 050	45 28 097	34 06 137	64 32 214	34 23 251	25 22 310
167	62 04 358	57 10 050	46 18 097	34 40 138	64 03 216	33 36 252	24 44 310
168	62 03 357	57 48 050	47 07 098	35 13 139	63 33 218	32 49 252	24 06 310
169	62 00 356	58 25 049	47 56 099	35 44 140	63 02 220	32 01 253	23 28 311
170	61 56 355	59 03 049	48 45 099	36 16 141	62 29 222	31 14 254	22 50 311
171	61 52 354	59 40 049	49 34 100	36 47 142	61 56 223	30 26 255	22 13 311
172	61 47 354	60 17 048	50 23 101	37 17 143	61 21 225	29 38 255	21 36 312
173	61 41 353	60 54 048	51 12 102	37 46 144	60 45 227	28 50 256	20 59 312
174	61 34 352	61 31 047	52 01 102	38 14 146	60 09 228	28 01 257	20 22 312
175	61 26 350	62 07 047	52 49 103	38 42 147	59 31 230	27 13 257	19 45 313
176	61 18 350	62 43 046	53 38 104	39 09 148	58 53 231	26 24 258	19 09 313
177	61 08 349	63 19 046	54 26 105	39 35 149	58 14 233	25 36 258	18 33 314
178	60 58 348	63 55 045	55 14 106	40 00 150	57 34 234	24 47 259	17 57 314
179	60 47 347	64 30 044	56 02 107	40 25 151	56 53 235	23 58 260	17 21 314

Figure 5.6 Specimen page from *H. O. 249*, Vol. I

latitude of 34°N and a longitude that yields LHAΥ = 15°. Then data (Hc and Zn) are available for the set Capella, Rigel, Diphda, Fomalhaut, Enif, Deneb, and Kochab. These stars are selected for their apparent brightness and azimuths that will give a good cut for lines of position in a definitive fix. The selection is limited, however, and reliance upon direct computation by calculator is much to be preferred. (The writer, incidentally, has found this volume useful in providing preliminary information as to Hc's and azimuths of selected stars likely to be available for twilight observations.)

A word of caution here—since each star will be observed at a different time, the assumed longitude taken so as to yield an even degree of LHAΥ will differ for each star that is observed. However, note that no interpolation is required in using Vol. 1, *H. O. 249*. Simply assume a position giving an even degree of latitude and an even degree of LHAΥ. But as in all stellar observations, one must correct his sextant observation for refraction, index error, and dip.

NOTES

Note 5.1
Among these methods was that of the haversine, which dealt with half-angle computations:

Haversine $\theta = \frac{1}{2}$ versine $\theta = \frac{1}{2}(1 - \cos\theta)$

Though in wide use from the seventeenth and eighteenth centuries on, they are of little use to the navigator today. Their advantage lay in the fact that for any set of values θ, 0° to 180°, there is a unique haversine, thereby eliminating ambiguity for angles greater than 90°.

Compendia for sight reduction methods can be found in Bowditch, *American Practical Navigator*, and C. H. Cotter, *The Complete Nautical Astronomer*.

For the most part navigators then, as now, were not facile mathematicians. Working with the basic trigonometric formulae entailed two complications: one, trigonometric formulae involving both multiplication and addition (for example, the law of cosines) could not be handled in any straightforward way by logarithms; and two, there was inherent ambiguity when angles greater than 90° were involved.

The modern pocket calculator usually overcomes both these so-called complications.

Note 5.2
There are several inexpensive calculators on the market that perform trigonometric functions: Casio, Radio Shack, Sharp, and Texas Instruments, for example, all produced basic calculators for under fifteen dollars in 1985.

There are, to be sure, expensive programmable calculators designed either specifically for navigation or for the sets of sequential operations that navigation requires (e.g., Tamaya NC-77, Plath Navicomp, Hewlett-Packard). However, in the writer's opinion the limited time-saving (a matter of an entry or two) is clearly not worth the added expense.

On the other hand, it may be worth a few extra dollars to obtain a "scientific calculator" that performs statistical functions. Computing means and variances is essential to any serious study of the magnitude and nature of observational error.

Note 5.3
For the reader unfamiliar with trigonometry, the basic ideas are easy to grasp. Invention of the subject is attributed to the Greek astronomer Hipparchus (circa 120 B.C.) although tabular and computational refinements are attributed to Renaissance mathematicians.

In the right triangle of Figure 5.7, the capital letters represent the interior angles of the triangle, the lower-case letters the sides. The trigonometric functions are simply ratios of the sides to the angles.

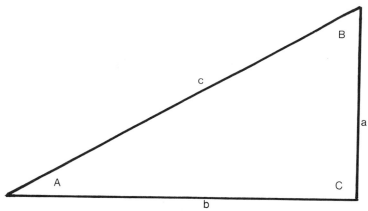

Figure 5.7 Right triangle

Thus for the angle A we may define the functions as follows:

$$\text{sinc A (sin A)} = \frac{a}{c} \text{ or } \frac{\text{side opposite}}{\text{hypotenuse}}$$

$$\text{cosine A (cos A)} = \frac{b}{c} \text{ or } \frac{\text{side adjacent}}{\text{hypotenuse}}$$

$$\text{tangent A (tan A)} = \frac{a}{b} \text{ or } \frac{\text{side opposite}}{\text{side adjacent}}$$

$$\text{cotangent A (cot A)} = \frac{b}{a}$$

$$\text{secant A (sec A)} = \frac{c}{b}$$

$$\text{cosecant A (csc A)} = \frac{c}{a}$$

The cotangent, secant, and cosecant are simply the reciprocals of the tangent, cosine, and sine, respectively, and are not keyed on the calculator except by virtue of the $\boxed{1/x}$ key.

With a table of trigonometric functions and partial information concerning the constituents of the right triangle (Figure 5.7), missing information can be inferred. For example, if we know angle A and side a we can infer side c and, in turn, side b (by virtue of cos A), etc. Furthermore, for

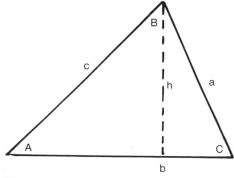
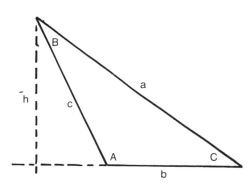

Figure 5.8 Oblique triangle

any non-right angle triangle, whether acute (Figure 5.8a) or obtuse (Figure 5.8b), we can apply the basic principles of the right triangle by constructing altitudes h to form right triangles such as ABD and BDC.

Both surveying (plane trigonometry) and navigation (spherical trigonometry) make use of relatively basic operations. Two laws of trigonometry that are fundamental follow.

The *law of sines* states that *for any triangle, the sides are proportional to the sines of the opposite angles:*

$$\frac{a}{\sin A} = \frac{b}{\sin B} = \frac{c}{\sin C} \qquad \text{(Formula 5.5)}$$

Thus, if we know two sides of a triangle, Figure 5.8a, and the angle opposite one of the sides, we can determine the angle opposite the other. Then, in turn, we can infer the third angle (the sum of the interior angles is 180°) and thus the remaining side by the law of sines.

The *law of cosines* states that *in any triangle the square of any side is equal to the sum of the squares of the other two sides minus twice the product of those two sides times the cosine of their included angle:*

$$a^2 = b^2 + c^2 - 2bc \cos A \qquad \text{(Formula 5.6)}$$

In general this means that any time we know two sides of a given triangle and the included angle, we can determine the third side. And by transposing Formula 5.6 we can determine the value of A if we know the values of the three sides. The law of cosines assures us that we can thereby determine all angles of a triangle if the sides are known. Indeed, if we know two sides and the included angle of a given triangle, we can determine all constituents of the triangle.

Spherical Trigonometry: So much for plane surfaces. In spherical trigonometry the derivation of these laws is complicated by the fact that all lines of the triangle are arcs of great circles. Furthermore, the sum of the angles of a spherical triangle may exceed 180° (e.g., any triangle with two of its vertices on the equator).

Law of Sines: In Figure 5.9 we have a pyramidal wedge cut out of a sphere. XYZ represents the spherical triangle as subtended from the sphere's center at O. Inside this slice we can construct two right triangles in dihedral planes such that the angles XAO, XBO, XPA, and XPB are all right angles. Now z is an arc of a great circle commensurate with angle XOA in the plane triangle XOA. And though z is an arc we can write:

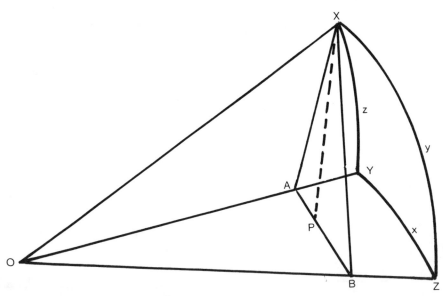

Figure 5.9 Plane triangles within sphere

$$\sin z = \sin XOA = \frac{AX}{OX}$$

Furthermore, angle Z in the spherical triangle XYZ is commensurate with the angle XBP in the plane triangle. Hence:

$$\sin Z = \frac{XP}{XB}$$

Combining the two expressions yields the equation:

$$\frac{\sin z}{\sin Z} = \frac{AX \cdot XB}{OX \cdot XP}$$

Following a similar procedure for arc y and angle Y we obtain:

$$\frac{\sin y}{\sin Y} = \frac{XB \cdot AX}{XP \cdot OX} = \frac{\sin x}{\sin X}$$

Other manipulations give the law of sines for spherical triangles:

$$\frac{\sin x}{\sin X} = \frac{\sin y}{\sin Y} = \frac{\sin z}{\sin Z}$$

In the nautical triangle (Figure 5.11), note that if we know *HA*, codeclination, and coaltitude, we can use the law of sines to determine azimuth angle Z. This is the basis for deriving Formula 5.3 in the text.

Law of Cosines: The law of cosines for spherical trigonometry presents a somewhat more

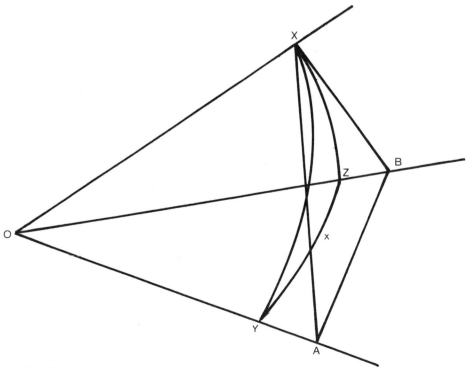

Figure 5.10   Plane triangle tangent to sphere

complicated derivation. Figure 5.10 again presents the pyramidal wedge of a sphere, giving the spherical triangle XYZ. We now construct a plane triangle tangent at X, as projected to XAB external to the sphere. Angles OXA and OXB are thereby right angles. The derivation of the law of cosines proceeds by noting that arc x is congruent with angle AOB. And spherical angle X is congruent with angle AXB. This enables us to write a law-of-cosines expression for triangles AOB and AXB:

$$AB^2 = OA^2 + OB^2 - 2 \cdot OA \cdot OB \cdot \cos x$$
$$AB^2 = AX^2 + BX^2 - 2 \cdot AX \cdot BX \cdot \cos X$$

These are simultaneous equations which we may now reduce by subtracting one from the other. Collecting terms and applying the Pythagorean theorem eventually yields:

$$\cos X = \frac{OA \cdot OB \cdot \cos x - OX^2}{AX \cdot BX}$$

Since all arc measures in the spherical triangle XYZ have congruent equivalences in the plane triangles XOA, XOB, and AOB, the expression above eventually can be written as:

$$\cos X = \frac{\cos x - \cos y \cos z}{\sin y \cdot \sin z}$$

or $\cos x = \cos y \cos z + \sin y \sin z \cos X$

Note 5.4

$$\sin Z = \frac{\sin t \cos d}{\cos Hc} \qquad\qquad \text{(Formula 5.3)}$$

is derived from law of sines (see Note 5.3). In Figure 5.11:

$$\frac{\sin \text{co-Dec.}}{\sin Zn} = \frac{\sin \text{co-h}}{\sin t}$$

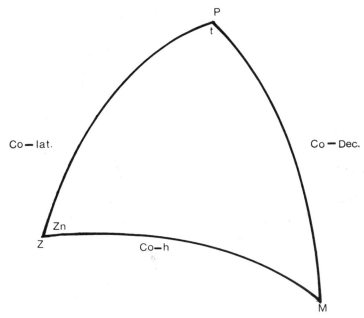

Figure 5.11 Navigational triangle

But:

$$\sin \text{co-Dec.} = \sin (90 - d) = \cos d$$
$$\sin \text{co-h} = \sin (90 - h) = \cos h$$

Hence, substituting, we obtain Formula 5.3.

The expression:

$$\cos Z = \frac{\sin d - \sin L \sin Hc}{\cos L \cos Hc} \qquad \text{(Formula 5.2)}$$

is initially derived from the law of cosines (see Note 5.3). For Figure 5.11:

$$\cos Z = \frac{\cos (\text{co-Dec.}) - \cos (\text{co-h}) \cos (\text{co-L})}{\sin (\text{co-L}) \sin (\text{co-h})}$$

Since:

$$\cos (\text{co-Dec.}) = \sin d$$
$$\cos (\text{co-L}) = \sin L$$
$$\cos (\text{co-h}) = \sin Hc$$

we obtain Formula 5.2 above.

The fundamental formula for altitude Hc is also derived from the law of cosines:

$$\cos t = \frac{\cos (\text{co-h}) - \cos (\text{co-Dec.}) \cdot \cos (\text{co-L})}{\sin (\text{co-Dec.}) \sin (\text{co-L})}$$

Substituting the functions of complementary angles gives:

$$\cos t = \frac{\sin Hc - \sin d \sin L}{\cos d \cos L}$$

Transposing for Hc yields the equation:

$$\sin Hc = \sin d \sin L + \cos d \cos L \cos t \qquad \text{(Formula 5.1)}$$

Note 5.5 Alternatives to the Conventional Methods of Computing h and Z

The following alternatives derive from Napier's rules for solving right spherical triangles. Such rules are introduced early into works on spherical trigonometry and can be used to prove the laws of sines and cosines for oblique triangles.

Visualize our familiar navigational triangle with the orthogonal projection of the body M onto the observer's meridian PZ as in Figure 5.12a and b. The orthogonal projection of M onto PZ means that the line MR is perpendicular to the line PZ. In the first case, PZ is extended to intercept MR; in the second case, the point R falls within PZ. In both cases the angle PRM is a right angle and the triangles PRM and ZRM are both right spherical triangles. As in the text, L', d', and h' are colatitude, codeclination, and coaltitude; L, d, and h are latitude, declination, and altitude.

In order to solve for altitude h and azimuth angle Z we need first to compute the values of two arcs: PR, which is the polar distance of our orthogonal point R, and MR, which is the distance of R from M.

From Napier's rules we may easily derive the following formulae:

$$PR = \tan^{-1} \frac{\cos t}{\tan d} \qquad \text{(Formula 5.7)}$$

$$MR = \sin^{-1} (\cos d \sin t) \qquad \text{(Formula 5.8)}$$

Solving for altitude h we have:

$$h = \sin^{-1} [\sin (L + PR) \cos MR] \qquad \text{(Formula 5.9)}$$

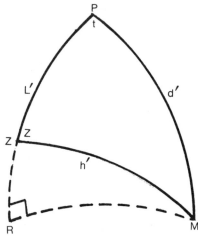
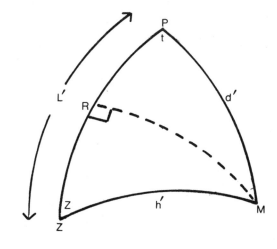

Figure 5.12   Navigational triangle

and for azimuth angle Z:

$$Z = \cos^{-1} \frac{\tan h}{\tan (L + PR)} \qquad \text{(Formula 5.10)}$$

(Note that the quantities L and d are latitude and declination and not their complementary values, as in Figure 5.12. All conversions are by virtue of the fact that the trigonometric co-functions of complementary angles are equal.)

In computing Z it is helpful to note:

a) if PM > PZ, then Z > 90°;
b) if PM < PZ, then Z < 90°.

There are two cases in which PM will be greater than PZ: one, if declination is same name but less than latitude; and two, if declination is contrary in name to latitude. Also if declination is contrary in name to latitude, PR as computed by Formula 5.7 will be negative. In such a case subtract the computed value from 180°.

We can apply the above to the examples in the text.

Example 1:   t = 44.35°, d = 19.42°N, and L = 28.70°N. Computing PR, MR, h, and Z, we have:

$$PR = \tan^{-1} \frac{\cos 44.35}{\tan 19.42} = 63.76 \qquad \text{(Formula 5.7)}$$

$$MR = \sin^{-1} (\cos 19.42 \sin 44.35) = 41.24 \qquad \text{(Formula 5.8)}$$

$$L + PR = 92.46°$$

$$h = \sin^{-1} (\sin 92.46 \cos 41.24) \qquad \text{(Formula 5.9)}$$
$$= 48.70° = 48°42'$$

$$Z = \cos^{-1} \frac{\tan 48.70}{\tan 92.46} \qquad \text{(Formula 5.10)}$$
$$= 92.8°$$

Example 2:   t = 35.32°, d = 16.11°S, and L = 46.28°N.

$$PR = \tan^{-1} \frac{\cos 35.32}{\tan - 16.11} = -70.50 \rightarrow 109.50° \qquad \text{(Formula 5.7)}$$

$$MR = \sin^{-1} (\cos - 16.11 \sin 35.32) = 33.74° \qquad \text{(Formula 5.8)}$$

$$L + PR = 46.28 - 70.50 + 180 = 155.78°$$

$$h = \sin^{-1}(\sin 155.78 \cos 33.74) = 19.95° \qquad \text{(Formula 5.9)}$$

$$Z = \cos^{-1}\frac{\tan 19.95}{\tan 155.78} = 143.8° \qquad \text{(Formula 5.10)}$$

Note that when the computed PR is negative, we must add that negative value to 180 to get a positive value. Since PR is an arc we should express it as a positive value.

Finally, consider a third example where L and d are same name but L < d.

Example 3:   t = 36.5°, d = 22.4°N, and L = 18.8°N.

$$PR = \tan^{-1}\frac{\cos 36.5}{\tan 22.4} = 62.85°$$

$$MR = \sin^{-1}(\cos 22.4 \sin 36.5) = 33.36°$$

$$L + PR = 81.65°$$

$$h = \sin^{-1}(\sin 81.65 \cos 33.36) = 55.73°$$
$$= 55°44'$$

$$Z = \cos^{-1}\frac{\tan 55.73}{\tan 81.65} = 77.56$$

Checking these results by Formulae 5.1 and 5.2, we find that:

$$h = \sin^{-1}(\sin 18.8 \sin 22.4) + (\cos 18.8 \cos 22.4 \cos 36.5)$$
$$= 55.73°$$

and

$$Z = \cos^{-1}\frac{\sin 22.4 - (\sin 18.8 \sin 55.73)}{(\cos 18.8 \cos 55.73)}$$

$$= 77.56°$$

It may be of interest to note that the writer timed himself in a casual computation of h and Z by both methods. In each case the computations took a bit less than two minutes. But alas, in both cases, the first time through, there were computational errors. Moral: check and double-check! Thus the navigator's devotion to "eternal vigilance."

A check for all sight-reduction computations whether by the methods described in the text or those given in this note is found by satisfying the following equation:

$$\frac{\sin t \cos d}{\cos h \sin Z} = 1 \qquad \text{(Formula 5.11)}$$

After computing h and Z, plug them into above equation. If the result is not 1, then look for an error in computing h or Z.

An advantage of the right-triangle solutions above is that they lend themselves to the computation of ex-meridian latitude (see Chapter 8). For such computations ZR must also be determined; though it is not required for computing h and Z, ZR is found by following either of these formulae:

$$ZR = \cos^{-1}\frac{\sin h}{\cos MR} \qquad \text{(Formula 5.12)}$$

$$ZR = \cos^{-1}\frac{\sin h \cos PR}{\sin d} \qquad \text{(Formula 5.13)}$$

CHAPTER SIX

The Navigator's Sextant

A celestial line of position is only as good as the sextant sight. Little wonder then that the navigator has a possessive fondness for his sextant. He is no more likely to lend it out than he would his toothbrush. When the second mate, traditionally the chief navigation officer, boards his ship his luggage may go up in a cargo net, but his sextant is coddled aboard by hand.

The modern sextant evolved from the gnomon (a shadow pin), the cross staff, and the astrolabe (*cf.* Note 6.1). The astrolabe, albeit the most sophisticated of the precursors of the sextant, is devoid of optical complications. Its working principle is easy to visualize. Consider, for example, an ordinary half-circular protractor: bisect the base and suspend it at that point along with a line and a plumb bob (Figure 6.1), add a sighting tube along the base of the protractor, and you have an astrolabe for measuring altitude. Construct a rotating base for the supporting arm and a compass rose and have, in addition, means for measuring azimuth.

Astrolabes of ancient designs were adopted for navigational purposes in the late fifteenth century. The reflecting quadrant, which introduced mirror optics into sighting, dates from designs by John Hadley, an early eighteenth-century astronomer. The great Sir Isaac Newton is known to have designed a double-mirror instrument with essentially the same optical scheme as is found in today's sextants.

PARTS OF THE SEXTANT

A photograph of the writer's sextant is presented in Figure 6.2. It was obtained from a retired sea captain who had purchased it new in 1941. In all important respects this remains a modern instrument.

In brief the structural detail and components are as follows:

A. The sextant frame, an alloy with desireable expansion characteristics.
B. Limb and arc of sextant whose face is graduated for altitude and whose base is cut to receive the gear of the micrometer tangent screw H. In this instrument the scale is inlaid with silver.
C. The rotatable index arm which moves one-half degree about its pivot (under D) to every one degree of arc on the scale of B.
D. The index mirror fixed to the rotatable index arm, i.e., the polished mirror that is adjusted to pick up and deliver the image of the observed body.
E. The fixed horizon glass, half of which (that next to the frame) is silvered mirror, the other half clear (to permit direct sighting of the horizon).
F. Shade glasses for index mirror. These are indispensable for viewing the sun.

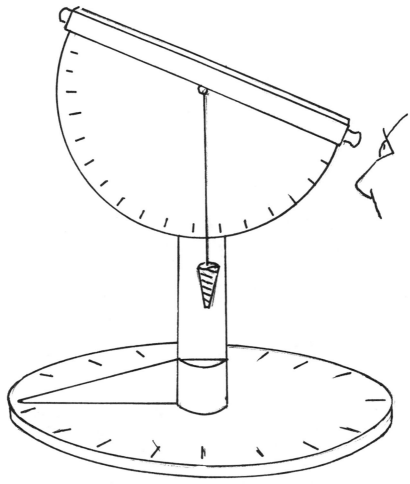

Figure 6.1 Simple astrolabe

G. Shade glasses for horizon. These are desirable when the sun's reflection upon the sea apron is unpleasantly distracting.

H. Micrometer drive and scale. One full turn moves the index arm one-half degree while showing a drum scale of one degree. The scale is in minutes of arc with a vernier fixed reference permitting readings to 0.2' of arc.

I. Clamp screw. Closure of clamp disengages the tangent screw so that index arm can be moved freely.

J. Telescope. Threaded into an adjustable collar, it can be removed easily for directly taking a sight. A second telescope, an inverting type with less light absorption, is sometimes provided.

K. Handle. For the right hand; also encloses batteries for light L.

L. Light, illuminating micrometer drum and scale.

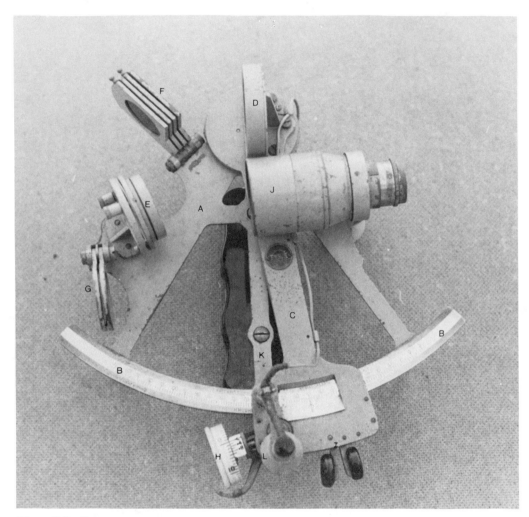

Figure 6.2   Sextant

OPTICAL PRINCIPLES

Although the sextant is capable of measuring arcs of up to 100° and more, the arc of the frame itself is barely 60°. Because of the optics, every degree of actual arc on the index arm is equal to 2° of altitude. The optical system is shown in Figure 6.3.

The optical principles of the sextant have nothing to do with the optics of the telescope. (The telescope serves merely to magnify the image that is reflected from the mirrors.) The basic optical principle of the sextant concerns the mirror. For every plane mirror we can erect an axis perpendicular to the mirror. This is the so-called *normal* of the mirror. Any beam of light striking the mirror does so at some angle to the mirror. The basic principle states that the angle of reflection is equal to the angle of incidence as shown at mirrors D and E, Figure 6.3.

The solid lines in our figure designate the actual tracks of light. The broken lines are projections of either the normals, or the planes of the mirrors, or the paths of

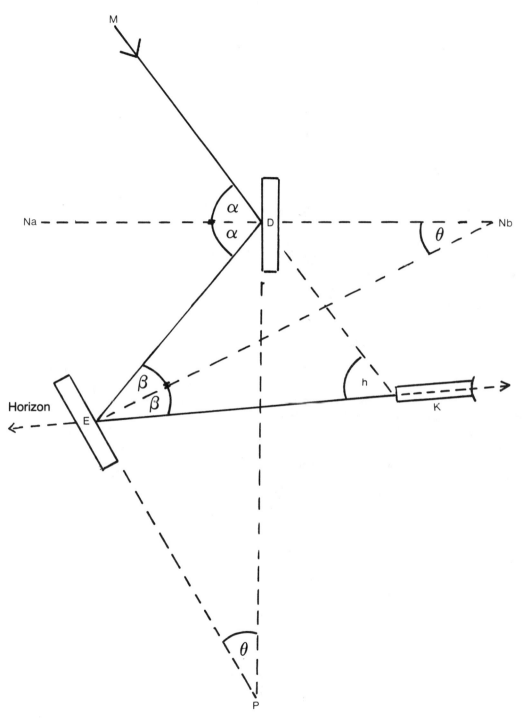

Figure 6.3   Sextant: optical principles

intercepted light. K represents the eyepiece of the sextant and the line EK is the line of sight on the horizon. Hence the light from M projected through the mirror to intercept EK makes the angle h, or altitude of the body.

Consider first the interior angles of the triangle DENb. Angle DENb is β, angle DNbE is θ, and angle EDNb is $180° - \alpha$. Since the sum of these angles is $180°$ we find that:

$$\theta = \alpha - \beta$$

By virtue of the same logic, in the triangle DEK:

$$h = 2\alpha - 2\beta$$

or substituting from above:

$$h = 2\theta$$

Note now that:

$$DNbE = EPD = \theta$$

since the sides of the first angle are perpendicular to the sides of the second angle. Now angle EPD is simply the angle between the rotatable index mirror and the fixed horizon mirror. Since it is equal to θ, and the altitude is equal 2θ, we can see that the altitude is twice the angle through which the index arm and mirror move.

SEXTANT PRACTICE

Though not easy to master, sextant observations are in principle quite simple. The observer takes the instrument in his right hand and rotates the index arm and mirror until the reflected image as seen through the eyepiece is observed to be in conjunction with the horizon. As a rule the observer begins by setting the index arm at an angle approximating the altitude of the body. If the image is seen above the horizon then he must increase the angle of altitude in order to bring that image down to the horizon. If the image is below the horizon, the image will be brought up to the horizon by decreasing the angle of altitude.

Stars and planets are treated as pinpoints of light. When the image of a star or planet is just intercepted by the horizon line the observation is marked and the time of observation is noted. In Figure 6.4 the arcs through the star and the sun (or full moon) indicate that the sextant is rocked, to bring the body to the horizon. This is known as "swinging the arc." By swinging the arc the observer can determine when the horizon mirror is positioned precisely at a right angle to the horizon. Furthermore, the point in the swing when the image of the observed object just kisses the horizon provides the accurate measure of altitude.

In observing the sun one must first make a suitable selection of glass shades to soften the intensity of light that comes directly from the sun and to suppress its glare upon the horizon sea. The observation is taken when the image of either the upper or the lower limb of the sun is just tangent to the horizon. Generally, it is the lower limb that is used; but, at times, when the sun appears "woolly" behind the haze of a light overcast, it may be advisable to observe the conjunction of the center of the sun and the horizon. At times, especially during early morning hours, the horizon line may be

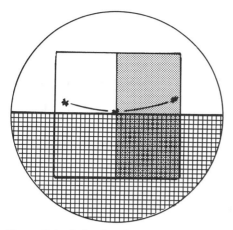 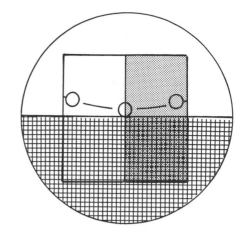

Figure 6.4 Swinging the arc

obscured. A horizon shade, especially if it is of polarized glass, may help to delineate the horizon. However, one can always delay his observation until later in the day when the horizon is likely to clear.

For the small boat navigator there is another problem in locating the horizon. As a rule he is quite close to the water, his eye level seldom being more than ten or twelve feet above the water's surface. In a seaway, nearby rollers will peak to obscure the true horizon. The observer must then anticipate wave patterns, letting the crest of the wave subside so that he catches the true horizon in the distance. Catching the tops of rollers results in an underestimation of altitude.

Locating the moon or sun or the planets and brighter stars through the sextant eyepiece offers little difficulty. The observer estimates the altitude, presets his sextant, and then scans along the observed azimuth axis. However, with lower magnitude stars and daylight observations of planets, one may need to precompute an Hc and the true azimuth in conjunction with the DR position. The observer then carries out a systematic scan until he is sure he has the object in focus.

There are two other common ways of readying the sextant for observation. One is to bring the star down to the horizon, the other is to bring the horizon up to the star. In the former case the observer sets his instrument at zero altitude and sights directly at the star. He then slowly lowers the instrument while rotating the index arm so that the reflected image remains in the horizon mirror. Then when the horizon also comes into view through the unsilvered part of the horizon glass, the observer is ready to make his observation. In the second case, the observer looks directly at the star through the horizon glass and operates the index arm and mirror to pick up the horizon. To do this he inverts the instrument, holding it in his left hand. He then rotates the index arm forward to pick up the horizon as reflected in the index mirror. With the two, the star and the horizon, in apparent conjunction in the horizon glass, the observer reinverts the sextant and proceeds with his observation.

It is often thought that if a shoreline obscures the working horizon then an observation cannot be taken. This is not necessarily the case. If the observer is sufficiently far offshore, the natural visual horizon may interpose itself without distortion. A table in Bowditch,* for example, indicates that for an eye level 10 feet above the sea the horizon is only 3.6 nautical miles distant. Thus, an observer 4 miles offshore could observe a body rising or setting over land and still be sure he has a true horizon in view.

From the relatively stable bridge of a large ship, the navigator often relies upon a single timed observation. With experience and a friendly sea the small boat navigator might do the same. However, a more reliable procedure is to average a number of observations over a short time span. Here it is advantageous to have the help of a crew member. After preliminary preparations the navigator gets set to observe. On the half minute he starts to shoot, reading off sextant altitudes whenever he gets a satisfactory sight. He continues to take sights and record them through to the next half minute.† His time of observation is then the minute midway between his start and stop times. The altitude assigned to that time is the average of the sightings (*cf.* Note 6.2).

SEXTANT CORRECTIONS

Some sextant corrections are required because of intrinsic properties of astronomical observation. Some are necessitated by the properties of the particular instrument. And some may be required because of the unique character or habits of the observer.

Intrinsic Corrections

Dip: Nearly everyone has experienced the fact that the higher the vantage point the farther one can see to sea. The corollary of this is that the higher the vantage the lower the horizon. Indeed, even from the afterdeck of a diminutive sailing vessel, one looks down on the horizon. The visual horizon is thereby below the true horizon which we use as reference in our nautical computations. If, for example, we sighted along a levelled transit we would get the true horizon. The difference between the apparent or visual horizon and the true horizon is known as *dip*. The more elevated the vantage point (E) the greater the dip (Figure 6.5).

Since the sextant sights on the visual horizon and not on the true horizon, dip corrections must always be made on sextant observations. A table of dip corrections (height by dip correction) can be found on the inside cover of the *Nautical Almanac*. Such corrections are negative ones, hence they are always subtracted.

Refraction: Though light from a source such as a star or the sun radiates in all directions, the particular navigator will observe it as travelling in a straight line. As light passes from a less to a more dense medium, as in the case of our star- or sunbeam, it is deflected, i.e., *refracted*, downward toward the observer. Figure 6.6 in exaggerated form shows light from a stellar source entering the earth's atmosphere. The oblique lines show the linear property of the beam of light, the horizontal lines describe wave fronts representing a section of the ambient radiation. The observer is at B. He sees the object ☆ as being projected to the celestial sphere along the line BAA'. The angle R is the angle

---

American Practical Navigator, Vol. II, Table 8.

†The writer has found that a stopwatch is of great assistance whether timing a single shot or averaging. In the single shot, the stopwatch is started in synchrony with the radio time signal from WWV or the chronometer and is stopped at the instant of getting the sighting. In averaging, the assistant says "Start!" to the navigator, and simultaneously starts the stopwatch precisely on the half minute according to the radio time signal or the chronometer.

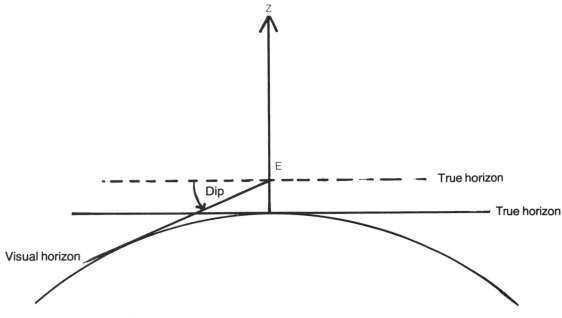

Figure 6.5   Dip angle

of refraction and represents the deflection of the star's apparent position from its real position.

Figure 6.6 shows an abrupt break between outer space and the earth's atmosphere. Actually refraction is a complex affair involving the gradient-like character of atmosphere—its humidity, temperature, and other local conditions. Mean refractions have been worked out for standard temperature and atmospheric conditions. For the nautical navigator altitude correction tables for refraction can be found in the *Nautical Almanac*, Figure 6.7. There is one table for stars and planets, another for the sun (with different values for sighting the upper and lower limbs), and still another for the moon. Since the correction tables for sun and moon are composite ones it is difficult to separate out the single factor of refraction. However, reference to the tables for stars and planets shows that refraction angle R in Figure 6.6 varies from approximately -5 minutes of arc for altitudes of $10°$, to 1 minute at $45°$, to zero correction at $90°$. (Correction for refraction is always subtracted.)

Semidiameter: In the case of the sun or the moon one usually sights on either the lower or the upper limb of the body. In either case the point of tangency on the body is half a diameter from its center. However, it is the center of the body that serves as reference for its positional coordinates. Consequently, if we shoot the lower limb of the sun or the moon we must add the semidiameter to our sextant reading; if the upper limb is observed, the semidiameter value is subtracted.

Figures 6.7 and 6.8 present specimen pages from the *Nautical Almanac*. The correction tables for the sun, Figure 6.7, include semidiameter and refraction. The differences in the corrections for the upper and lower limbs are due to the differential effects of refraction on the two limbs. The corrections for the moon, Figure 6.8, include dip, refraction, semidiameter, parallax, and augmentation (see "Applying Sextant Corrections" later in this chapter).

Semidiameter corrections for other bodies, including the planet Venus with its conspicuous phases, are insignificant and can be ignored.

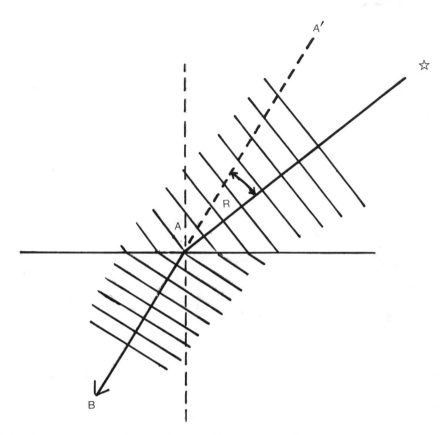

Figure 6.6 Refraction at interface of dense and less dense mediums

There are rare occasions, e.g., a misty horizon with a hazy sun, when the center of the sun is brought into conjunction with the horizon. In such cases the observation is corrected for refraction but not semidiameter. Refraction corrections are not given separately for the sun in the *Nautical Almanac* but can be obtained by subtracting SD, at the bottom of the daily entry column for the sun, from the lower-limb correction as applied to apparent altitude, Table A2. That is to say, the altitude correction Table A2 for the sun includes the combined corrections for semidiameter and refraction.

Parallax: Parallax is the difference in angle between the altitude measured at the center of the earth and that measured at the surface of the earth. With sufficiently refined instruments, the moon, sun, planets, and nearer stars should show detectable parallactic displacement. In navigational practice only the parallax of the moon need be taken into account.

Figure 6.9 shows the effect of parallax; hp is the altitude of the moon at the surface of the earth, and hg is the altitude at the center. The angle p is equal to the difference between the two angles and, as a correction, must be added to hp in order to get hg. As can be seen from Figure 6.9 the angle p will change as the moon moves from the horizon to the zenith. Toward the zenith the value of p diminishes toward zero. At the horizon, i.e., at moonrise or moonset, the value of p will be at the maximum. Parallax of the moon on the horizon is known as horizontal parallax, HP. It is the value recorded in the

ALTITUDE CORRECTION TABLES 10°-90°—SUN, STARS, PLANETS

OCT.—MAR.	SUN	APR.—SEPT.	STARS AND PLANETS		DIP		
App. Alt.	Lower Limb / Upper Limb	App. Alt. / Lower Limb / Upper Limb	App. Alt. / Corrⁿ	App. Alt. / Additional Corrⁿ	Ht. of Eye / Corrⁿ	Ht. of Eye	Ht. of Eye / Corrⁿ

```
  OCT.—MAR.  SUN  APR.—SEPT.     STARS AND PLANETS              DIP

App. Lower Upper  App. Lower Upper   App.          App. Additional  Ht.of      Ht.of   Ht.of
Alt. Limb  Limb   Alt. Limb  Limb    Alt.  Corrⁿ   Alt.  Corrⁿ      Eye  Corrⁿ  Eye     Eye   Corrⁿ

  °  ′              °  ′                °  ′                        m            ft.      m
 9 34 +10·8 −21·5  9 39 +10·6 −21·2   9 56 −5·3       1982        2·4 −2·8     8·0    1·0 − 1·8
 9 45 +10·9 −21·4  9 51 +10·7 −21·1  10 08 −5·2      VENUS        2·6 −2·9     8·6    1·5 − 2·2
 9 56 +11·0 −21·3 10 03 +10·8 −21·0  10 20 −5·1    Jan. 1–Jan. 3  2·8 −3·0     9·2    2·0 − 2·5
10 08 +11·1 −21·2 10 15 +10·9 −20·9  10 33 −5·0                   3·0 −3·1     9·8    2·5 − 2·8
10 21 +11·2 −21·1 10 27 +11·0 −20·8  10 46 −4·9     °  ′          3·2 −3·2    10·5    3·0 − 3·0
10 34 +11·3 −21·0 10 40 +11·1 −20·7  11 00 −4·8     6 + 0·5       3·4 −3·3    11·2    See table
10 47 +11·4 −20·9 10 54 +11·2 −20·6  11 14 −4·7    20 + 0·6       3·6 −3·4    11·9       ←
11 01 +11·5 −20·8 11 08 +11·3 −20·5  11 29 −4·6    31 + 0·7       3·8 −3·5    12·6     m
11 15 +11·6 −20·7 11 23 +11·4 −20·4  11 45 −4·5                   4·0 −3·6    13·3    20 − 7·9
11 30 +11·7 −20·6 11 38 +11·5 −20·3  12 01 −4·4   Jan. 4–Feb. 7   4·3 −3·7    14·1    22 − 8·3
11 46 +11·8 −20·5 11 54 +11·6 −20·2  12 18 −4·3                   4·5 −3·8    14·9    24 − 8·6
12 02 +11·9 −20·4 12 10 +11·7 −20·1  12 35 −4·2     °  ′          4·7 −3·9    15·7    26 − 9·0
12 19 +12·0 −20·3 12 28 +11·8 −20·0  12 54 −4·1     4 + 0·6       5·0 −4·0    16·5    28 − 9·3
12 37 +12·1 −20·2 12 46 +11·9 −19·9  13 13 −4·0    12 + 0·7       5·2 −4·1    17·4
12 55 +12·2 −20·1 13 05 +12·0 −19·8  13 33 −3·9    22 + 0·8       5·5 −4·2    18·3    30 − 9·6
13 14 +12·3 −20·0 13 24 +12·1 −19·7  13 54 −3·8                   5·8 −4·3    19·1    32 −10·0
13 35 +12·4 −19·9 13 45 +12·2 −19·6  14 16 −3·7   Feb. 8–Feb. 14  6·1 −4·4    20·1    34 −10·3
13 56 +12·5 −19·8 14 07 +12·3 −19·5  14 40 −3·6                   6·3 −4·5    21·0    36 −10·6
14 18 +12·6 −19·7 14 30 +12·4 −19·4  15 04 −3·5     °  ′          6·6 −4·6    22·0    38 −10·8
14 42 +12·7 −19·6 14 54 +12·5 −19·3  15 30 −3·4     6 + 0·5       6·9 −4·7    22·9
15 06 +12·8 −19·5 15 19 +12·6 −19·2  15 57 −3·3    20 + 0·6       7·2 −4·8    23·9    40 −11·1
15 32 +12·9 −19·4 15 46 +12·7 −19·1  16 26 −3·2    31 + 0·7       7·5 −4·9    24·9    42 −11·4
15 59 +13·0 −19·3 16 14 +12·8 −19·0  16 56 −3·1                   7·9 −5·0    26·0    44 −11·7
16 28 +13·1 −19·2 16 44 +12·9 −18·9  17 28 −3·0   Feb. 15–Mar. 2  8·2 −5·1    27·1    46 −11·9
16 59 +13·2 −19·1 17 15 +13·0 −18·8  18 02 −2·9                   8·5 −5·2    28·1    48 −12·2
17 32 +13·3 −19·0 17 48 +13·1 −18·7  18 38 −2·8     °  ′          8·8 −5·3    29·2
18 06 +13·4 −18·9 18 24 +13·2 −18·6  19 17 −2·7    11 + 0·4       9·2 −5·4    30·4    ft.
18 42 +13·5 −18·8 19 01 +13·3 −18·5  19 58 −2·6    41 + 0·5       9·5 −5·5    31·5    2 − 1·4
19 21 +13·6 −18·7 19 42 +13·4 −18·4  20 42 −2·5                   9·9 −5·6    32·7    4 − 1·9
20 03 +13·7 −18·6 20 25 +13·5 −18·3  21 28 −2·4   Mar. 3–Mar. 28 10·3 −5·7    33·9    6 − 2·4
20 48 +13·8 −18·5 21 11 +13·6 −18·2  22 19 −2·3                  10·6 −5·8    35·1    8 − 2·7
21 35 +13·9 −18·4 22 00 +13·7 −18·1  23 13 −2·2     °  ′         11·0 −5·9    36·3   10 − 3·1
22 26 +14·0 −18·3 22 54 +13·8 −18·0  24 11 −2·1    47 + 0·2      11·4 −6·0    37·6   See table
23 22 +14·1 −18·2 23 51 +13·9 −17·9  25 14 −2·0                  11·8 −6·1    38·9      ←
24 21 +14·2 −18·1 24 53 +14·0 −17·8  26 22 −1·9   May 13–Dec. 31 12·2 −6·2    40·1    ft.
25 26 +14·3 −18·0 26 00 +14·1 −17·7  27 36 −1·8                  12·6 −6·3    41·5   70 − 8·1
26 36 +14·4 −17·9 27 13 +14·2 −17·6  28 56 −1·7    42 + 0·1      13·0 −6·4    42·8   75 − 8·4
27 52 +14·5 −17·8 28 33 +14·3 −17·5  30 24 −1·6                  13·4 −6·5    44·2   80 − 8·7
29 15 +14·6 −17·7 30 00 +14·4 −17·4  32 00 −1·5     MARS         13·8 −6·6    45·5   85 − 8·9
30 46 +14·7 −17·6 31 35 +14·5 −17·3  33 45 −1·4   Jan. 1–Jan. 30 14·2 −6·7    46·9   90 − 9·2
32 26 +14·8 −17·5 33 20 +14·6 −17·2  35 40 −1·3                  14·7 −6·8    48·4   95 − 9·5
34 17 +14·9 −17·4 35 17 +14·7 −17·1  37 48 −1·2     °  ′         15·1 −6·9    49·8
36 20 +15·0 −17·3 37 26 +14·8 −17·0  40 08 −1·1    60 + 0·1      15·5 −7·0    51·3  100 − 9·7
38 36 +15·1 −17·2 39 50 +14·9 −16·9  42 44 −1·0                  16·0 −7·1    52·8  105 − 9·9
41 08 +15·2 −17·1 42 31 +15·0 −16·8  45 36 −0·9   Jan. 31–June 18 16·5 −7·2   54·3  110 −10·2
43 59 +15·3 −17·0 45 31 +15·1 −16·7  48 47 −0·8                  16·9 −7·3    55·8  115 −10·4
47 10 +15·4 −16·9 48 55 +15·2 −16·6  52 18 −0·7     °  ′         17·4 −7·4    57·4  120 −10·6
50 46 +15·5 −16·8 52 44 +15·3 −16·5  56 11 −0·6    41 + 0·2      17·9 −7·5    58·9  125 −10·8
54 49 +15·6 −16·7 57 02 +15·4 −16·4  60 28 −0·5    75 + 0·1      18·4 −7·6    60·5
59 23 +15·7 −16·6 61 51 +15·5 −16·3  65 08 −0·4   June 19–Dec. 31 18·8 −7·7   62·1  130 −11·1
64 30 +15·8 −16·5 67 17 +15·6 −16·2  70 11 −0·3                  19·3 −7·8    63·8  135 −11·3
70 12 +15·9 −16·4 73 16 +15·7 −16·1  75 34 −0·2     °  ′         19·8 −7·9    65·4  140 −11·5
76 26 +16·0 −16·3 79 43 +15·8 −16·0  81 13 −0·1    60 + 0·1      20·4 −8·0    67·1  145 −11·7
83 05 +16·1 −16·2 86 32 +15·9 −15·9  87 03 −0·1                  20·9 −8·1    68·8  150 −11·9
90 00             90 00              90 00  0·0                  21·4         70·5  155 −12·1
```

App. Alt. = Apparent altitude = Sextant altitude corrected for index error and dip.

Figure 6.7 Specimen pages from *Nautical Almanac*

ALTITUDE CORRECTION TABLES 0°–35°—MOON

App. Alt.	0°–4° Corrⁿ	5°–9° Corrⁿ	10°–14° Corrⁿ	15°–19° Corrⁿ	20°–24° Corrⁿ	25°–29° Corrⁿ	30°–34° Corrⁿ	App. Alt.
00	0° 33·8	5° 58·2	10° 62·1	15° 62·8	20° 62·2	25° 60·8	30° 58·9	00
10	35·9	58·5	62·2	62·8	62·1	60·8	58·8	10
20	37·8	58·7	62·2	62·8	62·1	60·7	58·8	20
30	39·6	58·9	62·3	62·8	62·1	60·7	58·7	30
40	41·2	59·1	62·3	62·8	62·0	60·6	58·6	40
50	42·6	59·3	62·4	62·7	62·0	60·6	58·5	50
00	1° 44·0	6° 59·5	11° 62·4	16° 62·7	21° 62·0	26° 60·5	31° 58·5	00
10	45·2	59·7	62·4	62·7	61·9	60·4	58·4	10
20	46·3	59·9	62·5	62·7	61·9	60·4	58·3	20
30	47·3	60·0	62·5	62·7	61·9	60·3	58·2	30
40	48·3	60·2	62·5	62·7	61·8	60·3	58·2	40
50	49·2	60·3	62·6	62·7	61·8	60·2	58·1	50
00	2° 50·0	7° 60·5	12° 62·6	17° 62·7	22° 61·7	27° 60·1	32° 58·0	00
10	50·8	60·6	62·6	62·6	61·7	60·1	57·9	10
20	51·4	60·7	62·6	62·6	61·6	60·0	57·8	20
30	52·1	60·9	62·7	62·6	61·6	59·9	57·8	30
40	52·7	61·0	62·7	62·6	61·5	59·9	57·7	40
50	53·3	61·1	62·7	62·6	61·5	59·8	57·6	50
00	3° 53·8	8° 61·2	13° 62·7	18° 62·5	23° 61·5	28° 59·7	33° 57·5	00
10	54·3	61·3	62·7	62·5	61·4	59·7	57·4	10
20	54·8	61·4	62·7	62·5	61·4	59·6	57·4	20
30	55·2	61·5	62·8	62·5	61·3	59·6	57·3	30
40	55·6	61·6	62·8	62·4	61·3	59·5	57·2	40
50	56·0	61·6	62·8	62·4	61·2	59·4	57·1	50
00	4° 56·4	9° 61·7	14° 62·8	19° 62·4	24° 61·2	29° 59·3	34° 57·0	00
10	56·7	61·8	62·8	62·3	61·1	59·3	56·9	10
20	57·1	61·9	62·8	62·3	61·1	59·2	56·9	20
30	57·4	61·9	62·8	62·3	61·0	59·1	56·8	30
40	57·7	62·0	62·8	62·2	60·9	59·1	56·7	40
50	57·9	62·1	62·8	62·2	60·9	59·0	56·6	50

H.P.	L U	L U	L U	L U	L U	L U	L U	H.P.
54·0	0·3 0·9	0·3 0·9	0·4 1·0	0·5 1·1	0·6 1·2	0·7 1·3	0·9 1·5	54·0
54·3	0·7 1·1	0·7 1·2	0·7 1·2	0·8 1·3	0·9 1·4	1·1 1·5	1·2 1·7	54·3
54·6	1·1 1·4	1·1 1·4	1·1 1·4	1·2 1·5	1·3 1·6	1·4 1·7	1·5 1·8	54·6
54·9	1·4 1·6	1·5 1·6	1·5 1·6	1·6 1·7	1·6 1·8	1·8 1·9	1·9 2·0	54·9
55·2	1·8 1·8	1·8 1·8	1·9 1·9	1·9 1·9	2·0 2·0	2·1 2·1	2·2 2·2	55·2
55·5	2·2 2·0	2·2 2·0	2·3 2·1	2·3 2·1	2·4 2·2	2·4 2·3	2·5 2·4	55·5
55·8	2·6 2·2	2·6 2·2	2·6 2·3	2·7 2·3	2·7 2·4	2·8 2·4	2·9 2·5	55·8
56·1	3·0 2·4	3·0 2·5	3·0 2·5	3·0 2·5	3·1 2·6	3·1 2·6	3·2 2·7	56·1
56·4	3·4 2·7	3·4 2·7	3·4 2·7	3·4 2·7	3·4 2·8	3·5 2·8	3·5 2·9	56·4
56·7	3·7 2·9	3·7 2·9	3·8 2·9	3·8 2·9	3·8 3·0	3·8 3·0	3·9 3·0	56·7
57·0	4·1 3·1	4·1 3·1	4·1 3·1	4·1 3·1	4·2 3·1	4·2 3·2	4·2 3·2	57·0
57·3	4·5 3·3	4·5 3·3	4·5 3·3	4·5 3·3	4·5 3·3	4·5 3·4	4·6 3·4	57·3
57·6	4·9 3·5	4·9 3·5	4·9 3·5	4·9 3·5	4·9 3·5	4·9 3·5	4·9 3·6	57·6
57·9	5·3 3·8	5·3 3·8	5·2 3·8	5·2 3·7	5·2 3·7	5·2 3·7	5·2 3·7	57·9
58·2	5·6 4·0	5·6 4·0	5·6 4·0	5·6 4·0	5·6 3·9	5·6 3·9	5·6 3·9	58·2
58·5	6·0 4·2	6·0 4·2	6·0 4·2	6·0 4·2	6·0 4·1	5·9 4·1	5·9 4·1	58·5
58·8	6·4 4·4	6·4 4·4	6·4 4·4	6·3 4·4	6·3 4·3	6·3 4·3	6·2 4·2	58·8
59·1	6·8 4·6	6·8 4·6	6·7 4·6	6·7 4·6	6·7 4·5	6·6 4·5	6·6 4·4	59·1
59·4	7·2 4·8	7·1 4·8	7·1 4·8	7·1 4·8	7·0 4·7	7·0 4·7	6·9 4·6	59·4
59·7	7·5 5·1	7·5 5·0	7·5 5·0	7·5 5·0	7·4 4·9	7·3 4·8	7·2 4·7	59·7
60·0	7·9 5·3	7·9 5·3	7·9 5·2	7·8 5·2	7·8 5·1	7·7 5·0	7·6 4·9	60·0
60·3	8·3 5·5	8·3 5·5	8·2 5·4	8·2 5·4	8·1 5·3	8·0 5·2	7·9 5·1	60·3
60·6	8·7 5·7	8·7 5·7	8·6 5·7	8·6 5·6	8·5 5·5	8·4 5·4	8·2 5·3	60·6
60·9	9·1 5·9	9·0 5·9	9·0 5·9	8·9 5·8	8·8 5·7	8·7 5·6	8·6 5·4	60·9
61·2	9·5 6·2	9·4 6·1	9·4 6·1	9·3 6·0	9·2 5·9	9·1 5·8	8·9 5·6	61·2
61·5	9·8 6·4	9·8 6·3	9·7 6·3	9·7 6·2	9·5 6·1	9·4 5·9	9·2 5·8	61·5

DIP

Ht. of Eye	Corrⁿ	Ht. of Eye	Ht. of Eye	Corrⁿ	Ht. of Eye
m		ft.	m		ft.
2·4	−2·8	8·0	9·5	−5·5	31·5
2·6	−2·9	8·6	9·9	−5·6	32·7
2·8	−3·0	9·2	10·3	−5·7	33·9
3·0	−3·1	9·8	10·6	−5·8	35·1
3·2	−3·2	10·5	11·0	−5·9	36·3
3·4	−3·3	11·2	11·4	−6·0	37·6
3·6	−3·4	11·9	11·8	−6·1	38·9
3·8	−3·5	12·6	12·2	−6·2	40·1
4·0	−3·6	13·3	12·6	−6·3	41·5
4·3	−3·7	14·1	13·0	−6·4	42·8
4·5	−3·8	14·9	13·4	−6·5	44·2
4·7	−3·9	15·7	13·8	−6·6	45·5
5·0	−4·0	16·5	14·2	−6·7	46·9
5·2	−4·1	17·4	14·7	−6·8	48·4
5·5	−4·2	18·3	15·1	−6·9	49·8
5·8	−4·3	19·1	15·5	−7·0	51·3
6·1	−4·4	20·1	16·0	−7·1	52·8
6·3	−4·5	21·0	16·5	−7·2	54·3
6·6	−4·6	22·0	16·9	−7·3	55·8
6·9	−4·7	22·9	17·4		57·4
7·2	−4·8	23·9	17·9	−7·5	58·9
7·5	−4·9	24·9	18·4	−7·6	60·5
7·9	−5·0	26·0	18·8	−7·7	62·1
8·2	−5·1	27·1	19·3	−7·8	63·8
8·5	−5·2	28·1	19·8	−7·9	65·4
8·8	−5·3	29·2	20·4	−8·0	67·1
9·2	−5·4	30·4	20·9	−8·1	68·8
9·5		31·5	21·4		70·5

MOON CORRECTION TABLE

The correction is in two parts; the first correction is taken from the upper part of the table with argument apparent altitude, and the second from the lower part, with argument H.P., in the same column as that from which the first correction was taken. Separate corrections are given in the lower part for lower (L) and upper (U) limbs. All corrections are to be **added** to apparent altitude, *but 30' is to be subtracted from the altitude of the upper limb.*

For corrections for pressure and temperature see page A4.

For bubble sextant observations ignore dip, take the mean of upper and lower limb corrections and subtract 15' from the altitude.

App. Alt. = Apparent altitude = Sextant altitude corrected for index error and dip.

Figure 6.8 Specimen pages from *Nautical Almanac*

ALTITUDE CORRECTION TABLES 35°–90°—MOON

App. Alt.	35°–39° Corrⁿ	40°–44° Corrⁿ	45°–49° Corrⁿ	50°–54° Corrⁿ	55°–59° Corrⁿ	60°–64° Corrⁿ	65°–69° Corrⁿ	70°–74° Corrⁿ	75°–79° Corrⁿ	80°–84° Corrⁿ	85°–89° Corrⁿ	App. Alt.
00	35° 56.5	40° 53.7	45° 50.5	50° 46.9	55° 43.1	60° 38.9	65° 34.6	70° 30.1	75° 25.3	80° 20.5	85° 15.6	00
10	56.4	53.6	50.4	46.8	42.9	38.8	34.4	29.9	25.2	20.4	15.5	10
20	56.3	53.5	50.2	46.7	42.8	38.7	34.3	29.7	25.0	20.2	15.3	20
30	56.2	53.4	50.1	46.5	42.7	38.5	34.1	29.6	24.9	20.0	15.1	30
40	56.2	53.3	50.0	46.4	42.5	38.4	34.0	29.4	24.7	19.9	15.0	40
50	56.1	53.2	49.9	46.3	42.4	38.2	33.8	29.3	24.5	19.7	14.8	50
00	36° 56.0	41° 53.1	46° 49.8	51° 46.2	56° 42.3	61° 38.1	66° 33.7	71° 29.1	76° 24.4	81° 19.6	86° 14.6	00
10	55.9	53.0	49.7	46.0	42.1	37.9	33.5	29.0	24.2	19.4	14.5	10
20	55.8	52.8	49.5	45.9	42.0	37.8	33.4	28.8	24.1	19.2	14.3	20
30	55.7	52.7	49.4	45.8	41.8	37.7	33.2	28.7	23.9	19.1	14.1	30
40	55.6	52.6	49.3	45.7	41.7	37.5	33.1	28.5	23.8	18.9	14.0	40
50	55.5	52.5	49.2	45.5	41.6	37.4	32.9	28.3	23.6	18.7	13.8	50
00	37° 55.4	42° 52.4	47° 49.1	52° 45.4	57° 41.4	62° 37.2	67° 32.8	72° 28.2	77° 23.4	82° 18.6	87° 13.7	00
10	55.3	52.3	49.0	45.3	41.3	37.1	32.6	28.0	23.3	18.4	13.5	10
20	55.2	52.2	48.8	45.2	41.2	36.9	32.5	27.9	23.1	18.2	13.3	20
30	55.1	52.1	48.7	45.0	41.0	36.8	32.3	27.7	22.9	18.1	13.2	30
40	55.0	52.0	48.6	44.9	40.9	36.6	32.2	27.6	22.8	17.9	13.0	40
50	55.0	51.9	48.5	44.8	40.8	36.5	32.0	27.4	22.6	17.8	12.8	50
00	38° 54.9	43° 51.8	48° 48.4	53° 44.6	58° 40.6	63° 36.4	68° 31.9	73° 27.2	78° 22.5	83° 17.6	88° 12.7	00
10	54.8	51.7	48.2	44.5	40.5	36.2	31.7	27.1	22.3	17.4	12.5	10
20	54.7	51.6	48.1	44.4	40.3	36.1	31.6	26.9	22.1	17.3	12.3	20
30	54.6	51.5	48.0	44.2	40.2	35.9	31.4	26.8	22.0	17.1	12.2	30
40	54.5	51.4	47.9	44.1	40.1	35.8	31.3	26.6	21.8	16.9	12.0	40
50	54.4	51.2	47.8	44.0	39.9	35.6	31.1	26.5	21.7	16.8	11.8	50
00	39° 54.3	44° 51.1	49° 47.6	54° 43.9	59° 39.8	64° 35.5	69° 31.0	74° 26.3	79° 21.5	84° 16.6	89° 11.7	00
10	54.2	51.0	47.5	43.7	39.6	35.3	30.8	26.1	21.3	16.5	11.5	10
20	54.1	50.9	47.4	43.6	39.5	35.2	30.7	26.0	21.2	16.3	11.4	20
30	54.0	50.8	47.3	43.5	39.4	35.0	30.5	25.8	21.0	16.1	11.2	30
40	53.9	50.7	47.2	43.3	39.2	34.9	30.4	25.7	20.9	16.0	11.0	40
50	53.8	50.6	47.0	43.2	39.1	34.7	30.2	25.5	20.7	15.8	10.9	50

H.P.	L U	L U	L U	L U	L U	L U	L U	L U	L U	L U	L U	H.P.
54.0	1.1 1.7	1.3 1.9	1.5 2.1	1.7 2.4	2.0 2.6	2.3 2.9	2.6 3.2	2.9 3.5	3.2 3.8	3.5 4.1	3.8 4.5	54.0
54.3	1.4 1.8	1.6 2.0	1.8 2.2	2.0 2.5	2.3 2.7	2.5 3.0	2.8 3.2	3.0 3.5	3.3 3.8	3.6 4.1	3.9 4.4	54.3
54.6	1.7 2.0	1.9 2.2	2.1 2.4	2.3 2.6	2.5 2.8	2.7 3.0	3.0 3.3	3.2 3.5	3.5 3.8	3.7 4.1	4.0 4.3	54.6
54.9	2.0 2.2	2.2 2.3	2.3 2.5	2.5 2.7	2.7 2.9	2.9 3.1	3.2 3.3	3.4 3.5	3.6 3.8	3.9 4.0	4.1 4.3	54.9
55.2	2.3 2.3	2.5 2.4	2.6 2.6	2.8 2.8	3.0 2.9	3.2 3.1	3.4 3.3	3.6 3.5	3.8 3.7	4.0 4.0	4.2 4.2	55.2
55.5	2.7 2.5	2.8 2.6	2.9 2.7	3.1 2.9	3.2 3.0	3.4 3.2	3.6 3.4	3.7 3.5	3.9 3.7	4.1 3.9	4.3 4.1	55.5
55.8	3.0 2.6	3.1 2.7	3.2 2.8	3.3 3.0	3.5 3.1	3.6 3.3	3.8 3.4	3.9 3.6	4.1 3.7	4.2 3.9	4.4 4.0	55.8
56.1	3.3 2.8	3.4 2.9	3.5 3.0	3.6 3.1	3.7 3.2	3.8 3.3	4.0 3.4	4.1 3.6	4.2 3.7	4.4 3.8	4.5 4.0	56.1
56.4	3.6 2.9	3.7 3.0	3.8 3.1	3.9 3.2	3.9 3.3	4.0 3.4	4.1 3.5	4.3 3.6	4.4 3.7	4.5 3.8	4.6 3.9	56.4
56.7	3.9 3.1	4.0 3.1	4.1 3.2	4.1 3.3	4.2 3.3	4.3 3.4	4.3 3.5	4.4 3.6	4.5 3.7	4.6 3.8	4.7 3.8	56.7
57.0	4.3 3.2	4.3 3.3	4.3 3.3	4.4 3.4	4.4 3.4	4.5 3.5	4.5 3.5	4.6 3.6	4.7 3.6	4.7 3.7	4.8 3.8	57.0
57.3	4.6 3.4	4.6 3.4	4.6 3.4	4.6 3.5	4.7 3.5	4.7 3.5	4.7 3.6	4.8 3.6	4.8 3.6	4.8 3.7	4.9 3.7	57.3
57.6	4.9 3.6	4.9 3.6	4.9 3.6	4.9 3.6	4.9 3.6	4.9 3.6	4.9 3.6	4.9 3.6	5.0 3.6	5.0 3.6	5.0 3.6	57.6
57.9	5.2 3.7	5.2 3.7	5.2 3.7	5.2 3.7	5.2 3.7	5.1 3.6	5.1 3.6	5.1 3.6	5.1 3.6	5.1 3.6	5.1 3.6	57.9
58.2	5.5 3.9	5.5 3.8	5.5 3.8	5.4 3.8	5.4 3.7	5.4 3.7	5.3 3.7	5.3 3.6	5.2 3.6	5.2 3.5	5.2 3.5	58.2
58.5	5.9 4.0	5.8 4.0	5.8 3.9	5.7 3.9	5.6 3.8	5.6 3.8	5.5 3.7	5.5 3.6	5.4 3.6	5.3 3.5	5.3 3.4	58.5
58.8	6.2 4.2	6.1 4.1	6.0 4.1	5.9 3.9	5.9 3.9	5.8 3.8	5.7 3.7	5.6 3.5	5.5 3.5	5.4 3.5	5.3 3.4	58.8
59.1	6.5 4.3	6.4 4.3	6.3 4.2	6.2 4.1	6.1 4.0	6.0 3.9	5.9 3.8	5.8 3.6	5.7 3.5	5.6 3.4	5.4 3.3	59.1
59.4	6.8 4.5	6.7 4.4	6.6 4.3	6.5 4.2	6.4 4.1	6.2 3.9	6.1 3.8	6.0 3.7	5.8 3.5	5.7 3.4	5.5 3.2	59.4
59.7	7.1 4.6	7.0 4.5	6.9 4.4	6.8 4.3	6.6 4.1	6.5 4.0	6.3 3.8	6.2 3.7	6.0 3.5	5.8 3.3	5.6 3.2	59.7
60.0	7.5 4.8	7.3 4.7	7.2 4.5	7.0 4.4	6.9 4.2	6.7 4.0	6.5 3.9	6.3 3.7	6.1 3.5	5.9 3.3	5.7 3.1	60.0
60.3	7.8 5.0	7.6 4.8	7.5 4.7	7.3 4.5	7.1 4.3	6.9 4.1	6.7 3.9	6.5 3.7	6.3 3.5	6.0 3.2	5.8 3.0	60.3
60.6	8.1 5.1	7.9 5.0	7.7 4.8	7.6 4.6	7.3 4.4	7.1 4.2	6.9 3.9	6.7 3.7	6.4 3.4	6.2 3.2	5.9 2.9	60.6
60.9	8.4 5.3	8.2 5.1	8.0 4.9	7.8 4.7	7.6 4.5	7.3 4.2	7.1 4.0	6.8 3.7	6.6 3.4	6.3 3.2	6.0 2.9	60.9
61.2	8.7 5.4	8.5 5.2	8.3 5.0	8.1 4.8	7.8 4.5	7.6 4.3	7.3 4.0	7.0 3.7	6.7 3.4	6.4 3.1	6.1 2.8	61.2
61.5	9.1 5.6	8.8 5.4	8.6 5.1	8.3 4.9	8.1 4.6	7.8 4.3	7.5 4.0	7.2 3.7	6.9 3.4	6.5 3.1	6.2 2.7	61.5

Nautical Almanac and serves as the basis for computing the parallax correction for the moon.

Instrumental Corrections

Unlike the intrinsic corrections which apply to all observations, instrumental corrections are unique to a particular instrument. As a rule an instrumental error is constant, and once known, a correction can be routinely applied. An instrument with a known constant error can be just as reliable, and just as informative, as a perfect instrument. Some instrument errors can be removed by adjustments. There are manuals, including *Bowditch*, which instruct the navigator on how to adjust an instrument (in most cases, the alignment of the mirrors) but unless he is expert in fine tuning he would be well advised to leave such matters to the specialist.

Index error is that due to a lack of parallel alignment between the index and horizon mirrors. If we set the micrometer drum (index arm) to zero then we should have perfect alignment between the image as seen through the horizon glass and that reflected by the index mirror. To check, set the micrometer drum to zero and focus on a horizontal line such as the horizon, or an extended roofline. If the two images in the horizon glass do not align, there is index error, Figure 6.10.

To determine the magnitude of the error, align the two images, then read the micrometer drum. When the error is positive it is said to be "on the arc," and the correction is subtracted. When the error is negative, or "off the arc," the correction is added. Index error should be checked at regular intervals.

Other errors include perpendicularity of the mirrors and telescope alignment. Although adjustments to right the mirrors are fairly simple ones, those to correct alignment should be left to the specialty shops. However, should one be able to check his own instrument against another of known accuracy, e.g., a theodolite, then a table of instrument corrections could be determined and systematically applied (see below).

Personal Errors

In the lore of documenting individual differences psychologists like to speak of the discovery of the personal equation. As the story goes, Maskelyne, astronomer royal of Greenwich, 1796, dismissed his assistant Kinnebrook because he, the assistant, was observing the times of stellar transit almost one second later than the royal astronomer, an intolerable amount of error. Bessel, another astronomer, undertook the study of these errors and thereby established the foundations for the theory of errors. In short, some errors among observers were found to be systematic, others random, so that any given observer might show a systematic bias (his personal equation) plus a random error component.

Figure 6.11 portrays the simplified version of personal error. Let μ be the true measure of an altitude. Then the distribution centered about the arithmetic mean $\overline{X}$ represents, at least theoretically, the distribution of the particular observer's observation. There is a random component represented by the spread of the distribution (the so-called error variance) and the systematic component represented by the difference between μ and $\overline{X}$. The theory of errors lends itself to sophisticated statistical treatment; however, the navigator as observer need only be cognizant of the underlying principles of error: one, he should be aware of the two components of personal error; and two, he should attempt systematically to minimize their effects.

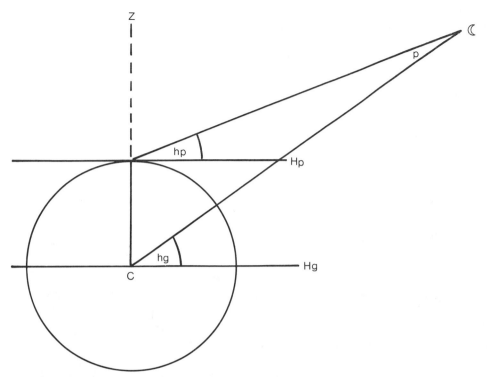

Figure 6.9   Parallax

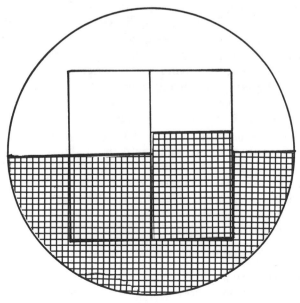

Figure 6.10   Index error

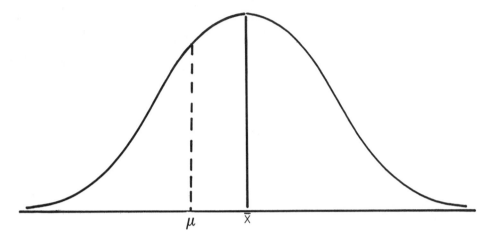

$\mu \qquad \bar{X}$

Figure 6.11   Theoretical distribution of observer error

The simplest procedure is to take an extensive set of observations under conditions where the correct altitude to be observed is known (*cf*. Note 6.3). Plotting the discrepancies between the observed and the correct altitudes (Ho − Hc) will yield information similar to that in Figure 6.12, namely, a frequency distribution of observational error, $E = $ Ho − Hc. Now if the mean of the errors $\bar{X}e$ is zero there is no systematic error. But if $\bar{X}e$ is greater or less than zero there is systematic error and we can reduce its impact by making a constant correction based directly on the magnitude of $\bar{X}e$. However, correcting for systematic error does not eliminate the scatter, or variability, of the distribution. The random component of error remains. We can, though, minimize the impact of the random error by averaging. Rather than relying on a single observation, we should take a set of observations over a brief time span, say, one or two minutes. The average of all observations would be assigned to a time midpoint in the time span. Our expectation is that the average of random errors is zero. Hence, our procedure should be, first, to correct each observation in the set of observations for systematic error. Then by averaging over the set of corrected observations we should minimize the random component of error (*cf*. Note 6.4).

Practically every novice in the art of sextant observation falls prey to systematic error. More likely than not, he or she consistently brings the reflected image below the horizon, declaring an appropriate tangent just as the "body wets a limb." Others may be of a more gentle sort, letting the body skip across the horizon without its "lipping the dew." With practice one may overcome systematic error but the random component will always remain. The best way to contend with random error is to average a set of observations.

APPLYING SEXTANT CORRECTIONS

In order to obtain Ho, the true observed altitude, two sets of corrections need to be applied to the sextant observations Hs. One is the set of corrections applying to all observations, all celestial bodies. The other is the set that applies to the specific type of bodies, i.e., sun, moon, planets, stars. With practice, the making of corrections becomes routine.

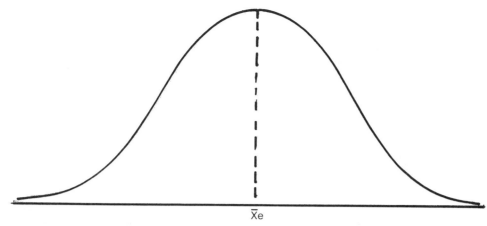

$\overline{X}e$

Figure 6.12   Error distribution: Ho − Hc

General Corrections

These must be applied to all observations:

Instrument Error Correction, I: Most instruments have been tested by the maker and the sextant case will often include a note as to the magnitude of error at various elevations. For older instruments, the observer may have to determine instrument error through systematic checks against observations of known accuracy.

Index Error Correction, IC: A separate instrument error readily determined by aligning the horizons as observed through both the horizon and the index mirrors. The index correction Ic is opposite in sign to the index error.

Personal Error Correction, PC: The consistent bias in a particular observer's sights is most readily obtained by computing the average error in a set of shots where each shot, with all other corrections applied, is compared against a known true altitude.

Dip, D: A separate table for dip corrections is provided in the *Nautical Almanac.* These corrections are always subtracted and apply to all observations regardless of the body.

Particular Corrections

These are applied to specific bodies:

Corrections for Sun Observations: In addition to the general corrections (I, IC, PC, D) above, there are other corrections that apply specifically to the sun and are incorporated into "Altitude Correction Tables—Sun" in the *Nautical Almanac* (see Figure 6.7). The corrections incorporated into a single value in this table include those for:

Refraction, R
Semidiameter, SD
Solar parallax, P
Irradiation, J

Solar parallax, like lunar parallax, is due to the fact that an observation is made on the surface of the earth, not at the center. *Irradiation* is an illusory effect generated by the contrast of a bright sky against the dark horizon, the sun's diameter appearing larger and the horizon appearing depressed. Solar parallax and irradiation effects are so small as to be negligible for the practical navigator. Nevertheless, they are included in the correction tables.

Corrections for Moon Observations: As with all bodies the general corrections (I, IC, PC, D) must be applied. In addition, correction for the following errors must be made:

Refraction, R
Semidiameter, SD
Augmentation, A
Horizontal parallax, HP

"Altitude Correction Tables—Moon" (see Figure 6.8) are somewhat more complicated than those for the sun. The top half of the table gives the combined correction for R, SD, and A.

Augmentation, A, is a nearly negligible factor due to the fact that the optical image of the moon is greater, because the moon is nearer at the zenith than it is on the horizon. (Incidentally, the well-known "moon illusion" in which the moon appears larger on the horizon than at the zenith is quite apart from *augmentation*. This illusion, which occurs in spite of augmentation, is due purely to psychological factors operating in human perception and has no effect upon sextant observation.)

The bottom half of the moon correction tables concerns correction for parallax. In the daily pages of the *Nautical Almanac* (see Figure 3.7) hourly values are given for HP. Horizontal parallax, HP, is the maximum value of parallax when the moon is on the horizon. The actual correction for parallax as given in the correction table is a function of HP and the apparent altitude, ha:

$$\text{corr.} = \text{HP} \times \cos \text{ha}$$

in which ha values are taken separately for the upper, U, and lower, L, limbs. Details for applying the moon altitude corrections are spelled out in the legend of the tables, Figure 6.8.

Corrections for Stars and Planets: As with the moon and sun the general corrections (I, IC, PC, D) must be made. In addition a correction for refraction R is made according to the "Altitude Correction Tables—Stars, Planets" (see Figure 6.7). Because of the great distance of the superior planets and all stars, parallax effects are negligible. This is not the case for the relatively near planets, Mars and Venus. Hence, the above tables include a small additional correction for parallax and phase to be applied to observations of Venus and Mars.

Examples: All observations were taken by the observer with a personal error (correction) $+2'$, and combined instrument and index error $-3'$. Corrections are recorded in a format that is widely used whether sight reduction is by tables or by calculator. Find the corrected observed altitude Ho.

Example 1: On May 16, 1982, the lower limb of sun was observed with hs = 56°32′ from a height of 11 feet.

Sun ($\odot$)			
IC	-3	hs	56°32′
PC	$+2$	corr.	$+11'$
D	-3.3	Ho	56°43′
$\odot$ corr.	$+15.3$		
corr. total	$+11$		

Example 2:   On February 26, Venus was observed with hs = 21°56′ from a height of 10 feet.

Venus			
IC	−3′	hs	21°56′
PC	+2′	corr.	−06′
D	−3.1′	Ho	21°50′
main corr.	−2.4′		
add'l corr.	+0.5′		
corr.	−6.0′		

Example 3:   On May 18, 1982, the upper limb of the moon was observed with hs = 34°57′ from a height of 14 feet, GMT = 0800, HP = 57.3′.

Moon			
IC	−3′	hs	34°57′
PC	+2′	corr.	+25.4′
D	−3.6′	Ho	35°22.4′
corr.	+56.6′		
HP:U	+3.4′		
UL −30	−30′		
corr. total	+25.4		

Since the upper limb of the moon was observed, the UL correction, −30′, is mandatory.

Example 4:   On May 17, 1982, Polaris was observed with hs = 36°18′ from a height of 12 feet.

Polaris			
IC	−3′	hs	36°18′
PC	+2′	corr.	−5.7′
D	−3.4′	Ho	36°12.3′
corr. R*	−1.3′		
corr.	−5.7′		

RELATIVE BEARINGS BY SEXTANT

There are occasions in coast pilotage when it is desirable to take relative bearings between objects on a shore. Since the sextant does in fact measure the "bearing" of a celestial body perpendicular to the horizon, it can also be used to measure angles between objects on shore. The observer sights one object as on the fixed horizon and the other object as reflected in the index mirror akin to a celestial object. To use the sextant in this way we rotate the frame to the horizontal. Now we sight through the telescope to view one object through the clear part of the horizon mirror. We next rotate the index arm until we bring the reflected image of the second object into juxtaposition with the

---

*This is the correction for refraction and does not include the adjustment for determining latitude from the Ho of Polaris. See Chapter 8 for Polaris latitude correction.

directly sighted object. Taking these horizontal bearings is simplified if we adopt the procedures for bringing the star down to the horizon.

Arc distance between any two stars as seen from earth remains constant, the intragalactic distances being what they are. Thus if we determine the great-circle arc (distance) between two stars, then a relative bearing between the two will provide a sextant check (*cf.* Note 6.5).

NOTES

Note 6.1
Early altitude-measuring instruments date from the astrolabes of Greek antiquity, although the gnomon, or shadow pin, had been utilized earlier to infer latitude from knowledge of the sun's altitude.

Early astrolabes consisted of metal plates with insertable disks so engraved as to represent conspicuous celestial configurations according to time. Initially, they were used to make inferences only concerning time. However, the addition of an alidade, or sighting arm, increased the astrolabe's utility and it soon achieved renown as the astronomer's most valuable instrument.

The simple astrolabe shown in Figure 6.1 of the text is for all significant detail a model of an instrument designed by Tycho Brahe (1546–1601), that great Danish astronomer known above all else for his observational skill. It was he who made the work of Kepler possible and who, among other things, gave the name *sextant* to an instrument utilizing both a fixed and a moving sight.

Prior to an age of instrumentation, the gnomon was used to measure the altitude of the sun or moon. The altitude of the sun is obtained simply by comparing the height of the gnomon with its shadow, with the ratio converted to angle. By projecting the shadow of the gnomon along a graduated rule, one can easily construct a shadow astrolabe, and with a table of tangents easily convert that scale to altitude, Figure 6.13.

The seaman's *cross-staff*, invented early in the fourteenth century by Levi ben Gershon, is essentially a variation on the shadow astrolabe but makes use of sightings rather than shadows. The cross-staff (Figure 6.14) has a scaled horizontal base and a vertical transom that slides along

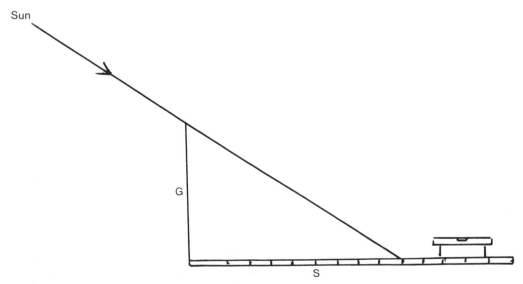

Figure 6.13   Shadow astrolabe with levelling bubble

the horizontal. By sighting down the horizontal to the horizon and across the top of the transom to the body, the observer obtains an altitude whose tangent is the ratio between the appropriate vertical and horizontal measures.

The cross-staff appears to have come into general use among navigators only after the early sixteenth century. Later instruments, rustic as they may seem, had horizontal scales (the transversary) graduated in terms of degrees.

The Arabian *kamal* is a variation on the cross-staff and is used to this day by some Red Sea and East African navigators of dhows. The kamal shown in Figure 6.15 consists of a simple rectangular board with a severally knotted cord attached to it through a hole in the middle. The board is held at arm's length and the navigator sights over the corners P and H to intersect simultaneously the polestar and the horizon. The extension of knots gives an indication of the altitude of Polaris. In practice the navigator sights by holding a knot at the eye or in the teeth and observing over P when H is tangent with the horizon. If knot B, say, is associated with the latitude of some destination and Polaris is sighted above point P, then the navigator is at a latitude greater than that of the destination associated with knot B. If Polaris is sighted below P then the navigator is at a latitude lower than that of the destination.

In his classic *The Raft Book,* Harold Gatty speculated that early Polynesian navigators may have used bamboo tubes, gourds, or coconuts as fixed sighting vehicles for measuring altitude. In principle the arrangement was a simple one of three sighting ports: one as the eyepiece, one for viewing the horizon, and one for the body, as in Figure 6.16. It was a nice conjecture on Gatty's part. Unfortunately, no subsequent research has been able to verify that the early Polynesians ever used instruments of any kind for estimating altitude. They used stars for directional purposes, to be sure, but when it came to estimating altitude, their eyeballs were the only instruments.

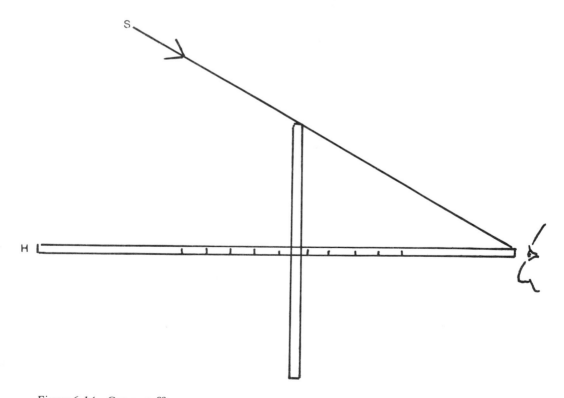

Figure 6.14   Cross-staff

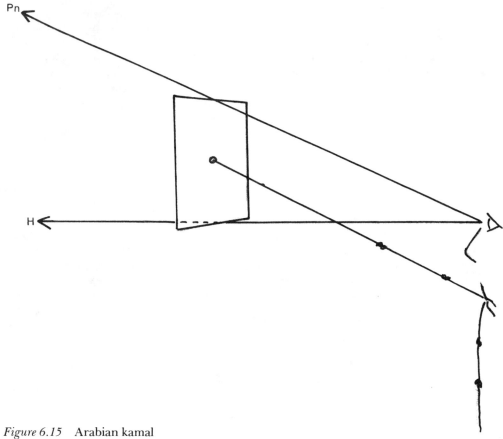

Figure 6.15   Arabian kamal

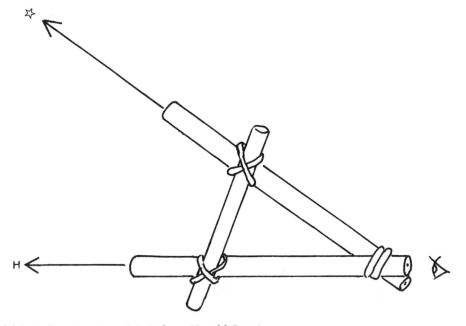

Figure 6.16   Polynesian "astrolabe" (from Harold Gatty)

It is all the more remarkable that these Polynesian navigators sailed by altitude estimates mostly in areas where no sighting of a polar star was possible. Hence, they appear to have had knowledge both of the seasonal and diurnal (nocturnal) trajectories of the stars.

The most sophisticated and accurate of the pre-sextant instruments was the *backstaff*. It operated along the principles of the cross-staff and the shadow astrolabe, yet it was sighted toward the horizon in opposition to the true bearing of the sun. It was invented in 1595 by John Davis, who is said to have been the only inventor of an altitude-measuring instrument who was also a seaman. The schematic for the most sophisticated of these backstaffs is presented in Figure 6.17.

All solid lines represent fixed structures. Along the arcs AB and CD are movable sighting vanes or adjustable apertures. H is a fixed horizon vane with a slit which, on the one hand, allows sighting of the horizon and, on the other, permits the detection of the angle at which the projected beam intersects (bisects) the screen. S is the adjustable shade vane permitting the passing of a linear beam of light from the sun. E is the adjustable sight vane through which the observer sights with his back to the sun (hence, the name backstaff).

To operate the backstaff the observer sets S to give an angle ϕ somewhat less than the altitude of the sun. Then sighting through E he adjusts the vane to an angle θ such that the horizon is sighted through the aperture H and the beam of light (first sighted on the background of H) just intersects the aperture. The altitude is thereby the simple addition of the angles of the two movable vanes.

Altitude $= \theta + \phi$

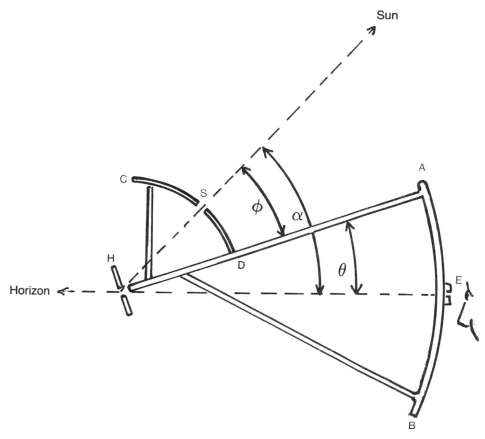

Figure 6.17   Backstaff

The modern sextant was successively perfected by John Hadley (1682–1744), Robert Hook (1635–1703), Sir Isaac Newton (1642–1727), and Nevil Maskelyne (1732–1811), all gentlemen scientists, as it were, rather than veterans of the poopdeck. In basic design the modern sextant has remained unchanged over the past two centuries. What has changed, of course, are the technical improvements of optics, metallurgy, and machining. To be sure, a notable improvement occurred when the micrometer drum for reading minutes of arc replaced the traditional vernier scale.

Note 6.2

There was a time in air navigation when the navigator had to rely upon celestial navigation. That time has all but passed. In place of a horizon sextant he used one incorporating a bubble chamber in its optics. When the bubble of the sextant is centered, the instrument is level with the horizon. A sight is then obtained when the reflected image of the object appears within the centered bubble. Such instruments are very convenient for use in night observations. However, the bubble is very sensitive to acceleration effects, therefore most bubble sextants incorporate some kind of mechanical averager. The navigator usually takes a succession of observations over a period of one minute. He notes the midpoint of the time span of sightings and then reads off his latitude from the recorded average.

With aircraft nowadays relying almost wholly on electronic aids to navigation, the bubble sextant has all but become a museum piece. Bubble attachments are, however, available for some of the more expensive marine sextants (e.g., the Plath). Still, those who have the bubble sextant will doubtless testify that the rollicking deck of a sailboat is not the ideal platform for centering a bubble in its chamber.

Note 6.3

A common procedure for determining personal error is simply to compare observed altitude against expected altitude as calculated for a given time span at the observer's specific location. The matter of calculating altitude for a specific set of geographic coordinates is made simple by utilizing the calculator and Formula 5.1. There is no need for the tediously precise interpolations that use of sight reduction tables would entail.

One first plots a curve of expected altitudes Hc over the time span of observation. Against this curve one then plots his own observations according to time, after appropriate corrections are made for dip, instrument error, refraction, semidiameter, and parallax, if they apply. The difference between the calculated altitude Hc and the observed altitude Ho will then be an indication of personal error. It is advisable to check for personal error over the practicable range of observations, and also separately for observations of the sun, moon, and planets.

Figure 6.18 presents the curve of expected altitude for a given location and time span. Against this curve are plotted the observations, Ho's, of two fictitious observers. Note that observer A has a persistent positive error but the variability in his error is less than that of observer B. Observer B, on the other hand, has a persistent negative error.

To determine correction for personal error the observer takes the arithmetic averages of all errors, i.e., the mean of all errors, and applies that mean in reverse sign. Subsequently, the average of all Ho's corrected for personal error will yield an average error of zero. For example, were observers A and B in Figure 6.18 to make appropriate corrections for their respective Ho's, their corrected Ho's would tend now to coincide with the curve of expected altitude. However, the fit of corrected observed altitudes to expected altitude would not be perfect. Some residual or random error would remain. This random component of error is not something we can correct for in any systematic way. The best we can do is to be aware of how large the random component of error can be.

What the reader is exposed to here is an elementary introduction to the theory of error, a subject appropriately belonging to theoretical and applied statistics. Some appropriate statistical measures are:

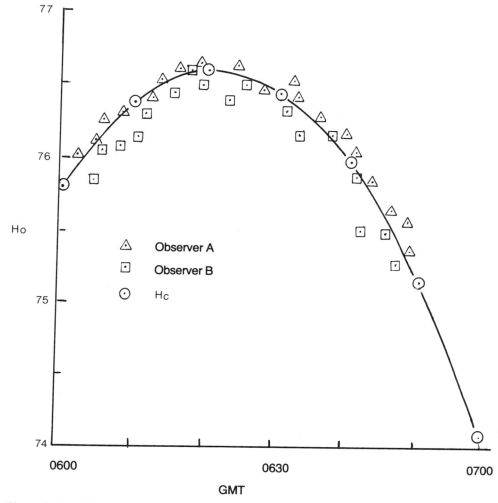

Figure 6.18   Altitude curve for Arcturus: at Pt. Loma Lt., 32°40′N, 117°14′W, May 18, 1982

1. the mean, $\overline{X}$,

$$\overline{X} = \frac{\sum_{i=1}^{N} Xi}{N}$$

where the symbol $\sum_{i=i}^{N} Xi$ designates the sum of all X's (i.e., measures of error) from 1 through the total of N such measures.

2. the average deviation, $\overline{D}$,

$$\overline{D} = \frac{\sum_{i=i}^{N} \left| Xi - \overline{X} \right|}{N}$$

where the vertical bars indicate all $X_i - \overline{X}$ values are to be treated as positive.

3. the standard deviation, SD,

$$SD = \sqrt{\frac{\sum\limits_{i}^{N}(X_i - \overline{X})^2}{N}}$$

If the fund of our original data is the set of all errors, say, of observer A in Figure 6.18, then the mean $\overline{X}$ would be the average error (the correction to be applied) and the average deviation $\overline{D}$ would give the average residual component of error. The standard deviation fits into a much larger rubric of statistical treatments which need not concern us here. It should be noted, however, that several of the inexpensive calculators, e.g., the TI-35, include provisions for entering a set of data and giving $\overline{X}$ and SD directly.

A final comment here—only the most serious student of navigation need go into the statistical treatment of error. It should be sufficient to know one's personal error and the magnitude or range of the random component (e.g., how likely is it that an observation will be as much as 5 miles off?).

Note 6.4

One of the difficulties for the occasional navigator is getting sextant practice. If he has a shoreline available out his front window or lives aboard a vessel suitably anchored in an open bight, he can practice at will. Aside from that, those small devices known as artificial horizons are not too satisfactory.

If, however, one is serious about practice, there are other alternatives. The one described here involves the borrowing of a transit or theodolite. An area of some expanse is required, say 50 feet or more.

1. Set up an observer's platform and mount your transit such that the leveled eyepiece is precisely at your eye level.
2. On the perimeter of your working area set up a line of rigid stakes all at least the equal of your eye level in height, Figure 6.19.
3. Make sure the telescope of the transit is level. Now, sighting on the stakes, place a mark on each of them exactly at the height of the transit level, i.e., at a point level with the eyepiece on the transit.
4. Attach to each of the points marked on the stake a line, taut as you can make it, to form a true horizon line. (Nonstretch dacron tape or line, found in marine or outdoor stores, will do.)

This no-sag line visible through your horizon mirror is now your *sea horizon*. Sight on the sun, bring it down to kiss the tape or line, and you will have an appropriate reading of sextant altitude. Two cautions: the line horizon must not sag, consequently a number of stakes should be used; and two, the observer's eye when taking the observation must always be at the height of the original transit sightings.

The important thing is to assure a level horizon line. There is a ready alternative which eliminates the possibility of sag. Find a setup similar to that above, with an evenly surfaced wall (or building) in the background. Now, again sighting with a transit, lay out a horizontal line on the building everywhere even with your eye level.

With suitable subdued illumination of your self-built horizon, sightings can be made both night and day. If observers of different heights are to use this fabricated horizon, it would be a simple matter to construct a crutch to control the sextant height while taking an observation.

Note 6.5

Taking a bearing between two stars is not an easy task. The plane of the sextant frames is aligned along that of the great circle intersecting the two stars. One star will be seen in the horizon mirror,

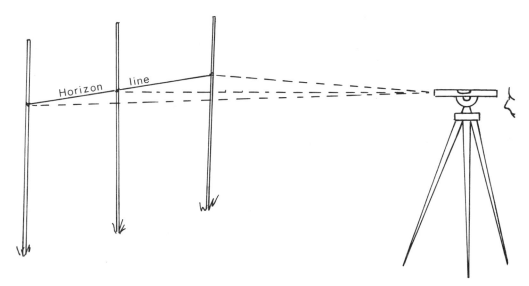

Horizon line

Figure 6.19   A true horizon line with a transit

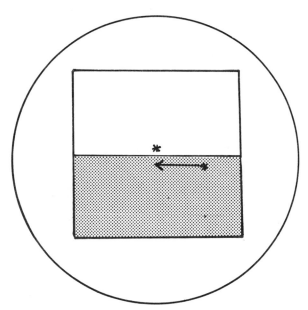

Figure 6.20   Sextant bearing between two stars

the second must be brought into conjunction with the first by reflection in the horizon glass, Figure 6.20.

However, bringing that second star down to the first through the field of intervening stars can be difficult. Consequently, it is better that we precompute the arc distance between the two stars, and then set the precomputed arc on the micrometer drum of the sextant.

Two stars and the elevated pole will yield an astronomical triangle similar to the familiar nautical triangle. In Figure 6.21, Pn is the elevated pole, M1 is the first star, and M2 is the second. The distance PnM1 is the codeclination of M1; that of PnM2, the codeclination of M2. The angle M1PnM2 is the difference in hour angle between the two stars.

Since M1 and M2 move uniformly across the heavens as if fixed to the celestial sphere, the hour angle difference between the two is simply the difference in their respective sidereal hour angles. With two sides of the triangle and their included angle known, the third side (i.e., the arc distance between M1 and M2) is found by the law of spherical cosines:

cos arc = ([sin Dec. M1 × sin Dec. M2] + [cos Dec. M1 × cos Dec. M2
        × cos (SHA M1 − SHA M2)])   (Formula 6.1)

The discerning reader will find this identical to the nautical triangle, with M1 replacing Z and arc distance being equal to coaltitude.

Example: Rigel and Sirius. From the 1982 *Almanac:*

	Rigel	*Sirius*
Dec.	8°13.4'S	16°41.6'S
SHA	281°34.8'	258°54.5'
Diff. in SHA	22°40.3'	

Converting the odd minutes to decimals, we follow the procedure similar to that of computing Hc (Chapter 5). Utilizing Formula 6.1 we find arc distance between Rigel and Sirius to be 23°40.2'.

To get a check on sextant error we first apply corrections for index and personal errors. Since two stars are involved, correction for refraction is difficult to determine. Refraction is applied to altitude above horizon. Unless the two stars are directly one above the other on the same true

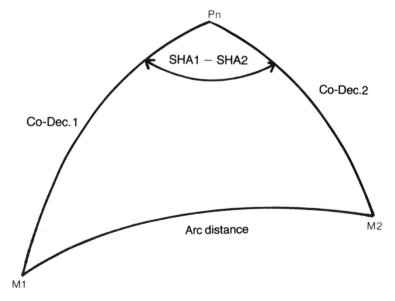

Figure 6.21   Celestial triangle for arc-distance between two stars

azimuth we cannot simply subtract the smaller from the larger refraction. However, if we should take two stars with altitudes within 10° or less of one another, or stars whose altitudes are above 30° where refraction effects become comparatively insignificant, then we can safely ignore corrections for refraction. Comparing our corrected sextant bearing with the precomputed distance will give us sextant error.

Suppose in our example we take a sextant bearing between Rigel and Sirius when both are near our own meridian. Since their altitudes are nearly the same at that time, we can ignore refraction effects. Suppose our index error correction is $-2'$ and our known personal error correction is $-3'$. If our sextant bearing between the two stars is 23°44', we know our instrument error to be:

Sextant	23°44'
corr.	−05'
Sextant (corr.)	23°39'
True arc	23°40.2'
Sextant error	− 1.2'

Hence, a correction of +1.2 would be made to compensate for instrument error.

CHAPTER SEVEN

Star Identification

With but a few exceptions all of the celestial objects visible to the naked eye are from the relative proximity of our own galaxy. Since our galaxy, a spiral one some 100,000 light years across, contains approximately 100,000 million stars, it is a generous provider of beacons for the night. However, it may come as a surprise to the reader that of this bounty only about 6,000 stars, the moon, and five of the planets are discernable to the unaided eye. And of these, the navigator can get by observing the moon, four of the planets, and twenty or so of the brighter stars including, of course, our sun.

Now the stars of our familiar skies are distinctive in three conspicuous ways: one, they vary in brightness; two, they maintain comparatively fixed relations (contrary to the planets); and three, they can be nicely arranged into those configurations and constellations that give to the skies their seasonal structure. For identification of stars, all three factors are important.

BRIGHTNESS OR APPARENT MAGNITUDE

Any person who makes a practice of looking at the night sky soon learns that the evening star, Venus, is the brightest of the planets, that Sirius in the winter sky is brighter than all the surrounding stars, and that the North Star, Polaris, is pale by comparison. Venus, of course, is a planet and owes its brightness to reflected light. However, the stars, like the sun, generate their own light through radiation. As seen from the earth their apparent brightness is due, first, to their size, secondly, to their distance, and thirdly, to their age and the character of their radiation.

The navigator is not much concerned with the physical characteristics of celestial objects as such, only their relative brightness and spatial relations. He is really only concerned with relatively bright objects that are easy to identify. The planets Venus, Mars, Jupiter, and Saturn qualify. They are relatively bright with a steady, unflickering glow. And they are distinguishable from stars in that they wander within the zodiac against a fixed stellar background. The so-called navigational stars qualify because they too are relatively bright. And since they are bright relative to the stellar background, they can be easily structured into patterns and constellations.

The rating of brightness, or apparent magnitude, as judged from earth, goes back to Hipparchus and Ptolemy. The original scale was set up to accommodate everything from the very brightest star, Sirius, down to those barely detectable by the eye. The original scale of magnitude was a simple judgmental one. Observers sorted all visible stellar objects into six categories of perceived brightness. According to early practice, Sirius would have been in category one, and the faintest stars in category six. However, with the perfection of photometry, true luminosities (brightness recorded by photoelectric cells) could be ascertained. Psychological judgments could then be correlated against the actual physical luminosities (*cf.* Note 7.1).

What emerged is an arbitrary scale of brightness that is a blend of traditional judgment and modern photometric measurement. Hence, stars belonging traditionally to any one of the six ancient categories were subject to further gradation. For example, Sirius, the brightest star in the heavens, and Polaris, a conspicuous but much less bright star, both belonged to category one according to ancient judgment. But according to contemporary judgments of magnitude, Polaris is assigned a magnitude of +2.1 and Sirius −1.6, with the lower value assigned to the brighter object. Negative magnitudes are necessitated by the fact that the old category-one stars and objects themselves varied greatly in brightness. Some idea of the range of magnitude can be observed in the data of Table 7.1.

Table 7.1
Magnitudes of Some Celestial Objects

Object	Magnitude	
Sirius	−1.6	
Jupiter	−2.0	
Venus	−4.0	
Full moon	−12.6	
Sun	−26.7	
Rigel Kentaurus	+0.1	(third brightest star)
Faintest star (unaided eye)	+6.0	
Faintest star (200″ telescope)	+20.0	

In his celestial observation, the navigator makes use of only the brightest stars. Table 7.2 presents the ordering of the 20 brightest stars. All are useful to the navigator but do not exhaust the catalogue of navigational stars (see the *Nautical Almanac* for a list of 57).

Of our 20 brightest stars, Sirius, Rigel Kentaurus, Procyon, and Altair are among our nearest stellar neighbors, being approximately 4 to 16 light years away. On the other hand, Betelgeuse, Rigel, and Deneb are somewhat more distant, approximately 500 to 1,400 light years away. Since the sun is roughly 30,000 light years from the center of our galaxy, all of our bright navigational stars are relatively nearby objects.

COLOR OF STARS

Although the great preponderance of stars appear to have uniform twinkle and color, there are significant color differences that help in identification. The astronomer makes inferences concerning age, mass, and temperature of stars in terms of spectral analysis. And the casual observer soon learns the gradations from bluish white to red that can be associated with given stars.

Table 7.2
The Twenty Brightest Stars

Star	SHA*	Dec.*	Magnitude	Distance (lt. yrs.)
Sirius	258°55′	16°42′S	−1.6	8.7
Canopus	264°07′	52°41′S	-0.9	98.
Rigel Kentaurus	140°24′	60°46′S	0.1	4.3
Vega	80°55′	38°46′N	0.1	26.5
Arcturus	146°17′	19°17′N	0.2	36
Capella	281°10′	45°59′N	0.2	45
Rigel	281°35′	8°13′S	0.3	900
Procyon	245°25′	5°16′N	0.5	11.3
Betelgeuse	271°27′	7°24′N	Var 0.1 to 1.2	520
Achernar	335°45′	57°20′S	0.6	118
β Centauri (Hadar)	149°21′	60°17′S	0.9	490
Altair	62°31′	8°49′N	0.9	16.5
α Crucis (Acrux)	173°36′	62°60′S	1.1	370
Aldebaran	291°17′	16°28′N	1.1	68
Spica	158°56′	11°04′S	1.2	220
Antares	112°55′	26°24′S	1.2	520
Pollux	243°57′	28°04′N	1.2	35
Fomalhaut	15°50′	29°43′S	1.3	22.6
Deneb	49°48′	45°13′N	1.3	1600
Regulus	208°09′	12°03′N	1.3	84

Table 7.3 lists a few of the more conspicuous color identifications.

Table 7.3
Spectral Categories

Color	Stars
Blue	Rigel, Spica, Achernar
White	Sirius, Vega, Fomalhaut
Yellow	Capella, Canopus, Procyon, (Sun)
Orange	Aldebaran, Arcturus
Red	Antares, Betelgeuse

Saturn, Mars, Venus, and Jupiter are also distinguishable by color, but the redness of Mars, for example, is due to the reflecting properties of its surface, not its radiant energy.

STELLAR POSITIONS

As we have seen, stars are given coordinates that fix their positions in the celestial sphere. The coordinates for navigational astronomy are sidereal hour angle and

---

* Taken from 1982 *Nautical Almanac.*

declination, the equivalents of longitudinal and latitudinal measure. For purposes of observational astronomy, right ascension (360° − SHA, converted to time) is often preferred.

Actually the stars are not fixed. Our galaxy is a nebula in which stars move in a spiral vortex, those at the center being more densely packed and moving with comparatively greater radial velocities. As we move out away from the center along the spiral arms, the radial velocities diminish. As a result stars near the sun appear to move pretty much in unison while those more distant will show detectable displacement from any fixed set of coordinates. Because of the immense distances, however, proper motion, or the angle of displacement against the celestial background, is nearly imperceptible. Star maps of today differ hardly at all from those of antiquity.

However, there are small annual parallactic effects due to the excursional extremes of the earth's orbit about the sun. A check of the pages of the *Nautical Almanac* shows that the SHA's for most of the listed navigational stars may oscillate as much as one minute of arc through the year while declinations change somewhat less. Surprisingly, an error of as much as one minute of arc in SHA may result in an error of one nautical mile in plotting an LOP.

Perhaps the most effective means of identifying a given star is to precalculate its altitude from a knowledge of its SHA and declination, and the GHA of Aries. If the sky is mottled, hazy, or otherwise partially obscured this may be the only reliable means of identification. By presetting the precomputed Hc in the sextant with corrections appropriately applied, one may easily pick up the intended star by sweeping the sextant slowly across the horizon in the direction of the star's azimuth.

STAR CHARTS

The most effective means of learning the stars is through study and application of star maps or charts. These come in several forms. The *Nautical Almanac* includes four star charts: two of these are polar stereographic projections, one for the northern hemisphere, one for the southern; the other two are square grid charts with boundaries 30° to either side of the equinoctial (one is for SHA, 0–180°, the other, 180°–360°). *Bowditch* and *Dutton* both present sets of star charts, covering northern and southern hemispheres for all seasons of viewing. There are also several commercial star atlases and guides readily available.

There are two difficulties with all such atlases and charts. The first is that a chart is laid out flat before the reader. He is looking down at the stars rather than up. As a consequence east and west are reversed from the traditional terrestrial mapping. To use the chart effectively it should be held overhead. The second problem is that star charts tend to show the whole of a visible sky or the whole of the celestial canopy, whereas the viewer sees only a segment of the sky within the boundaries of his purview. He would have to sweep the entire heavens to get the full picture. A star globe might present a more faithful projection but it too suffers from the observer's looking down rather than up from within its center. The ideal vehicle for learning stars is a planetarium, where one looks up to see the sky projected as it is really seen. Furthermore, the projector can simulate the sky for any locale, at any season.

However, this ideal aside, I have found the detachable star chart in the *Air Almanac* (see Figure 2.8) to be as good as any that are available. It is constructed on a simple two-way grid, declination by sidereal hour angle. Thus by referring to the list of navigational stars in the *Nautical Almanac* we can easily determine their locations by the pertinent data, SHA and declination. As in the case of the Mercator projection, representations of areas in the polar regions are distorted. But since the polar constellations (the Big and Little Dippers, Cassiopeia in the north, and Crux in the south) are readily identified, this is not an overriding flaw. On the other hand, constellations and patterns in midlatitudes (declinations) are well represented and one can use the chart easily to find the salient patterns. Traditionally stars have been clustered according to the historic constellations; however, star identification is aided greatly by our following directional lines, sweeping curves, and geometric constructions that transcend the individual constellations.

Suppose, for example, we begin our study of star identification by looking at the summer sky (see Figure 7.1). It will be dominated by a large and conspicuous right triangle overhead formed by three bright stars, Deneb, Vega, and Altair (all three, incidentally, belonging to different constellations). Vega will be the brightest of the three, but its most distinguishing characteristic is its appendage of a small but nearly perfect parallelogram. From Deneb in the southwesterly direction hangs the clearly discernible Northern Cross. The sky at this time of the year is not particularly rich in

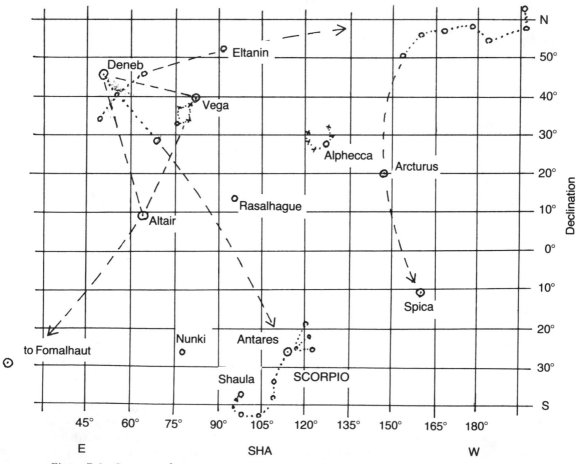

Figure 7.1   Summer sky

bright navigational stars, but if one follows a slight southeasterly sweep deep into the southern sky he may pick up Fomalhaut.

To the south and west of this triangular threesome is Scorpio, reowned for looking much like its eponym. At the base of the head is found the great Antares, perhaps the reddest of navigational stars.

One need hardly mention Ursa Major and Ursa Minor, the Big and Little Dippers. One pours into the other, with Polaris at the end of the smaller handle. Here, too, Cassiopeia, the wandering "W," is found always diametrically opposed to the Big Dipper with Polaris interposed. Although its constituent stars, Ruchbah, Caph, and Schedar, are relatively low magnitude they stand so conspicuously apart from other stars they are easily identified.

In the autumn sky, Pegasus comes into view, high in the northern sky and not at all looking like a horse. Four stars, Scheat, Markab, Alpheratz, and Algenib, compose a large square with the head or kite's tail running northeast from Alpheratz. This group is an excellent locater. The line from Scheat through Markab unmistakably points south to lonely Fomalhaut. Alpheratz and Algenib point south to Diphda (Deneb Kaitos) a star that is frequently used in autumn observations. From the kite tail off Pegasus there is a set of minor stars (Mirach, Almach, and Mirfak) leading into the most distinctive arc in the whole of the sky—in a long graceful sweep first to the northeast to pick up Capella, one of the vertices in an irregular quadrilateral, then easterly to pick up the twins Castor and Pollux, then southerly to Procyon and on to Sirius, the brightest of all the stars. If one is far enough south, he can continue a southerly sweep on past Sirius to Canopus, second only to Sirius in brightness (see Figure 7.2).

Within this sweeping curve that now dominates the winter sky is found the most striking of all constellations, Orion. The three stars in Orion's buckle are unmistakable. They fit into a neat configuration that resembles another kite with a small tail, all enclosed by a larger rectangle with Betelgeuse (an orange giant so large that it would nearly swallow the lesser planetary orbits of our solar system) and Rigel at diametric corners. This complex of stars neatly straddles the equinoctial with the northernmost star in Orion's buckle being over the celestial equator.

The Big Dipper presents another distinguished pointer system (see Figure 7.3). In spring it is high in the northern sky. Not only do Merak and Dubhe on the edge of the cup point to Polaris, but the same line projected south intercepts Regulus and Alphard, a star of somewhat lesser magnitude farther to the south. Following the handle of the dipper, the arc that sweeps south intercepts two very conspicuous stars, Arcturus and Spica.

With a bit of ingenuity the observer can establish his own geometric configurations as aids to identifying stars of lesser magnitude.

We have said nothing of the skies far to the south. So long as the navigator plays within the relatively benign limits of the southeast trade winds on his trip around the world, most of the familiar constellations will remain within his view. But if he has an inclination to frolic in the "forties" he will learn to rely upon a number of first-magnitude stars all within 8° of the 60°S declination line. In the southern summer sky, Canopus will be seen as continuing the southerly sweep from Sirius. These two stars seen in reasonable proximity are the two brightest in the skies. Rising some few hours earlier Achernar can be seen at about the same declination as Canopus. Most conspicuous of all will be the Southern Cross, followed by Hadar and Rigel Kentaurus.

Both the north and south polar regions are outside the galactic equator, that region marked by the Milky Way. Therefore, these regions are relatively deficient in distinguishable constellations. In the north we have the two dippers and Cassiopeia; in the

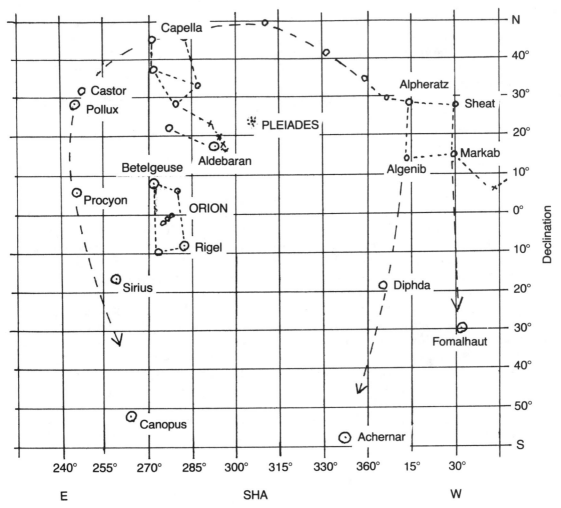

Figure 7.2   Autumn and winter sky

south, we have the renowned Southern Cross, the false cross, and Centaurus. At the approach of the southern autumn, Crux will be seen in the midnight sky. It offers a rather compact facsimile of a cross, which, to some, is not as figurally impressive as the false cross some three hours to the west. Seeing the two for the first time an observer might mistake one for the other. However, the two bright stars in the real cross, Acrux and Gacrux, clearly separate the two. An hour or so to the east and at the same celestial latitude is another pair, in the constellation of Centaurus, Rigel Kentaurus and Hadar, both among the brightest of stars.

One of the impressive features of the southern skies does not involve stars; or rather, it involves the apparent absence of stars. Near the Southern Cross is a dense black cloudlike area that appears to be devoid of stars. Such dark nebulae are known as "coalsacks" and are thought to be due to the absorption of light by some intervening gaseous cloud. By coincidence another such cloud can be found in the northern cross, close to Deneb.

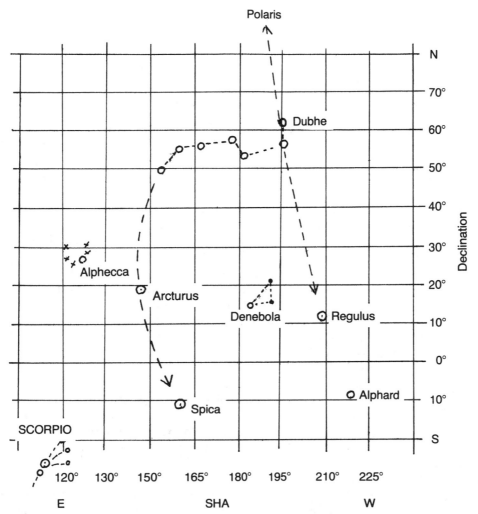

Figure 7.3   Big Dipper as a pointer system

The Milky Way is a clear feature of a starlit sky but is not particularly helpful in identifying navigational stars. On a clear moonless night away from the ambient light and smog of the cities, one sees the galactic equator swinging north through the northern cross to intercept Cassiopeia and south in the summer skies to engulf the whole of Scorpio. Although the Milky Way runs through Cassiopeia southeasterly to intercept Crux, and then northeasterly to embrace Scorpio and Cygnus, most of the brighter stars and constellations are just outside its plane. This is due primarily to the great density of material that acts as a screen to conspicuous detail within the galactic plane itself. In fact, one can detect dark gaps in the Milky Way that are thought to be due to the absorption of light by large masses of gas and dust.

TWILIGHT: SUNRISE AND SUNSET

There are occasions when ambient moonlight will illuminate a horizon suitably for taking sextant observations. However, the moon will often put a shimmering glare on the water that tends to give an apparent horizon below the true one. Consequently the best time for observing the planets and stars is during nautical twilight, that relatively brief period when both the celestial body and the horizon can be seen clearly in the sextant's telescope.

Twilight, technically, is divided into three periods. *Civil twilight* exists during the period just before sunrise and just after sunset, specifically, when the sun is from 0° to 6° below the horizon. This is a period when the horizon can be clearly seen and during which most navigators prefer to take star and planet observations. A word or two of caution, however—during the earliest part of civil twilight the ambient light of the sky will conceal stars of lesser magnitude. Hence, one will require a sextant telescope of considerable power to pick up a star of the magnitude of Polaris (2.1).

The duration of twilight varies with latitude and the seasons. Twilight lengthens as we ascend to higher latitudes. At any given latitude twilight is longest at the solstices (June 21 and December 21) and shortest at the equinoxes (March 21 and September 21) with only marginally longer durations in summer than in winter.

Nautical twilight technically is the period during which the sun is between 0° and 12° below the horizon. During much of this period one may yet get a good horizon but as twilight deepens the horizon becomes murky. A comparatively more powerful sextant telescope will prolong the definition of the horizon.

The third twilight period is known as *astronomical twilight* and covers the span of time when the sun is between 0° and 18° below the horizon. Of interest to astronomers but not the navigator, most of this period is too dark for horizon observations. One may pick up telltale signs of dawn in this period or the fleeting track of a satellite, but not the horizon.

When is the best time for taking one's twilight observations? This comes with experience. The navigator soon learns the optimal time for taking his star and planet shots. Generally the horizon will be clear during civil twilight and conditionally so during mid-nautical twilight contingent upon air clarity, the true azimuth of the body, and, of course, cloud cover. However, only the very brightest of stars and planets will be visible at the onset of civil twilight (P.M.). Unfortunately, as twilight deepens and stars of lesser magnitude become visible, the horizon loses its definition. With a sextant scope of modest power the navigator can usually count on a period of at least 20 to 25 minutes for taking his twilight observations.

Twilight observations are generally facilitated by predetermining the altitudes and azimuths of the bodies to be observed. This can be done with sight reduction tables, actual computations, or, perhaps most easily, a star finder (see below). Powerful sextant scopes are helpful in magnifying the sources of faint light. However, the more powerful the telescope the more limited the field. If the navigator must accommodate his observations to the relatively quick motions of a sailboat it may be to his advantage to use a sextant scope of comparatively lesser power but larger field. Recall, too, that taking observations in the morning twilight is helped by the fact that the visible heavens precede sunrise; at evening twilight, we must wait for the telltale configurations to emerge.

Tabular Treatment: Sunrise, Sunset, Twilight

Perhaps the simplest method for finding our twilight information is to go to the tables in the daily pages of the *Nautical Almanac* (see Figure 3.7). One simply enters the tables at the appropriate latitude and picks off the local time for sunrise, sunset, and the end or onset of twilight. To find the duration of nautical twilight we subtract the onset of nautical twilight from that of sunrise. For example, for May 17, 1982, at latitude 35°N, nautical twilight begins at 0353 local time and sunrise is at 0455. Therefore, the duration of nautical twilight will be 62 minutes. Finding sunrise or sunset is of course straightforward, and interpolating for odd degrees of latitude is relatively simple.

Computational Treatment

There are times when precision greater than that of the daily tables is desirable, especially in the determination of sunrise and sunset. In such cases, in fact, in all cases, it is convenient to resort to direct computation via the hand calculator. Furthermore, the computational procedure fits in well with the problem of converting solutions in local time to those in zone or Greenwich time.

Our basic formula for altitude,

$$\sin Hc = \sin L \sin d + \cos L \cos d \cos HA \qquad \text{(Formula 5.1)}$$

is ready-made for determining the time of sunrise or sunset. At such times the sun's altitude is theoretically zero. Hence, the term sin Hc becomes zero and we obtain:

$$\cos HA = -\ \frac{\sin L \sin d}{\cos L \cos d} = -\tan L \tan d \qquad \text{(Formula 7.1)}$$

The theoretical time for the rising and setting of a celestial body is a simple function of the observer's latitude and the body's declination.

However, in the case of the sun (or the moon) the situation is complicated, first, by the fact that rising and setting are defined by the conjunction of the upper limb of the body and the horizon, and second, by the effects of refraction. Refraction effects vary with altitude, being at their maximum when the body is at the horizon. For all bodies, refraction at the horizon is 34' (standard condition). This constitutes a correction to be subtracted from the observation. Thus when a body (a star, for example) is first observed to emerge from the eastern horizon it is actually 34' below the horizon. For the sun, then, at sunrise, the upper limb is actually 34' below the horizon and its center is another 16' below, due to the distance of its semidiameter. Thus at sunrise the center of the sun is actually 50' (or 0.83°) below the horizon. Therefore, we assign an altitude Hc = −0.83° to our fundamental Formula 5.1 to obtain:

$$\cos HA = \frac{(\sin -0.83) - (\sin L \sin d)}{\cos L \cos d} \qquad \text{(Formula 7.2)}$$

This formula covers both sunrise and sunset. The hour angle solved for is that between the observer and the sun at the time of sunrise. It is actually the angle the sun must travel before it is directly overhead, or the time to local noon. Therefore, to obtain the local time of sunrise we subtract that hour angle from 180°, or that hour angle converted to time from 12 hours.

Note again that the times of sunrise and sunset are local times. Local time is a function of our specific longitude. Normally we carry zone time on our ship's clock, and Greenwich time on our chronometer. There are no clocks for local time. How do we convert local time to Greenwich or zone time so that we may have a precise notion of when the sun is to peek above the horizon at our location?

Converting local time to Greenwich time is straightforward if we know our location. We can assume that for any given day and latitude, the sun rises at any meridian as it does at Greenwich meridian except for a small variation due to changing declination. Therefore, if the sun rises at 0435 local time at a given latitude on Greenwich meridian it will do so at the same latitude on any other meridian. The time difference, then, between sunrise at Greenwich and that of the sea-wandering observer is simply the longitude of the observer, an hour angle, converted to time. (Note local mean time at Greenwich is identical with Greenwich mean time.)

There is, however, a complication that we must attend to when we use the calculator to determine precise times of sunrise and sunset. We convert hour angle to time by virtue of the sun moving at an apparently steady rate (15° per hour) which would be all very well if the true sun were on time with the ideal mean sun. Since that is not the case, we must correct our calculated time (the Greenwich mean time for sunrise) by the equation of time, which is to say, the amount of time the actual sun is ahead or behind the ideal mean sun that is used in basic computations. The equation of time as well as correction for refraction and semidiameter are incorporated into the daily tables of the *Nautical Almanac,* but not into Formula 7.2.

For May 18, 1982, 35°N latitude, we find by our *Almanac* (see Figure 3.7) that local mean time of sunrise is 0455. Let us now check this result by calculator. On or about sunrise at Greenwich on this date the declination of the sun is 19°28′N. Plugging this value into our calculator we compute from Formula 7.2:

$$HA = \cos^{-1} \frac{(\sin -0.83) - (\sin 35 \sin 19.47)}{\cos 35 \cos 19.47}$$

$$= 105.44°$$

Subtracting *HA* from 180° and converting to hours (by dividing by 15) we get 4h 58.2m. This is local mean time for the sunrise of the mean sun. To get sunrise of the true sun we now apply the equation of time. The equation of time for May 18 is 3m 40s. Since the position of the true sun (as verified from the *Almanac*) is in advance of the ideal mean sun, the equation of time will be subtracted from the sunrise of the mean sun. This gives us 04 54 32 as the sunrise of the true sun at 35°N latitude, LMT.

Examples: On May 16, 1982, our DR position at the approximate time of sunrise is estimated as 38°20′N, 124°30′W. Determine (1) sunrise, (2) sunset, and (3) onset of nautical twilight in the morning. Also (4) determine GMT for sunrise at the DR position.

In order to calculate the exact time of sunrise, we must know our latitude and the declination of the sun at the approximate time of sunrise, say, a time within plus or minus one-half hour of the true sunrise. We obtain latitude from a DR position for an approximate time of sunrise. To determine the declination of the sun we use our DR position and the *Almanac.* The *Almanac* gives us sunrise at Greenwich for a latitude equivalent to our own DR latitude. And our DR longitude indicates whether we are early or late on Greenwich and by how much.

Example 1:   Proceeding now with our example, our DR latitude as given is 38°20′N or 38.33°. Sunrise at Greenwich for our latitude is roughly 0448. But since our DR longitude is 124°30′W we are roughly 8 hours late on Greenwich. Hence our local sunrise will be somewhere between 1200 and 1300 GMT, May 16, 1982. Referring to the specimen pages from the *Almanac* (see Figure 3.7) we find the declination of the sun to be 19°05.5′N or 19.09°N.

Utilizing Formula 7.2 we now find:

$$HA = \cos^{-1} \frac{(\sin -0.83) - (\sin 38.33 \sin 19.09)}{(\cos 38.33 \cos 19.09)}$$
$$= 107.05°$$

And

$$LMT \text{ sunrise (mean sun)} = \frac{180° - 107.05°}{15}$$
$$= 4.86 \text{ hours} = 4h \, 51m \, 36s$$

For LMT of the true sun we apply the equation of time (i.e., 3m 42s). Reference to the tables for GHA of the sun shows the true sun to be in advance of the mean sun. Hence the equation of time will be subtracted:

$$LMT \text{ sunrise (true sun)} = 4h \, 51m \, 36s - 3m \, 42s$$
$$= 4h \, 47m \, 54s$$

Example 2: For the time of sunset, utilizing the same DR position as above, we will find the declination of the sun to be about $19°14'N$ (verify that the approximate time of sunset will be about 0300 GMT, May 17, 1982). Hence from Formula 7.2:

$$HA = \cos^{-1} \frac{(\sin -0.83) - (\sin 38.33 \sin 19.23)}{(\cos 38.33 \cos 19.23)}$$
$$= 107.18°$$

$$LMT \text{ sunset, mean sun} = \frac{180° + 107.18°}{15}$$

$$= 19.15h = 19h \, 9m$$
$$LMT \text{ sunset, true sun} = 19h \, 9m - 3 \, m \, 42s$$
$$= 19h \, 5m \, 18s$$

Note here that to obtain the hour angle associated with LMT for sunset we add 180° to our HA (Formula 7.2). And as for sunrise, we subtract the equation of time.

Example 3: The onset of nautical twilight in the morning is defined as the time at which the center of the sun is 12° below the horizon. Since neither refraction nor semidiameter is involved here, the formula for HA becomes:

$$\cos HA = \frac{(\sin -12) - \sin L \sin d}{(\cos L \cos d)} \qquad \text{(Formula 7.3)}$$

Hence,

$$HA = \cos^{-1} \frac{(\sin -12) - (\sin 38.33 \sin 19.09)}{(\cos 38.33 \cos 19.09)}$$

$$= 123.65°$$

$$LMT, \text{ nautical twilight} = \frac{(180° - 123.65°)}{15}$$
$$= 3.76 \text{ hours} = 3h \, 45m \, 36s$$

Subtracting the equation of time (3m 42s) we have:

$$LMT, \text{ nautical twilight} = 3h \, 41m \, 54s$$

Example 4:   To determine GMT of sunrise as actually observed at 38°20′N, 124° 30′W we use the formula:

$$GMT = LMT \begin{array}{c} + \text{ W longitude} \\ - \text{ E longitude} \end{array} \qquad \text{(Formula 7.4)}$$

where longitude is converted to time. Hence, utilizing the data from item 1:

$$GMT = 4\,h\,47m\,54s \; + \frac{124.5}{15}$$
$$= 13h\,5m\,54s$$

Thus precisely at 13 05 54 GMT we should expect to see the upper limb of the sun pierce the horizon.

It should be apparent from Example 4 that if we can determine the precise time of sunrise from a given position we ought also to be able to infer something about position from a precise timing of sunrise. Indeed we can, even if the procedure is somewhat tedious and an accurate knowledge of latitude is required (see Chapter 8). Knowing latitude and declination, we can determine LMT for sunrise. And getting the precise GMT of visual sunrise we can use Formulae 7.2 and 7.4 above to give us longitude. This is a procedure that is recommended for lifeboat navigation if the would-be survivor has remembered to bring along his chronometer and *Almanac*.

For greater precision and for computations concerning moonrise and moonset, see Note 7.2.

SELECTING STARS FOR OBSERVATION

Other things being equal we select those stars that are easy to identify, are sufficiently bright to be seen at twilight, and offer a set of angular differences in LOP's so as to yield a definitive fix. In this respect, precomputations are helpful. By predetermining Hc and Zn for a set of stars we can preset the sextant and orient ourselves with respect to taking the shot.

H. O. 249, Vol. 1
This is another helpful device for making preparations. Its tables are set up to give the Hc's and Zn's of a small set of stars for observation at a given latitude, and for a given LHA of Aries. One enters the tables, finds the set of stars that are convenient to observe, and selects those offering a desirable pattern of LOP's. This volume of *H. O. 249* is helpful even if one relies on the calculator for sight reduction.

Rude Star Finder
This star finder is also a helpful device. It is designed not so much for star finding or identification as it is for selecting an appropriate set of stars for observation. It is now produced under several different auspices but all varieties, so to speak, are identical, Figure 7.4.

The main plastic disc presents a polar projection of stars either from the northern or the southern hemisphere. The outer scale represents LHA of Aries and the major navigational stars are plotted according to their declinations and SHA's. A transparent plastic overlay presents the horizon system of the observer with a zenith corresponding to his latitude. By orienting this overlay with respect to the outer scale, LHA of Aries,

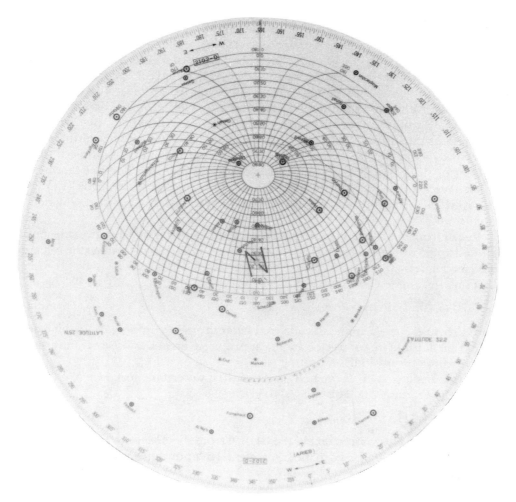

Figure 7.4 Rude Star Finder

the observer reads off prospective altitude and azimuths for the selected navigational stars. The accuracy is great enough to select stars by well-patterned azimuths and also for presetting altitudes in the sextant.

The star finder does help find stars, to be sure. However, it is not helpful in learning the configurations of stars and is only of limited assistance in identifying unknown stars.

In general, we want to observe stars that will give optimal azimuths in their LOP's. As we shall see in Chapter 10 this occurs when, in a three-star fix, the azimuths differ by 120°.

The *Rude Star Finder, H. O. 249,* Vol. 1 on stars, and finding Polaris correction all make use of the LHA of Aries. Recall that LHA is always measured westerly from the observer's longitude. Thus, comparing our longitude against the GHA of Aries will give the LHA of Aries.

IDENTIFYING STARS

In Chapter 3, in the discussion of time diagrams, we pointed out how conspicuous stars might be identified if we know how they can be oriented or placed with respect to known stars or planets. That is to say, if we know the declination and SHA or GHA of a familiar stellar object, then a conspicuous nearby object will have similar coordinates. That procedure is rather hit-and-miss. We now turn to a procedure whereby, if we can measure the altitude and true azimuth of a star at a given instant of time, we can then determine its declination and sidereal hour angle, those stellar fingerprints that will enable us to enter the *Nautical Almanac* for an unequivocal identification of the star. Furthermore, once we determine the declination and SHA of a body we can carry out the calculations of sight reduction without in fact our knowing the name of the body. What is in a name? Nothing, of course, if we do not know the body's declination and SHA.

Recall from our discussion of the nautical triangle that if we know two sides and the included angle we can utilize the basic laws of trigonometry to determine the remaining parts (see Figure 4.5).

Thus we find:

$$\sin d = (\sin L \sin h) + (\cos L \cos h \cos Z) \qquad \text{(Formula 7.5)}$$

where L, h, and Z are latitude, altitude, and azimuth angle, respectively. In this case, h is our sextant altitude (hs) corrected for the appropriate errors, and Z is azimuth angle as derived from observation.

To determine SHA of the body we must first determine its GHA. We transpose terms in the fundamental Formula 2.1 to give us:

$$\text{SHA}\star = \text{GHA}\star - \text{GHA}\Upsilon \qquad \text{(Formula 7.6)}$$

Hence, knowing GHA$\star$ and taking the GHAΥ from the *Almanac* we find SHA$\star$.

To find the GHA$\star$ we go to the fundamental relationship among GHA, longitude, and meridian hour angle:

$$\text{GHA}\star = \lambda \pm t \qquad \text{(Formula 7.7)}$$

Now meridian angle t is unknown. However, since we have already computed d, and since Z and h are observables we compute t by the formula:

$$\sin t = \frac{\sin Z \cos h}{\cos d} \qquad \text{(Formula 7.8)}$$

Hence, computing d and t and utilizing Formulae 7.6 and 7.7 we determine the declination and SHA of the body.

Example: On May 18, 1982, 0630 GMT, at DR position, 35°N, 124°W, a star is observed prior to meridian transit with Ho = 36°09′, and a true azimuth, Zn, of 100.5°. Solving for d, Formula 7.5:

$$\sin d = (\sin 35 \sin 36.15) + (\cos 35 \cos 36.15 \cos 100.5)$$
$$d = 12.58° = 12°35′$$

And solving for t:

$$\sin t = \frac{\sin 100.5 \cos 36.15}{\cos 12.58}$$
$$= 54.44° = 54°26′$$

(Note that since our position is north latitude and the hour angle of the body is to the east, $Z = Zn$; otherwise we convert Zn back to Z to plug into Formula 7.5).

Applying Formula 7.7 above we have:

$$GHA\star = 124 - 54°26' = 69°34'$$

Going to the specimen pages of the *Almanac* and using the increment of 30m for Aries (namely 7°31') we observe that at 0630 GMT:

$$GHA\ \Upsilon = 325°36' + 7°31' = 333°07'$$

Hence, from Formula 7.6 we find:

$$SHA\star = 69°34' - 333°07' = 96°27'$$

Checking the data for selected stars in the *Nautical Almanac* (see Figure 3.7) we find a star with nearly identical coordinates, namely Rasalhague (SHA = 96°28.2', d = 12°34.3'N).

To get nearly exact measures of d and SHA in the above we need accurate observations of altitude and true azimuth. We can count on the sextant for accuracy of altitude, but azimuth, whether taken by pelorus or bearing compass, will be comparatively inaccurate, say, accurate only to within a degree or two. However, that will be sufficient for discriminating among the 40 or so major navigational stars. And once we identify the body, then we can obtain the exact d and SHA from the *Almanac*.

PRECOMPUTING STAR ALTITUDE AND AZIMUTH

Generally the navigator knows the skies sufficiently well that he need not spend a great amount of time in identifying stars to observe. On a passage of any duration he will be familiar with the evening and morning stars. However, should the sky be partially obscured by cloud cover, identification may be a bit of a problem, one star peeping out here, another there, without the large configurations being visible. In such cases it is helpful to precompute altitudes and azimuths of the stars that one intends to observe.

The computations can be done at the navigator's leisure, morning, noon, or anytime, so long as the navigator can anticipate the time of observation and can project a reasonable DR position. Having precomputed a set of altitudes and azimuths the navigator can then locate his stars in the partially obscured skies by presetting his sextant and orienting himself directionally, so as to coincide with each star's true azimuth. The navigator soon learns that the practice of precomputing altitudes will facilitate both observational and computational work.

Example: On a voyage from San Diego to Hilo, Hawaii, our navigator estimates that his position on May 16, 1982, at the time of nautical twilight is approximately 25°20'N, 142°30'W. Nautical twilight is estimated to end at 1933 LMT (either by the *Almanac* or Formula 7.3). Hence, he plans to make his observations about 1920 LMT, or, by virtue of Formula 7.4, at 0450 GMT, May 17, 1982.

He plans to observe the following stars:

	SHA	*Dec.*
Alphecca	126°30.8'	26°46.5'N
Alphard	218°19.5'	8°35'S
Capella	281°10.1'	45°58.9'N

Utilizing the standard Formulae 2.1, 7.7, 5.1, and 5.2, the reader can verify that our navigator determined the following:

$GHA\Upsilon = 294°31.8' + 12°32.1' = 307°04'$

		t	Hc	Z	Zn
Alphecca	$(-)$	68.93°	28.87°	72.05°	72.05°
Alphard	$(+)$	22.90°	49.42°	143.74°	216.26°
Capella	$(+)$	85.73°	20.76°	47.82°	312.18°

Note that the photograph of the Rude Star Finder, Figure 7.4, is set with the template at 25°N and an $LHA\Upsilon$ of 165° appropriate to our example. A close inspection of Figure 7.4 will show that for Alphecca, Alphard, and Capella the data are in conformity with our computations.

NOTES

Note 7.1

The matter of rating brightness touches upon psychophysics, a subject well known to psychologists and astronomers alike. Almost by intuition one knows that a weight, say, of twenty pounds does not feel twice as heavy as one of ten pounds, or that a light that is rated at 100 watts is twice as bright as one rated at 50 watts. With a bit of care and practice we can separate the continuum of some given type of experience into graded categories, just as Ptolemy separated the brightness of stars into six categories or magnitudes of brightness. However, if we compare the scale of psychological judgment with the physical counterpart, the relation is not a simple one. Ernst Weber, an early experimenter in psychophysics, found that if one uses a "just noticeable difference" as the basis of a scale of judgmental differences then a constant ratio of increments to base energy was required as input for an increment to generate a noticeable difference. This is expressed in the ratio:

$$k = \frac{\Delta I}{I}$$

where I is some referent base for input in physical terms and ΔI is the amount of additional energy required for the perception of a noticeable difference. Weber's work was further refined by Gustav Fechner. The Weber-Fechner Law expresses the relationship between sensation (S) and stimulus energy (R):

$S = k \log R$

About this same time (1856) the astronomer Pogson, following up on work of Herschel, found that for judging magnitude, the ratio of apparent brightnesses between magnitudes is:

$k = 2.512$

This Pogson derived from an expression:

$m_2 - m_1 = k \log (l_1 \div l_2)$

where $m_2 - m_1$ is a difference of one magnitude and l_2 and l_1 are the corresponding brightness factors. On the basis of observational experience it was determined that:

$\log (l_1 \div l_2) = 0.4$

From the above we can then write:

$\log (l_j \div l_i) = 0.4 \ (m_j - m_i)$

where i and j designate difference in magnitude. Thus,

Diff. in magnitude	Ratio of brightness
1 magnitude	2.51
2	6.31
3	15.85
4	39.80
5	100.00

To compute magnitudes of stars one needs to determine the ratio of brightness between the object star and some established standard. In such a case astronomers use very sensitive photoelectric equipment to measure brightness between two stars. Also, one can compute difference in brightness from difference in magnitude. For example, Polaris has a magnitude of 2.1, Sirius -1.6; therefore, from a magnitude difference of 3.7 we find:

$$\log (1_s \div 1_p) = .4 \times 3.7 = 1.48$$

$$1_s \div 1_p = 30.20$$

That is to say, the brightness of Sirius is thirty times that of Polaris. Both, of course, are frequently used as navigational stars.

The astronomer's treatment of this subject is further complicated by his need to distinguish between brightness and apparent magnitude as measured from earth (as above) and *luminosity* and *absolute magnitude* as calculated for a standard distance. Thus, from the earth the sun is the brightest object in the heavens; but from the standard distance of 32.6 light-years (10 parsecs), it is a rather ordinary star, much less luminous, for example, than Deneb, Rigel, or Sirius.

From the time of Ptolemy, stars were grouped into six categories of magnitude. However, with the perfection of photographic and photoelectric equipment far more gradations could be made. Among the old category of first magnitude stars there are considerable variations as to brightness. Therefore, it became necessary to go below a magnitude of one into negative values. When planets, the moon, and the sun are judged, large negative magnitudes are required. So far as our navigational stars are concerned the range is hardly more than three to four magnitudes.

Note 7.2

Addendum on Rising and Setting: For more accurate calculations, dip and the exact value of the semidiameter (SD in the daily pages of the *Almanac*) should be incorporated into Formula 7.2. For sunrise-sunset:

$$HA = \cos^{-1} \frac{\sin (-34' - SD - dip) - (\sin L \sin d)}{(\cos L \cos d)} \qquad \text{(Formula 7.2')}$$

However, in sighting from the deck of a sailboat, the dip factor will be negligible and Formula 7.2 will give sufficient accuracy.

Since the semidiameter of the sun and the moon are nearly equal (always close to 16') Formula 7.2 should also suffice for moonrise and moonset. There is, however, the additional complication of parallax in the case of the moon. For the accurate determination of moonrise and moonset we have:

$$HA = \cos^{-1} \frac{\sin (-34' - SD + HP) - (\sin L \sin d)}{(\cos L \cos d)} \qquad \text{(Formula 7.9)}$$

where SD and HP of the moon are taken from the daily pages of the *Almanac*. *HA* applied to longitude will give us the GHA of the body at moonrise. And reference to the *Almanac* will give us the GMT for the appropriate GHA.

Example: As an exercise let us compute the time of moonrise at Greenwich, England (51°29'N, 0°W) on May 16, 1982, to check this against the tabular value of the *Nautical Almanac*.

Checking the specimen pages of the *Almanac* (see Figure 3.7) we find that for a latitude of 51°29'N moonrise on May 16, 1982, is approximately 01 43 LMT. Since LMT and GMT are identical at Greenwich the declination of the moon at moonrise is about 16°49'S (i.e., declination at hour 01 43 GMT) and HP is 55.5'. SD of the moon on May 16 is 15.2. Plugging the data into Formula 7.9 we have:

$$HA = \cos^{-1} \frac{\sin + .11 - (\sin 51.48 \sin - 16.82)}{(\cos 51.48 \cos - 16.82)} \qquad \text{(Formula 7.9)}$$

$$= 67.48° \quad = 67°29'$$

Thus at moonrise the moon will be 67°29' to the east of Greenwich, giving us a GHA of the moon at moonrise of 292°31'. Now entering the *Almanac,* we wish to find GMT for the moonrise such that the GHA of the moon is 292°31'. To do this we use the main entries for the moon and the table of increments.

At 0100 GMT, GHA of the moon is 282°07.7'; at 0200 GMT, GHA of the moon is 296°39.0'. Simple interpolation reveals that a GHA of 292°31' will occur at 0143. A more precise interpolation entails our having recourse to the table of increments in the *Almanac.* To find the exact GMT of moonrise we need to find the moment of time equivalent to 10°23' of *HA* of the moon (i.e., the difference between 282°08'GHA at 0100 GMT and 292°31' GHA at moonrise). Reference to the table of increments and correction (*v* correction, see Chapter 6, is applied in reverse direction) indicates that the time equivalent for the change of *HA* of 10°23' is 42m 53s. Hence, the exact time of moonrise at Greenwich on May 16, 1982, is 01 42 53 GMT.

CHAPTER EIGHT

Finding Latitude and Longitude

The system of mapping the world by latitude and longitude goes back to Greek antiquity. On the one hand, there was an interest in describing the systematic motions of celestial objects; on the other, there was the effort to compare celestial and terrestrial positions. The interrelating of these two concerns has made positional astronomy and celestial navigation possible.

Accurate determination of latitude is practically as old as the early records of maritime exploration. In the important details the methods of determining latitude by meridian transit and by observing the altitude of the polar star have remained unchanged through the centuries. However, determining longitude was quite a different matter. Not until the eighteenth century when the chronometer had finally been perfected were the navigator and the geographer able to make precise determinations of longitude. With the creation of reliable chronometers, the modern age of navigation was born. From that time on navigators were able to make independent determinations of latitude and longitude.

Nowadays the routine of plotting the running fix has all but supplanted the determination of latitude and longitude by special methods. Still, tradition dies hard, at least among old salts. Nothing is quite like the blush of honest pleasure that comes to the navigator who gets latitude and longitude from such time-honored methods as the meridian transit and the time sight. Such methods still have their place, and might very well constitute the core of the navigator's celestial navigation repertory.

Latitude by Meridian Passage

Latitude is the angle at the center of the earth between the equator and a geographic point on the earth's surface. It is readily apparent that if we know a star's altitude when that star is on the observer's meridian, and also know its declination (its latitude) then comparing altitude and declination should give us the observer's own latitude. Pytheas was known to have used this method in the fourth century B.C. and during one of the earliest voyages into the Atlantic he determined that he had reached a latitude near the present Arctic Circle. He relied on the gnomon, a shadow pin with a horizontal scale, for his observations.

Simply stated, the situation is this: since the observer's latitude and the body's declination have the equator as a common reference the observer can determine his own latitude from knowledge of the altitude of the body. The body must be in its culmination, i.e., its highest diurnal altitude, as it crosses the observer's meridian.

Let us consider the several possibilities of meridian transit. There are four possible cases of upper transit, that is, cases where the body crosses the upper branch of the observer's meridian, and one case in which the body may be viewed in lower transit.

Case 1

In this case the declination and latitude are the same name with declination less than latitude. For example, in Figure 8.1a, both body and observer are north of the equator, but the body is south of the observer at meridian transit. For latitude we have:

$$L = 90° - h + d \qquad \text{(Formula 8.1)}$$

where L is latitude, h altitude, and d declination. This formula holds regardless of whether the observer is north or south of the equator. The defining conditions are that L and d are same name and L is greater than d. L is the angle that the zenith Z makes with the equator E.

Example: An observer in the northern hemisphere finds the altitude of M at meridian passage to be 63°, declination d is 15°N. By Formula 8.1 the above latitude L is 42°N.

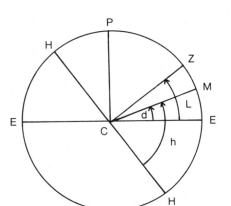

Figure 8.1a   Case 1: latitude by meridian transit

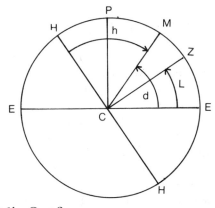

Figure 8.1b   Case 2

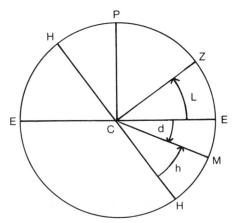

Figure 8.1c   Case 3

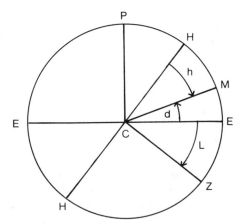

Figure 8.1d   Case 4

Case 2

Figure 8.1b presents the situation where L and d are the same name but d is greater than L. Again latitude L is the angle that zenith Z makes with the equator E.

$$L = d - (90° - h)$$
$$= d + h - 90° \qquad \text{(Formula 8.2)}$$

Example: At meridian transit the observer finds the altitude of M to be 74°, the declination of M is 42°N. Applying Formula 8.2, L is 26°N.

Case 3

Figure 8.1c presents the case where the latitude of the observer and the declination of the body are contrary in name; also, L is greater than d. Here the angle of latitude is:

$$L = 90° - h - d \qquad \text{(Formula 8.3)}$$

Example: An observer in north latitude observes the body M at transit with d of 14°S. Its observed altitude is 43°. Thus the observer's latitude is 33°N.

Case 4

In Figure 8.1d the observer and the body are contrary in name *but* L is south. The formula for latitude is the same as Formula 8.3 above.

$$L = 90° - h - d$$

Thus Formula 8.3 applies whenever L and d are contrary in name.

Example: An observer in south latitude observes body M at transit to have an altitude of 23°. The declination of M is 48°N. L is therefore 19°S.

Case 5

In the case of circumpolar body M, its transit may occur on the lower branch of the observer's meridian, that is to say, when its true azimuth in the northern hemisphere is 0°. Figure 8.1e illustrates the situation. Latitude is:

$$L = 90° - d + h \qquad \text{(Formula 8.4)}$$

This case is closely related to finding latitude by the polestar. If we take $(90° - d)$ as the codeclination or polar distance of M, then latitude is simply the observed altitude plus the polar distance.

Example: M with a declination of 62°N is observed in transit on the observer's lower branch. The observed altitude is 21°. Thus L is 49°N.

Our first four cases are summarized in Table 8.1.

Table 8.1

	d < L	d > L
L, d same name	L = 90° − h − d	L = d + h − 90°
L, d contrary name	L = 90° − h − d	L = 90° − h − d

The formulae in Table 8.1 are quite simple to apply. Since the emphasis in this book is on calculator computation there is a general trigonometric formula that covers all cases. Recall from Figure 4.4 that the nautical triangle includes the sides codeclination, coaltitude, and colatitude, and the angles t (hour angle) and Z (azimuth). At meridian transit the hour angle between the observer's meridian and that of the body is

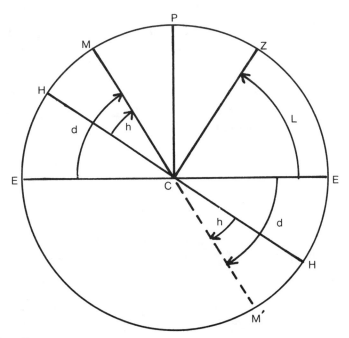

Figure 8.1e   Case 5

zero. Hence, with a bit of manipulation we can derive a basic formula for latitude that covers all cases:

$$L = \sin^{-1} (\sin d \sin h) \pm (\cos d \cos h) \qquad \text{(Formula 8.5)}$$

or

$$\sin L = \pm \cos (d \pm h) \qquad \text{(Formula 8.6)}$$

(The notation $\sin^{-1}$ indicates that the quantity in the brackets is the sine of the quantity L.)

In applying Formula 8.5 there are two rules to follow. The first rule applies to all calculator computations: if declination of the observed body is contrary in name to the observer's latitude enter the declination as a negative angle (change-of-sign entry, $\boxed{+/-}$).

The second rule applies only to Formula 8.5: if declination of the body and the observer's latitude are of the same name but declination is greater than latitude, the sign in Formula 8.5 is minus, in all other cases plus. However, in all cases of lower transit observations the sign is plus.

Formula 8.6 is the equivalent of 8.5. In all cases except that in which L and d are same name but d is greater than L:

$$\sin L = \cos (d - h) \qquad \text{(Formula 8.6a)}$$

In the case where L and d are same name but d is greater than L:

$$\sin L = -\cos (d + h) \qquad \text{(Formula 8.6b)}$$

However, when the body is observed in lower transit, our Case 5, use Formula 8.6a.

Determining the Time of Meridian Passage

For the accurate determination of latitude one needs to observe the body precisely at its culmination, the point at which it reaches maximum altitude relative to the observer. This is the point when the hour circle of the body and the observer's meridian coincide.

There are two ways of proceeding here. Consider, for example, a meridian observation of the sun. With a rough approximation of local noon, the observer begins taking sights prior to culmination and continues to take sights until his readings reach a maximum and then begin to diminish. A plot of his sightings would help to eliminate random variations or irregularities in the sightings. The maximum reading would then be the sight, the altitude h, corresponding to a culmination.

Another way of proceeding is to get a more precise indication of the time of meridian passage so as to limit the time span of observation. As local noon approaches the navigator will be able to estimate his longitude from his ongoing dead reckoning. If his course has been on the north-south axis, there is little change in longitude with time. If his course has been more along the east-west axis then he will use his DR to indicate where in his particular time zone he is (i.e., he'll know whether meridian passage will be before, near, or after his local zone time noon). Having an approximate longitude, he converts the east or west longitude to a corresponding GHA. Entering the *Nautical Almanac* he then determines the GMT that gives a GHA of the apparent sun identical with that of his longitude.

Example: On May 16, 1982, as local noon approaches, DR longitude is 132°30'W. Find time of meridian transit. We want to find the GMT that gives precisely a GHA of the sun equal to 132°30'.

GHA at 2000 GMT	120°55.4'
For a GHA of 132°30' the required increment	11°34.6'
Time equivalent (from Table of Increments)	46m 18s
GMT for meridian passage	20h 46m 18s

A longitude of 132°30'W is in the time zone nine hours slow on Greenwich (i.e., $132.5 \div 15$). Therefore, local zone time for meridian passage is approximately 11 46 18.

Note that the solution is the inverse of the procedure for determining GHA when time is known. Here we determine time from a knowledge of GHA. There is still an element of approximation here; a good estimate of longitude is required. Without that, we would be forced to determine culmination by means of continuous observation (*cf.* Note 8.1).

The procedures for determining meridian passage for stars, planets, and moon follow a pattern identical with that above. First, make a preliminary estimate of when transit should occur. Then determine a corresponding DR longitude and convert that longitude to GHA. And then, entering the appropriate columns of the *Nautical Almanac,* find the GMT yielding the identical GHA for the body.

Only in exceptional conditions of observation (good ambient light to define the horizon) are we likely to take a meridian observation of stars or planets. The moon, however, may offer a good horizon for observation at its culmination.

Example: On May 16, 1982, the meridian transit of the moon is expected when DR longitude λ is approximately 35°15'W. Find local time of transit.

GHA for λ	35°15'
at 0800 GMT, GHA (v = 12.4')	23°47'
Increment GHA to λ	11°28'
corr. v (reverse sign)	−10'
Increment GHA	11°18'
Time equivalent increment	47m 22s
GMT for transit	08h 47m 22s
Zone time (2 hours slow on Greenwich)	06 47 22

Note that in working from GHA to GMT we apply the moon's v correction in reverse sign.

LATITUDE BY POLARIS

One of the time-honored techniques for finding latitude is to observe the altitude of the polar star. This is complicated by the fact that our North Star, Polaris, is not positioned precisely at the pole of the earth's axis. Furthermore, the effects of precession, that 23½° wobble about a fixed ecliptic plane, means that Polaris will in time desert its place as polar beacon leaving the lamp unlit until some other star wanders by (cf. Note 8.2).

First, consider the ideal case where we assume the polestar to coincide directly with the pole. Since our polar star would then have a declination of 90°N, then, by virtue of Formula 8.4 we find:

L = h

An observation of the polar star thus gives us latitude directly. Graphically this is illustrated in Figure 8.2. Angle h is equal to angle L by virtue of the fact that the sides of the two angles are mutually perpendicular. As a matter of fact, however, Polaris is not located directly at the pole but has a circumpolar orbit of just under one degree. That is to say, its declination is just over 89°. The broken-line circle in Figure 8.2 shows the orbit in exaggerated form. The result of this departure from true north is that only twice during the sidereal day will the observed altitude of Polaris correspond with the altitude of the pole (roughly, but not precisely, when Polaris is due east or west of the pole). At other times when Polaris is in the northern sector, its altitude will be less than the altitude of the pole, and when it is in the southern sector its altitude will be greater. There are three factors which contribute to the discrepancy between the actual altitude of Polaris and that of the pole itself: (a) a main one due to the simple geometry of Polaris' orbit; (b) a second one due to the fact that from the observer's vantage the orbit is tilted, i.e., becomes elliptical; and (c) a third one due to precession of the equinoxes and a factor known as aberration (see *Bowditch*). In order to infer latitude directly from the altitude of Polaris we must make corrections for these three factors.

Correction Tables
Correction tables are found in both the *Nautical Almanac* and the *Air Almanac*. In both tables entry is made according to the LHA of Aries as computed for the time and place of observation. In the *Air Almanac* all corrections are combined into a single Polaris correction. In the *Nautical Almanac* the corrections are made in three parts. Instructions for combining and applying the separate corrections are included at the bottom of the table (cf. Note 8.3).

It should be noted that with a magnitude of only +2.1 Polaris is not among the brightest of stars. The best procedure for observing Polaris during twilight is to preset

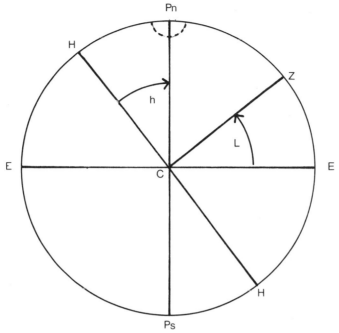

Figure 8.2   Latitude by Polaris

an altitude according to the DR position, where the altitude would be approximated by DR latitude plus or minus the appropriate Polaris corrections applied in the reversed sign.

OTHER METHODS FOR DETERMINING LATITUDE

The history of navigation abounds with methods for determining latitude. Clearly the preferred method for the nautical navigator is that of meridian passage. This, however, requires an observation at the exact moment of culmination. Since this may involve a protracted period of observation as well as some fussy precalculations, it may prove inconvenient for the navigator to catch the precise moment of transit.

Ex-Meridian Altitudes
There are a number of methods that enable the navigator to infer latitude from an altitude observation taken more or less near the time of transit. These fall under the heading of *ex-meridian* observations and generally involve computing rates of change in altitude as a function of time at and around the time of actual transit. Rates of change are relatively difficult to compute and apply, and although *Bowditch* presents a set of two tables (Tables 29 and 30) for determining such ex-meridian corrections, they are cumbersome to use. Fortunately, there is a comparatively simple method for determining ex-meridian latitude. It makes use of the right triangle method of sight reduction discussed in Note 5.5.

We repeat here Figure 5.12 which shows the navigational triangles with the orthogonal projection of the body M onto the observer's meridian PZ. (Note for all prime values, $L' = 90° - L$, etc.)

We now visualize t as meridian angle before or after meridian transit. It is apparent that if we can compute the values PR and ZR then a bit of arithmetic will give us our latitude L. In Figure 5.12A when declination d is less than L or is different in name:

$$L = 90° - (PR - ZR)$$ (Formula 8.7)

In Figure 5.12B where d is greater than L, but same name:

$$L = 90° - (PR + ZR)$$ (Formula 8.8)

Hence, if we can compute PR and ZR, we can determine latitude directly.

In Note 5.5 we found:

$$PR = \tan^{-1} \frac{\cos t}{\tan d}$$ (Formula 5.7)

$$MR = \sin^{-1} (\cos d \sin t)$$ (Formula 5.8)

Napier's rules for solving right spherical triangles in turn gives us:

$$ZR = \cos^{-1} \frac{\sin h}{\cos MR}$$ (Formula 5.12)

$$\text{or} \quad ZR = \cos^{-1} \frac{\sin h \cos PR}{\sin d}$$ (Formula 5.13)

It follows then that if we obtain an ex-meridian altitude Ho and can determine t and d, we can compute our latitude.

Example 1: Approximately 18 minutes after meridian transit the observed altitude of the sun is 80°12′. At the time of observation GHA of the sun is 75°54′, declination is 22°09′N, and DR longitude is 71°24′W. Find latitude.

We first determine t:

$$t = GHA - \lambda = 75.9 - 71.4 = 4.5°$$

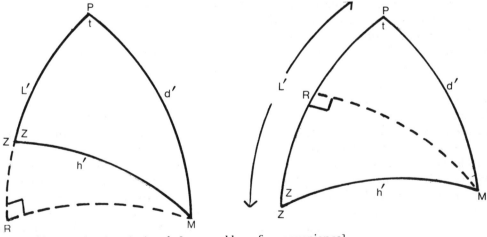

Figure 5.12   Navigational triangle [repeated here for convenience]

Computing PR:

$$PR = \tan^{-1} \frac{\cos 4.5}{\tan 22.15} = 67.79° \qquad \text{(Formula 5.7)}$$

And computing ZR:

$$ZR = \cos^{-1} \frac{\sin 80.2 \cos 67.79}{\sin 22.15} = 8.90° \qquad \text{(Formula 5.13)}$$

Hence for latitude:

$$L = 90 - (67.79 + 8.90) = 13.31° = 13°19'N \qquad \text{(Formula 8.8)}$$

Example 2: Approximately 22 minutes after transit the observed altitude of the sun is 58°51'. GHA of the sun is 157°09', declination is 8°45'S, and DR longitude is 151°39'W.

To find latitude:

$$t = 157.15 - 151.65 = 5.5°$$

$$PR = \tan^{-1} \frac{\cos 5.5}{\tan -8.75} = 81.21° \to 98.79 \qquad \text{(Formula 5.7)}$$

$$ZR = \cos^{-1} \frac{\sin 58.85 \cos 98.79}{\sin -8.75} = 30.72 \qquad \text{(Formula 5.13)}$$

Hence,

$$L = 90 - (98.79 - 30.72)$$
$$= 21.93° = 21°56'N \qquad \text{(Formula 8.7)}$$

Note that if PR is negative, add the negative value to 180° to obtain the corresponding positive value (*cf.* Note 5.4).

There are other methods for computing latitude directly (*cf.* Note 8.4), but this one has the advantage of being "robust." That is to say, it is relatively insensitive to uncertainties or error in DR longitude if the observation is taken near meridian transit.

Zero or 180° Azimuth Observations

Among cruising navigators the most common method of determining latitude involves plotting a latitude line from an assumed position that offers computational convenience. The navigator determines an approximate time for meridian passage, takes an observation sometime during that interval, and then assumes a longitude such that the hour angle t is zero. The true azimuth will then either be 0° or 180° and the LOP will plot as a segment of a line of latitude. The intercept will then represent the difference in latitude between the observer's actual and assumed positions. With $t = 0$ the fundamental formula for Hc at the meridian passage is:

$$Hc = \sin^{-1} (\sin L \sin d + \cos L \cos d) \qquad \text{(Formula 8.9)}$$

By a fundamental relation in trigonometry, Formula 8.9 reduces to:

$$Hc = \sin^{-1} \cos (L - d) \qquad \text{(Formula 8.10)}$$

(with the precaution that if declination is contrary in name to latitude we enter it with a change-of-sign key, $\boxed{+/-}$).

Example: On May 18, 1982, at approximately local noon our DR position is 12°36'S, 17°42'W. At 13 08 10 GMT a sextant observation with appropriate corrections gives us an Ho of 58°02'. Find our latitude.

At 13 08 10 GMT:

GHA 1300   15°54.7', d = 19°33'N
Increment 08'10"   2°02.5'
GHA   17°57.2'

Assume a longitude to give t = 0; hence, assumed position is 12°36'S, 17°57'W. Solving for Hc by Formula 8.7 above:

$$Hc = \sin^{-1} (\sin 12.6 \sin -19.55) + (\cos 12.6 \cos -19.55)$$
$$= 57.85° = 57°51'$$

Comparing Ho and Hc we get an intercept of 11'. Since the sun is north declination and we are south latitude the true azimuth is 360°. Hence the intercept is toward the body and our actual latitude is 12°25'S.

It should be emphasized, however, that accuracy of estimating latitude from a noon shot is contingent upon accuracy in estimating one's longitude. In effect this is to say we should have an accurate estimation of when local noon occurs so that our observation occurs either at or very near meridian passage. In the above example, an error of 8' in assuming meridian passage would introduce an error in Hc, hence estimate of latitude, of approximately 4 miles. On the other hand, an error in assumed longitude would not in and of itself be serious. For example, in the above problem, had we actually been at 17°32'W rather than 17°57'W where the sun actually was at the time of observation the error in our computed Hc would have been insignificant.

The point of all this is that it is important to observe the body as it reaches culmination—more important, say, than having a precise estimate of longitude. To make sure of observation at culmination it is advisable to continue to observe the body over a time bracket that safely includes local meridian passage.

Latitude from the Timing of Sunset

One of the classic methods of determining longitude involves the timing of sunset (see below). Less well known, or at least less utilized, is a procedure for determining latitude from the timing of sunset. Just as we can determine longitude at sunset given that latitude is known, so can we determine latitude given that longitude is known.

In Chapter 7, we found that visual sunset occurs when the center of the sun is actually 50' or 0.83° below the horizon. To find latitude at sunset, we must first determine the moment when the true altitude of the sun is 0°, that is, when its center exactly coincides with the horizon, irrespective of the factors of refraction and semidiameter that influence the apparent or visual sunset. If we ignore the effects of refraction the basic formula for the timing of the rising or setting of any body is:

$$t = \cos^{-1} - \frac{\sin L \sin d}{\cos L \cos d} \qquad \text{(Formula 7.1)}$$
$$= \cos^{-1} - (\tan L \tan d)$$

By rearranging terms we have:

$$\tan L = -\frac{\cos t}{\tan d} \qquad \text{(Formula 7.1')}$$

Thus if we know t and d at true sunset we can compute our latitude directly.

By timing the true sunset we can determine the GHA of the sun from the *Almanac*, also declination d. In order to determine meridian angle t we of course need to know our longitude λ. But, how do we determine actual sunset rather than visual sunset that occurs the moment the upper limb of the sun disappears below the horizon?

The answer is straightforward. We work upward, as it were, from the effects of refraction and semidiameter. Under standard conditions refraction at zero altitude is about 34', at 0°30' of altitude, about 31'. Semidiameter of the sun on the average is 16'. Combining those two factors (R − SD) would indicate that if the lower limb of the sun as sighted through the sextant yields an observed altitude Ho of 15', then the center of the true sun just intersects the horizon. Our procedure at that point is to preset a sextant altitude hs equivalent to an Ho of 15' and to time the instant the lower limb of the sun as seen through the sextant touches the horizon.

Note that in this procedure we must apply such corrections as dip, index error, etc., in reverse order to get from Ho = 15' to the equivalent sextant altitude hs. Moreover, we require both a precise timing of the moment that the sun lips the horizon and an accurate determination of longitude.

Later in this chapter we shall describe one means of getting an accurate determination of longitude prior to sunset (see "Prime Vertical Sights"). In the example that follows we merely assume that longitude at sunset is known.

Example: Our navigator is heading NW out of Cabo San Lucas intending to make San Diego on two long tacks. Figuring dip correction as −3, and index error as +1, he presets his sextant to hs = 0°19' (so that Ho= 0°15') for a timing of sunset. Precisely at 02 47 22 GMT, May 17, 1982, he observes the lower limb of the sun touching the horizon. A prior prime vertical sight advanced to time of sunset gives him a longitude of 122°15'W. At that time declination is 19°14'N. To find meridian angle t he computes:

$$t = GHA - \lambda$$

From the *Nautical Almanac* (see Figures 3.7 and 3.8) for GMT 02 47 22 May 17, GHA is found by:

GMT	GHA	d
02 00	210°55.4'	
47 22	11°50.5'	
02 47 22	222°46'	19°13.6'N

Hence:

$$t = 222°46' - 122°15' = 100°31' = 100.52°$$

Solving for latitude (Formula 7.1'):

$$L = \tan^{-1} - \frac{\cos 100.52}{\tan 19.23}$$

$$= 27.63° = 27°38'N$$

This coupled with his longitude of 122°15' gives him a sunset fix.

Again we emphasize that both an accurate timing of sunset and an accurate knowledge of longitude are required in this determination of latitude. For example in the present problem, a 4-second error in timing would have introduced a 1.5′ error in latitude.

LONGITUDE METHODS

Whereas finding latitude proved to be a relatively simple problem for early astronomers and navigators, finding longitude proved to be the most difficult problem in all of navigation. Latitude could be found with simple devices for measuring altitude such as the gnomon, the astrolabe, and the quadrant. There were no early instruments for measuring longitude, no tape measures, to be sure, and no chronometers. Thus until fairly recent times the measurement of longitude was mostly conjecture.

The measurement of longitude is inseparably bound to time, and time to the rotation of the earth. It takes the sun on the average twenty-four hours, noon to noon, to complete its apparent revolution. Thus it moves through 15° of arc in every hour. If we divide every hour into degrees and minutes of longitude, then a clock that keeps the sun's time should help us in finding longitude. Starting with the prime meridian, Greenwich, we can plot the sun's position, its longitude, by virtue of our clock. And knowing the sun's position as observed in transit by an observer, and knowing also the time of that transit we can determine the observer's longitude.

There are many proposals and methods of measuring longitude. All make use of accurate timing. Our discussion shall be confined to four that should perhaps be in the repertory of every navigator: one, the classical time sight; two, the traditional running fix; three, the sighting of an object on the prime vertical; and four, the timing of observed sunrise or sunset. There are other methods, such as that of lunar distance, but these are of historic interest only (*cf.* Note 8.5).

Time Sight
Until fairly recently the taking of a time sight was a standard procedure for determining longitude.

Consider our basic formula for sight reduction:

$$\sin Hc = \sin L \sin d + \cos L \cos d \cos t \qquad\qquad \text{(Formula 5.1)}$$

Rearranging terms will give us:

$$\cos t = \frac{\sin h - \sin L \sin d}{\cos L \cos d} \qquad\qquad \text{(Formula 8.11)}$$

Assuming accurate information on h, L, and d, we can determine the hour angle t between the observed body and the observer. And knowing t we can determine longitude λ.

Recall now that the GHA of a body is determined from the *Nautical Almanac* on the basis of accurate timing. If we know both GHA and hour angle east or west of the body we can easily combine the two to get longitude:

$$\lambda = GHA \pm HA \qquad\qquad \text{(Formula 8.12)}$$

Since t, the meridian angle, is *HA*:

$$\lambda = GHA \pm t \qquad\qquad \text{(Formula 8.12)}$$

It should be emphasized that small errors in h or L result in large errors in t, and hence in our estimate of λ. Consequently the navigator must be very sure of his latitude position. This is most likely to be the case soon after he finds his latitude by meridian transit. The standard procedure is to determine noon latitude and follow this in a couple of hours by the time sight.

Example: On May 17, 1982, during and around local noon we obtain an altitude hs of 79°51' at the apparent culmination of the sun. After applying corrections for index error ($-1'$), dip ($-3'$), and semidiameter and refraction ($+16'$), we obtain an Ho of 80°03'. For the time of our observation (GMT 2205), d = 19°25'N. Applying Formula 8.6a we find by calculator:

$$L = \sin^{-1} \cos (19.42 - 80.05) = 29.37° \text{ or } 29°22'N$$

Later, at 0046 GMT on May 18, we take a second sight and obtain hs = 52°03'; with corrections, Ho = 52°14'. We have been making good a course of 250° at 6 knots. Our latitude as projected from our earlier latitude shot is 29°16'N. For 0046 GMT, May 18, declination is 19°26'N and GHA is 192°25'. Applying Formula 8.11 for calculator computation we have:

$$t = \cos^{-1} \frac{(\sin 52.24) - (\sin 29.27 \sin 19.43)}{(\cos 29.27 \cos 19.43)}$$

$$= 40.25° = 40°15'$$

Then from Formula 8.12:

$$\lambda = 192°25' - 40°15' = 152°10'W$$

That, combined with our latitude as advanced from noon, gives us a position which should check out with a position obtained by advancing our noon line to the LOP determined from the 0046 GMT observation.

A variation of the time sight incorporates the method of a Sumner line (see Note 4.2). Suppose we are not all that sure of our latitude at the time of our time sight observation. Assume two latitudes within the limits of expected error and compute longitudes for each just as above. We then have two sets of coordinates: (L1, λ1) and (L2, λ2) pertaining to the two time sights. Connecting the two points will give us a Sumner line of position, but not a precise estimate of longitude.

Conventional Running Fix

Any conventional fix will give us a position with latitude-longitude coordinates. The intercept method as proposed by Marcq St. Hilaire is now standard. Either we can obtain a fix by taking nearly simultaneous observations of several bodies at night, or moon and sun in the day, or we can plot a running fix, taking two or more observations of the same or different bodies at different times, advancing all earlier lines of position to the time and LOP of the last observation. The usual procedure for the cruising sailor is to take a shot of the sun before noon, at noon, and possibly an hour or two after noon, all LOPs moved to the time of the noon shot. In the writer's experience well over half of the scores of navigators he has met in the Pacific have relied primarily on the noonday fix for their celestial navigation.

Prime Vertical Sights: Objects Bearing Due East or West

A conventional LOP plotted on a true azimuth line of 180° or 360° will give us a line of latitude. Similarly a conventional LOP plotted on a true azimuth of 90° or 270° will give us a line of longitude. How do we go about determining when to take an observation such that the true azimuth will be due east or west?

A great circle through our zenith and nadir and perpendicular to the horizon is known as a vertical circle. The vertical circle through the east and west points of the observer's horizon is his prime vertical circle. Hence the question is: when will a celestial body be on the prime vertical? In Note 8.4 it is pointed out that we can rewrite the fundamental law of cosines to focus on declination rather than altitude:

$$\sin d = \sin L \sin h + \cos L \cos h \cos Z \qquad \text{(Formula 8.13)}$$

Now if Z is 90° or 270° its cosine is zero and the end term drops out. Hence, from Formula 8.13 we get:

$$h = \sin^{-1} \frac{\sin d}{\sin L} \qquad \text{(Formula 8.14)}$$

Thus, the body will be on the prime vertical at the precise moment the observed altitude (as corrected) corresponds to that obtained by Formula 8.14. By taking periodic shots we can easily determine when the body we are observing will be on the prime vertical.

Example: Suppose my DR latitude is projected as 33°20'N and the declination of the sun 19°26'N. Then:

$$Hc = \sin^{-1} \frac{\sin 19.43}{\sin 33.33} = 37.26° = 37°16'$$

This is the precomputed altitude. Thus if our index correction is -1, dip is -3, and our main correction is $+15$, we have a total correction of $+11$ to add to hs to derive Ho. However, since we wish to get an Ho that corresponds with Hc above we subtract the correction from Hc. Thus an hs of 37°05' yields an Ho of 37°16'. And precisely at the moment we get a sextant reading of 37°05' for the lower limb of the sun, the sun is on our prime vertical. We could, of course, now plot an LOP by the usual intercept procedure assuming both latitude and longitude. However, there is available a direct procedure that requires neither intercept nor plotting. Formula 8.14 enables us to compute Hc for the moment the body is on the prime vertical. However, a familiar azimuth formula is:

$$\sin Z = \frac{\sin t \cos d}{\cos h} \qquad \text{(Formula 5.3)}$$

But for Z equal to 90° or 270°, $\sin Z = 1$; hence,

$$\sin t = \frac{\cos h}{\cos d} \qquad \text{(Formula 8.15)}$$

giving us our hour angle at the time the body is on the prime vertical. Combining Formulae 8.14 and 8.15 for computational purposes gives us:

$$t = \sin^{-1} \frac{\cos \left(\sin^{-1} \frac{\sin d}{\sin L} \right)}{\cos d} \qquad \text{(Formula 8.16)}$$

(For computation procedure, see Note 8.6.)

Then, applying our fundamental Formula 8.12 relating GHA, t, and λ, we solve for longitude.

Suppose, in the example above, the time at which our sextant reads $37°05'$ is 01 46 12 GMT, May 18, 1982. Solving for t via Formula 8.16 gives us:

$t = 57.56° = 57°34'$

From the *Nautical Almanac* (see Figures 3.7 and 3.8):

GHA 0100, May 18, 1982	$195°55'$
Increment 46m 12s	$11°33'$
GHA	$207°28'$
t	$57°34'$
λ	$149°54'W$

When the body is on the prime vertical its altitude changes more rapidly than it does when high on the observer's own meridian. Thus timing in the prime vertical case is likely to be more accurate than it would be during meridian passage (*cf*. Note 8.7).

The altitude change of any body is most rapid when it is on the observer's prime vertical. Not all bodies reach the prime vertical, however. For that to occur, the declination must be the same name and smaller than the observer's latitude.

Longitude by Sunrise and Sunset

In the previous chapter we mentioned that longitude can be determined from an accurate timing of sunrise or sunset. The method is recommended for lifeboat navigation (see *Bowditch* and *Dutton*) and works reasonably well in lower altitudes. However, it is subject to considerable error in the higher latitudes whenever the navigator is unsure of his latitude.

In brief, if we can determine a precise time of sunrise for a given latitude and know the GMT at the time of actual sunrise, then longitude is known by virtue of:

$$\lambda = GHA \pm HA \qquad\qquad\qquad \text{(Formula 8.12)}$$

where *HA* is hour angle that positions the sun at sunrise (or sunset). First, we determine the hour angle of the sun that will be associated with the latter's rising or setting at a given latitude (see Chapter 7). Second, we mark the time, GMT, that the upper limb of the sun either just pierces or falls beneath the horizon. Third, we convert that time to GHA of the sun by means of the *Nautical Almanac*. And fourth, we determine longitude by virtue of Formula 8.12.

Example: Just prior to sunrise on May 18, 1982, an observation of Polaris, duly corrected, gives us a latitude of $28°45'N$. Actual sunrise was observed to occur at 14 46 32 GMT. Find the longitude. In the morning of May 18, 1982, declination of the sun is $19°34'N$. With $d = +19.57°$ and $L = 28.75°$, we find by Formula 7.2 that hour angle at sunrise (mean sun) is:

$$HA = \cos^{-1} \frac{(\sin -.83) - (\sin 28.75 \sin 19.57)}{(\cos 28.75 \cos 19.57)}$$
$$= 102.27°$$

This is the hour angle of the mean sun at sunrise. To get the hour angle of the true sun we must apply the equation of time. The equation of time in the morning of May 18, 1982, is $-3m\ 40s$. Our table of increments and corrections in the *Nautical Almanac* shows this to be equivalent to 55' of arc. Hence, our *HA* adjusted for the equation of time is:

$$102°16' - 0°55' = 101°21'$$

Using the main entries of the *Nautical Almanac* and the increments for minutes and seconds, the GHA of the sun at 14 46 32 is:

		GHA
1400	GMT	30°54.7'
46	32	11°38'
1446	32	42°32.7'

Applying Formula 8.12:

$$\lambda = 42°33' + 101°21'$$
$$= 143°54'W$$

This method should only be used if we are very sure of our latitude. That is why determining latitude by Polaris prior to sunrise is the recommended procedure. On the other hand, if we were unsure of our latitude, say, an error of 10' of latitude at an assumed latitude of 40°N, our error in the determination of longitude would be on the order of 7 miles. For a fixed margin of error on latitude, the higher the latitude the greater the error in longitude.

NOTES

Note 8.1
This is the usual procedure: if we know our longitude at the approximate time of meridian transit, then we find the GMT at which the GHA of the body coincides with our longitude. What we are seeking is simply the time of local apparent noon (LAN).

There is another procedure for finding LAN sometimes used by ships' navigators who may wish to determine the time of transit well in advance. At some time in the morning well in advance of LAN, the time of transit, the navigator determines his longitude (either by DR or a sunline or other celestial LOP). At the time, GMT, he also determines the GHA of the sun. The difference between his longitude λ and the GHA of the sun is an hour angle t. Call this te. Determining the time of LAN then becomes a problem of interception. The time to transit is simply the time it takes the sun to close the angle te.

Recall that the ideal mean sun traverses the heavens at a rate of 15° per hour, i.e., 900' of arc per hour. However, there is also the speed of the ship along the east-west axis to consider. This component of speed will be added if the ship is on an easterly course, or subtracted if on a westerly course. Hence, the time to LAN is simply:

$$T = \frac{te}{900'/hr \pm \text{ship's speed on E-W axis (DLo)}} \qquad \text{(Formula 8.17)}$$

The time T added to GMT above yields the desired LAN.

Note that only if the vessel's true course is either west or east can it be plugged directly into Formula 8.17. If the course is in an intermediate quadrant, such as SW or NE, then the east-west component must be determined either graphically as a simple problem of vectors or directly by trigonometric means. For example, every course can be treated as a tangent between a N-S component of direction and speed and an E-W component.

Suppose our course is SW. Then from Figure 8.3 we can see that our true course is $270° - Z$ where:

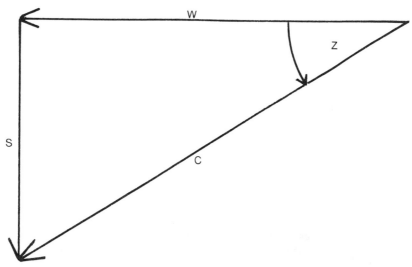

Figure 8.3   Components of speed

$$\tan Z = \frac{\text{S component}}{\text{W component}} \qquad \text{(Formula 8.18)}$$

To find the westerly component of our speed W in terms of DLo:

$$\text{E-W component} = C \cos Z \div \cos L \qquad \text{(Formula 8.19)}$$

where C is the component of speed along our true course vector and Z is the course angle between the N-S and E-W axes. Since the horizontal component of speed is westerly it will be subtracted from the sun's component (Formula 8.17).

Example: A prime vertical observation (see "Prime Vertical Sights" above) at 11 45 10 GMT, May 17, 1982, gives a longitude of 56°53'W with a corresponding DR position of 34°45'N, 56°53'W. We are making a true course of 125° at a speed of 12 knots. Find LAN, the time of meridian transit of the sun.

Referring to our specimen pages of the *Almanac* (Figures 3.7 and 3.8), we find:

	GMT	GHA
	11 00	345°55.2'
Increment	45 10	11°17.5'
	11 45 10	357°12.7'

Then,

$$\begin{aligned} te &= 56°53' + (360° - 357°13') \\ &= 59°40', \\ &= 3{,}580' \text{ of arc to close} \end{aligned}$$

To find our vessel's easterly component of closure, we use Formula 8.19 where Z, the angle of our course vector, is $125° - 90° = 35°$, and L is DR latitude.

$$\begin{aligned} \text{E component} &= 12 \cos 35 \div \cos 34.75 \\ &= 11.96' \text{ per hour} \end{aligned}$$

Hence, the time to close the hour angle to LAN is by Formula 8.17:

$$T = \frac{3,580}{900 + 11.96}$$

$$= 3.93h$$
$$= 3h\,55m\,48s$$

and

$$LAN = GMT + T$$
$$= 11\,45\,10 + 3\,55\,48$$
$$= 15\,40\,58\,GMT$$

Note that the easterly component of the vessel's speed is *added* to that of the sun, since the two components are converging.

Note 8.2

At the present time Polaris is getting closer to the celestial north pole. It will continue to do so until its orbit is 28′ instead of its present 48′. But a precessional orbit with a radius of $23\frac{1}{2}°$ sweeps a large area of the polar skies. In time (neither we nor our grandchildren need remain expectant) Deneb and Vega, both far brighter than Polaris, will occupy the polar chair. Meanwhile the southern lamp remains unlit. But patience is advised. In time Avior, in the false southern cross, will twinkle above the south pole offering direction and latitudinal succor to those on their way to Polynesia and New Zealand.

Note 8.3

Should the cruising sailor fancy Polaris shots he would do well to pick up a Polaris correction chart from the *Air Almanac*. Although the chart considers only the major correction due to the variation in declination, he would not be far off in ignoring supplementary corrections. He would also be advised to have a sextant with a powerful telescope and to preset the expected altitude. The only time he is likely to have a workable horizon is during twilight.

Latitude by Polaris is one of the oldest methods to be found in the navigator's repertory. However, the complexity of the problem of correcting for Polaris' wanderings is indicated in Figure 8.4. Consider first the major correction $a0$ as indicated in the *Nautical Almanac*. In our figure the line of sight is along the N-S axis through the pole P to the observer's zenith Z. As Polaris revolves diurnally about the circle in an apparent westerly direction its declination varies from the 90° line OwOe northerly and southerly as its position is projected laterally to the N-S axis. Thus when Polaris is at position M1 its position along the N-S axis is M′1. And its declination is less than 90° by the amount PM′1. This is the amount by which its altitude will be less than the observer's latitude, other factors being ignored. On the other hand, suppose Polaris is at M2; then its declination departs from 90° by the amount PM′2. But note that its position is closer to the observer's zenith position than when at M1. This means its altitude will be greater than it would be were it at P on the OwOe line. The correction applied to observed altitude, therefore, will be subtracted when Polaris is in the lower semicircle and added when in the upper semicircle. Since the N-S axis is the observer's meridian, and the line PM is the celestial meridian of Polaris when it is at M1, the angle t is a meridian angle. If the orbit of Polaris is 48′ then PM′, the magnitude of Polaris' correction when Polaris is at M1, will be:

PM′ = 48′ cos t

This, however, is not the only correction that must be made in order to infer the altitude of the true pole P from the altitude of Polaris in its diurnal orbit. Again let us refer to Figure 8.4. According to Polaris' orbit, the altitude of Polaris should be identical with that of the true pole P when it is in the position Ow and Oe. And every point on the line OwPOe is a point of equal altitude. But due to the fact there is an apparent tilt to the horizontal plane, the observer will observe an altitude of Polaris equal to that of the true pole only when Polaris is at W and E. In effect, on the N-S axis the location of Polaris is at W′ when observation will indicate it to be at P.

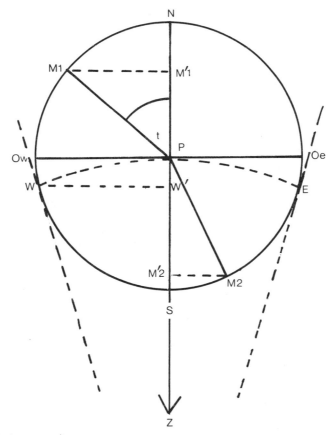

Figure 8.4 Polaris correction

Hence PW' will constitute the magnitude of the correction that should be made. The double arrow lines constitute the line of sight to apparent west and east as seen from the GP of our zenith. The closer the GP or zenith is to the true pole, the greater the effect PW'. It should be apparent that our second correction factor is one invariably to be subtracted ($a1$ in the *Nautical Almanac*).

The third correction ($a2$ in the *Nautical Almanac*) compensates for the effects of the earth's rotational motion: one, there is a small annual increment of precession of the polar axis, and two, the earth revolves in an orbit generating an effect known as aberration, an optical effect due to the fact that the earth is moving in the orbit relative to the stellar light source. Such effects are related to the earth's seasonal position in the orbit.

Considering all corrections, as the *Nautical Almanac* does, the main correction $a0$ is plus or minus dependent on Polaris' orbital position as generally indicated by the LHA of Aries. The $a1$ and $a2$ corrections are always subtractive. For computational purposes, however, all corrections are made *positive* by adding an appropriate constant to their respective values. The sum of the constants is $+1$ and the sum of the corrections will be $-1 + a0 + a1 + a2$.

A satisfactorily accurate calculator treatment of the Polaris correction can be achieved by assuming a plane circular orbit for Polaris (not the apparent elliptical one) and using a plane trigonometric function to determine vertical displacement of Polaris from the polar position. Apply the correction:

Latitude = Ho of Polaris − 48′ cos LHA Polaris (Formula 8.20)

where Ho is hs corrected for instrument error, dip, and refraction; 48′ is the polar orbit (i.e., polar distance or $90° - d$) of Polaris; and the LHA of Polaris is obtained from the following:

$$LHA = GHA\ Polaris\ \pm\lambda\ {}^{E}_{W}$$

with

$$GHA\ Polaris = GHA\Upsilon + SHA\ Polaris$$

Sidereal hour angle of Polaris varies considerably through the year. Its monthly value can be found in the *Nautical Almanac*.

Note 8.4

Another method, the *double-altitude* method, was outstanding in its simplicity, but not in its accuracy. We have seen that a line of position is a segment of a large circle of equal altitude of which the substellar point is the center. We also know how to locate a body's GP at any instant of time. Why not, then, take a globe of the earth and draw circles of equal altitude for a given body at two different times? The method goes back to Robert Hues who published a treatise on the subject in 1594. The intersection of the two circles would of course give not only latitude but a fix. The method, however, suffered from the fact that good chronometers essential for accurate location of the GP's were not available.

However, in these days of cheap chronometers and easy calculator computation a method of double-altitude observation can be revived. Consider again the well-worked nautical triangle.

The sides of our familiar PZM triangle are the complements of altitude of M, declination of M, and latitude of Z. With the appropriate information—two sides and the included angle—we can solve for altitude Hc as in Formula 5.2. If the two sides and their included angle are L, h, and Z we can write an equivalent form:

$$\sin d = \sin L \sin h + \cos L \cos h \cos Z \qquad\qquad\text{(Formula 8.21)}$$

Now suppose we write out this equation for two different observations on the same body, say, the sun. We can then write two equations, based on different observations, *both equal to sin d*. Solving these simultaneous equations eliminates the terms involving declination and we get:

$$\tan L = \frac{\sin L}{\cos L} = \frac{(\cos h2 \cos Z2) - (\cos h1 \cos Z1)}{(\sin h1 - \sin h2)} \qquad\text{(Formula 8.22)}$$

This is an interesting formula, since the solution for latitude requires knowledge only of altitude at two different times and the corresponding azimuths. As H. R. Mills, in *Positional Astronomy and Astro-Navigation Made Easy*, points out, we could use the formula in a set of two stellar observations, even if we did not know what star or object we were observing.

Unfortunately, a precise determination of azimuth is required, more precise than we could get by a pelorus or an astrocompass if sighting from a boat. The double altitude observation is of interest, however, if we are in need of a latitude observation and cannot rely on the ready availability of a meridian observation.

Example: Consider the following: we are sailing south off the California coast and have not had a reliable sun sight check on our DR position for 24 hours. On May 16, 1982, at 1800 GMT we obtain a sight which, corrected for index error, semidiameter, and refraction, gives us an Ho of $58°56'$. Exactly one hour later we obtain a second sight which, with corrections, gives an Ho of $69°11'$. What is our latitude? In order to utilize Formula 8.22 we need precise estimates of Z1 and Z2, the azimuths at the times of the first and second observations. Since, as is generally the case on small boats, we have no means of accurate azimuth sightings, we can compute these by assuming our DR position. And since the derivation of Formula 8.22 above requires our using the same latitude for both observations, we take a DR position midway between the times of our two observations for our computation.

The simplest formula for computing azimuth angle is:

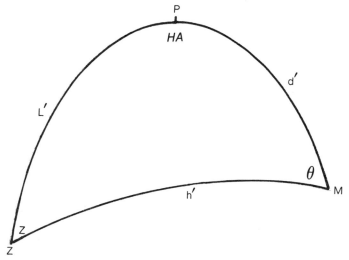

Figure 8.5 Celestial triangle

$$\sin Z = \frac{\sin HA \cos d}{\cos h} \qquad \text{(Formula 5.3)}$$

Our DR position at 1830 GMT, midway between our two observations, is 34°45′N, 121°10′W. For our first observation at 1800 GMT:

Ho   = 58°56′
GHA1 = 90°56′ (see Figure 3.7)
d   = 19°09′N
*HA*1 = 121°10′ − 90°56′ = 30°14′

Solving for Z:

$$Z = \sin^{-1} \frac{\sin 30.23 \cos 19.15}{\cos 58.93}$$

   = 67.16° or 112.84° since sin X = sin 180 − X.

We know that the sun is in the SE quadrant, therefore:

   Z1 = 112.84°

For our second observation:

Ho   = 69°11′
GHA2 = 105°56′ (see Figures 3.7 and 3.8)
d2   = 19°09′N
*HA*2 = 121°10′ − 105°56′ = 15°14′

Solving for Z2:

$$Z2 = \sin^{-1} \frac{\sin 15.23 \cos 19.15}{\cos 69.18}$$

   = 44.28° or 135.72°

The sun is still in our SE quadrant; hence Z2 = 135.72°. Finally, solving for latitude L via Formula 8.22 we have:

$$L = \tan^{-1} \frac{(\cos 69.18 \cos 135.72) - (\cos 58.93 \cos 112.84)}{(\sin 58.93 - \sin 69.18)}$$

$$L = 34.71° = 34°43'N$$

Two cautions, however—one, the derivation of Formula 8.22 is based on the assumption that the latitude does not change between the two observations. If, say, the two altitude observations are within one hour of one another, change in latitude will not be great and the effects will be minimal. The best results will obtain when the two observations are taken within a small interval of one another *and* when the altitudes are changing rapidly. (Rapidly changing altitudes occur just after rising and before setting.) And two, accuracy is contingent upon an accurate determination of azimuth angle Z. Had we rounded the azimuth to the nearest whole number in our example above, the obtained latitude would have differed by 4'.

Note 8.5

One of the earliest schemes for determining longitude involved observing the progressive path of an eclipse. From ancient times astronomers had perfected the explanation and prediction of eclipses. Suppose we know when an eclipse is to take place with respect to the prime meridian, or some other established reference. Then the timing of the eclipse at some other geographic point will give us an indication of the longitude of that place. Eclipse Island off Newfoundland takes its name from Captain Cook's precise determination of its longitude by virtue of observing an eclipse of the sun.

Another proposal, for which Galileo is responsible, involved the eclipses and occultations of Jupiter's moons, the four that are easily seen through a pair of good binoculars. Galileo made the discovery of these moons when he put the newly invented telescope to astronomical use. Each of Jupiter's main satellites has a different period of revolution. These periods range from 42 to 400 hours. During their revolutions the moons will be obscured either by eclipse or by occultation (when Jupiter's light obscures the moon passing in front of it).

It was apparent to Galileo that if one could describe in detail the temporal pattern of the eclipses and occultations of the various satellites, then by comparing time differences of an eclipse as viewed from two different reference points one could infer differences in longitude between the two points. A method for inferring longitude from a timing of the eclipses of Jupiter's moons was developed even before reliable chronometers became available. In fact the first edition of the British *Nautical Almanac,* 1767, included tables on the eclipses of Jupiter's moons.

Charles Cotter in *A History of Nautical Astronomy* reports one of the more imaginative if not ingenious proposals submitted as a candidate for the Parliamentary prize offered for solving the problem of longitude in 1714. Whiston and Ditton (credentials unlisted) proposed that along the familiar trade routes vessels be anchored and used as launch pads for telltale sky rockets so that the cruising navigator could readily locate position by sound and sight. Indeed, with today's deep sea buoys and observation platforms, the Whiston-Ditton proposal has a certain modern ring to it. But alas, they did not win a prize, for as one of the referees, Sir Isaac Newton, pointed out, one must first determine longitude in order to ascertain what the rocket was to token.

Prior to modern practice the most sophisticated method was that of determining longitude by lunar distance. The idea of determining longitude by observing distance between sun and moon was known in the sixteenth century; however, as one French observer was later to comment, those early solutions would require the mathematical genius of a Newton and the observational skill of a Halley.

In principle, the method of lunar distance is straightforward. From accurate descriptions of the different apparent motions of the moon and the sun, we ought to be able to infer time from an observation of angular distance between the two bodies. However, because of the refraction and the parallax of the moon the observed angular distance does not correspond to the true angular distance as measured at the center of the earth. To "clear the distance," that is, to correct the apparent angular distance to true angular distance, involved tedious computations. Such corrections might be on the order of a half-degree or more. Two sets of observations are taken: one of the apparent lunar distance, the other of the altitudes of the moon and the sun. After clearing the distance and determining GMT, the altitude observation allows one to determine his longitude, contingent, however, on an assumed latitude.

For details as to the complexities of the method, see Note 3.5.

Note 8.6

Formula 8.15 simply spells out the computational procedure for Formula 8.14 where the altitude h itself is to be computed. For our example:

d = 19.43N
L = 33.33

The bracketing in Formula 8.15 simply orders the sequence of operations. For this computation on my TI-30 calculator, the steps are as follows:

(19.43 [sin] [÷] 33.33 [sin]) [INV] [sin] [cos] [÷] 19.43 [cos] [=] [INV] [sin]

which gives 57.56°.

Note 8.7

The idea of relating accuracy in timing to rates of change in altitude is straightforward mathematically but becomes somewhat complicated when we consider errors of measurement. First, to determine rates of change in altitude with respect to time we differentiate the basic formula:

$$\sin Hc = \sin L \sin d + \cos L \cos d \cos HA$$

with respect to HA, the time factor. This gives us:

$$\frac{d\,h}{d\,HA} = \cos L \, \frac{\cos d \sin HA}{\cos h}$$

$$= \cos L \sin AZ \qquad\qquad \text{(Formula 8.23)}$$

which is the ratio expressing change in altitude as a function of change in hour angle. Change in hour angle is of course a matter of time.

In order to get comparable units, hour angle must be expressed in terms of arc, one minute of time being equal to 15′ of arc. Thus letting $dHA = 15′$ we get:

$$dh = (15 \cos L \sin Z)′ \text{ per minute of time} \qquad\qquad \text{(Formula 8.24)}$$

This gives the minutes change in altitude per minute change in time, where such change is a function of latitude and azimuth angle. Since the sine of $Z = 0$ when Z is 180° or 360° and 1 when Z is 90° or 270°, the rate of change ranges from zero at meridian passage to a maximum when the body is on the prime vertical.

For example, suppose our latitude is 33°30′N with the sun nearing meridian passage, Z = 177°. (Note that declination is not a factor.) Our dh would be only .65′ per minute of time. On the other hand suppose the sun were on the prime vertical with Z = 270°. Our dh would then be 12.51′ per minute of time. This much is straightforward: change of altitude is more rapid when the body approaches the prime vertical. But how does this relate to an observer whose observations are invariably subject to error?

Consider an observer with a probable error of ± 2′; that is, after all systematic corrections are made, 50 percent of his observations are within ± 2′ of the true altitude and 50 percent are outside ± 2′ of the true altitude. Figure 8.6 presents curves of altitude with respect to HA (a) when the sun is near meridian passage and (b) when it is near the prime vertical. The smooth curves indicate the plot of the true altitude of the sun as a function of hour angle. The external points are simply two observations, each with an error of +2′ of altitude. So far as the observer is concerned the errors would be random. The actual observation Ao above the circle is the observational error

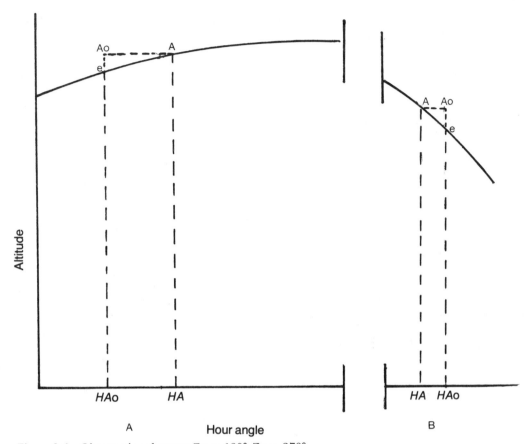

A   Hour angle   B

Figure 8.6   Observational error: Zn = 180°, Zn = 270°

at the time of the observation. The horizontal distance AoA is the error as translated in terms of hour angle. From the observation Ao the observer infers the hour angle associated with *HA*, not with *HAo* which would be the correct inference had there been no observational error. In Figure 8.6b the relative amount of error in inferring *HA* is clearly less than it is in Figure 8.6a. Whereas the vertical component of observational error is the same as that in Figure 8.5a, the horizontal component is smaller.

Although the navigator does not generally wish to make inferences concerning hour angle from an observation of altitude, there is one case for which the above argument is germane—that is, when he wishes to determine the time of meridian passage from the continuous sighting of the culminating body. Any small observational error can result in a substantial timing error of meridian passage.

It is also of interest to the navigator to know something about the rate of change of a body's azimuth. Differentiating the fundamental equation of the nautical triangle, this time Z with respect to *HA* gives us:

$$\frac{dZ}{dHA} = \frac{\cos d}{\cos h} \cos \theta$$

or

$$\text{Rate} = 15 \frac{\cos d}{\cos h} \cos \theta' \text{ per minute of time} \qquad \text{(Formula 8.25)}$$

In this case, θ is parallactic angle (see Figure 8.5) between the hour circle of the body and the vertical circle through the zenith and body, which needs to be calculated:

$$\sin \theta = \frac{\sin Z \cos L}{\cos d} \qquad \text{(Formula 8.26)}$$

The reader can verify that rate of change is greatest at the body's culmination when $Z = 0°, 180°$ and least on the prime vertical.

CHAPTER NINE

The Sailings: Course and Distance Checks

With the scandalous increase in U. S. chart prices the cruising sailor is advised to rely more and more on small-scale nautical charts, general purpose plotting sheets, and the volumes of *Coast Pilots* and *Sailing Directions*. Also a large pad of good quality tracing paper is a must. The reason for these chary ways becomes obvious. For example, if one were to order all the large-scale charts covering a routine voyage from California to Mexico, French Polynesia, Hawaii, and back, he might well be looking at a bill of over one thousand dollars.

To be sure, there are times when the cruising navigator will want detailed large-scale charts: for waterways encrusted with reef-strewn passages, for example, or for intricate harbor approaches (this is where the pad of tracing paper can be useful). But still, even for coastal cruising one can get by with small-scale charts and the combination of plotting sheets and the appropriate *Pilots* and *Sailing Directions*. For example, in a voyage from San Francisco to Panama the sailor might get by quite well on two small-scale Mercator charts, two volumes—a *Coast Pilot* and a *Sailing Directions*, and a pad of universal plotting sheets.

In such practice it is convenient to make use of the various "sailings," those techniques for computing course and distance on Mercator charts. First, we'll discuss the elementary sailings associated with basic dead reckoning and then move on to sailings of a more global nature—the great circle and rhumb line as applied to oceanic passages.

With the possible exception of polar navigation, the type of chart invariably used by the navigator is the Mercator. It will be recalled that on this chart all straight lines are rhumb lines, and though they are not shortest-distance lines (except along the north-south axis) they have the advantage of cutting all meridians at a constant angle. With respect to the traditional sailings this is a nice feature, but the fact that elongating latitude requires a mid-latitude distance scale offers a complication.

PLANE AND PARALLEL SAILING

For short distances we can treat the world as a plane surface and get fair approximations of course and distance by applying the fundamental functions of plane trigonometry. In Figure 9.1, P1 and P2 are points of departure and destination. Around these points we construct a right triangle, p being departure, l being difference of latitude, C being the course, and D the distance. From the fundamental formulae of the right triangle we have:

$$D = \frac{l}{\cos C} \qquad\qquad \text{(Formula 9.1)}$$

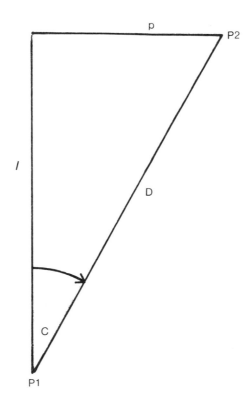

Figure 9.1   Plane sailing

$$\tan C = \frac{p}{l} \qquad\qquad\qquad\qquad\qquad \text{(Formula 9.2)}$$

$$l = D \cos C \qquad\qquad\qquad\qquad\qquad \text{(Formula 9.3)}$$

$$p = D \sin C \qquad\qquad\qquad\qquad\qquad \text{(Formula 9.4)}$$

Note that p, D, and l are distances. Solivng for D gives us distance run and l indicates difference of latitude D.Lat., with one nautical mile being equal to $1'$ of latitude. Although p is horizontal distance, it is not equivalent to difference in longitude (DLo). The earth is of course a sphere with lines of longitude converging at the poles. In order to convert p, departure, to DLo we resort to the formula of parallel sailing, that is, sailing east or west along the departure. For DLo we have:

$$DLo = \frac{p}{\cos L} \qquad\qquad\qquad\qquad\qquad \text{(Formula 9.5)}$$

Or, we can convert DLo into distance p by:

$$p = DLo \cos L \qquad\qquad\qquad\qquad\qquad \text{(Formula 9.6)}$$

with L being the latitude of the destination.

MID-LATITUDE SAILINGS

For short distances and tracks we can do quite well in our sailings by utilizing Formulae 9.1 through 9.6. However, the meridians of longitude do not converge at a constant rate. Therefore, for longer tracks and greater displacements in latitude we use mid-latitude Lm between point of departure and point of destination. Thus Formula 9.6 becomes:

$$p = DLo \cos Lm$$ (Formula 9.6′)

Example: Our point of departure is Santa Barbara (34°25′N, 119°41′W), our destination is San Diego (32°43′N, 117°11′W). Determine course and distance. For this we need l and p:

$$l = 34°25′ - 32°43′ = 1°42′ = 102′$$
$$DLo = 119°41′ - 117°11′ = 2°30′ = 150′ \text{ of longitude}$$

Our mid-latitude is 33.57°; applying Formula 9.6′ we obtain:

$$p = 150 \cos 33.57°$$
$$= 124.98′$$

Then, for course, Formula 9.2:

$$C = \tan^{-1} \frac{124.98}{102} = S50.78°E$$

or $TC = 180° - 50.78° = 129.22°$

For distance, use Formula 9.1:

$$D = \frac{102}{\cos 50.78} = 161.32′$$

Note that C is the course angle in the right triangle of Figure 9.1, not necessarily the true course TC.

Mid-latitude sailing can also be used for tracking.

Example: After sailing on a true course of 165° from San Diego (32°43′N, 117°11′W) for 300 miles, what is the DR position? In other words, we are to determine l and DLo.

$$l = D \cos C$$ (Formula 9.3)
$$= 300 \cos 15°$$
$$= 289.78′ \text{ where C is the course in the schema of Figure 9.1.}$$
$$= 289.78′ = 4°50′$$
$$p = D \sin C$$ (Formula 9.4)
$$= 300 \sin 15° = 77.65′$$

For mid-latitude:

$$32°43′ - (289.78′ \div 2) = 30°18′$$

$$DLo = \frac{p}{\cos Lm}$$ (from Formula 9.5)

$$DLo = \frac{77.65}{\cos 30.3}$$

$$= 89.94′ = 1°30′$$

Since l is 4°50' and DLo is 1°30' our DR position after running 300 miles from San Diego is 27°53'N, 115°41'W. Note that we have determined a DR position without recourse to chartwork.

TRAVERSE SAILING

Although the traditional sailings come under the heading of dead reckoning rather than celestial navigation, they are convenient adjuncts of celestial practice. With all celestial work we need a continuing record of DR position. Cases of special interest are those wherein we are changing tacks over a long distance, or are hove-to or jogging along during a blow, or are tacking downwind in any weather. Frequently, the navigator is too busy looking after the boat to take time for detailed course plotting.

Consider a case of a boat tacking to windward. In Figure 9.2 we show the DR track of the boat with a change of tack every four hours. At noon, the first day shown, the position is 28°50'N, 119°50'W.

At noon of the following day, the DR position plots at 30°21.5'N, 120°13.5'W.

The navigator could also have determined his position by traverse sailing—keeping a record of course sailed and log distance, but not bothering to plot the course. There are two means for doing this: one, keeping a record of course and distance (and also distance in the N-S and in the E-W directions by separate computations and then referring to Traverse Tables in *Bowditch*); and two, keeping a similar record with the help of a calculator and then calculating an overall latitude and longitude for the noon position of the second day.

Table 9.1 shows the results of our calculations:

Table 9.1

			dL		p	
Course	*Dist.*	*N+*	*S−*	*W+*	*E−*	
327°	21'	17.6'		11.4'		
062°	23.5'	11.0'			20.7'	
314°	19'	13.2'		13.7'		
017°	25'	23.9'			7.3'	
273°	15'	0.8'		15.0'		
341°	26'	24.6'		8.5'		
Subtotals		91.1'	0	48.6'	28.0'	
Net		91.1'		20.6'		

For the data in the dL column we use Formula 9.3, for data in the p column, we use Formula 9.4. Since we are interested in the cumulative results of our tacks we must counterbalance south against north by giving the south component a negative value, and similarly, west against east by giving east a negative value.

The cumulative results show a total gain in latitude of 91.1' (minutes or miles) giving a latitude, at noon on the scond day, of 30°21.1'N. To find our longitude we use Formula 9.5. Using our mid-latitude of 29.6° and a p of 20.6' we get 23.7' as our DLo between our first and second day positions. Hence, longitude on the second day is 120°13.7'W. Our positions by chart and by traverse sailing therefore check very well.

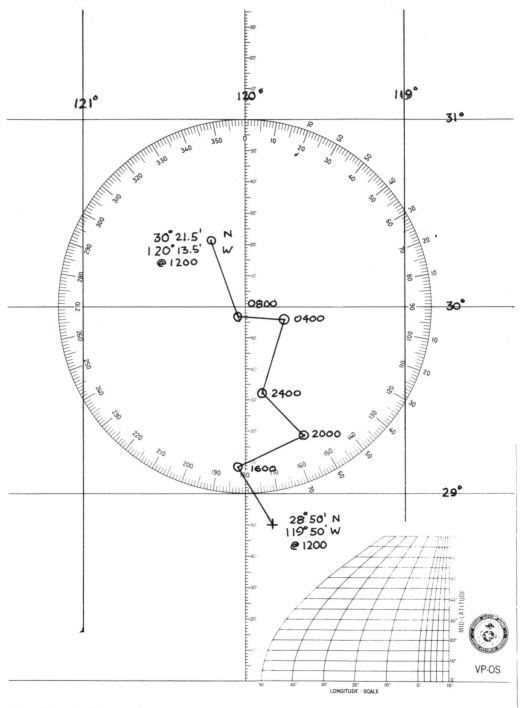

Figure 9.2   Tacking track

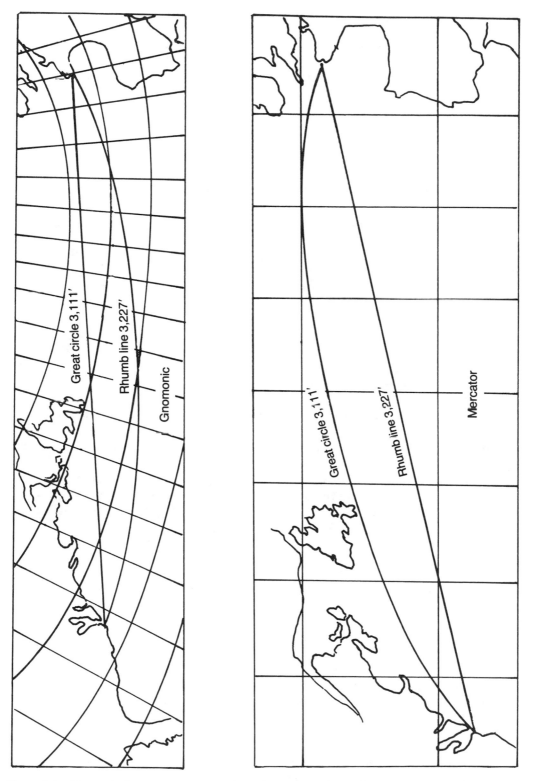

Figure 9.3 Great-circle course on gnomonic and Mercator charts (from Dutton, 1969)

In addition to the individual tack we can also include a track representing the effects of drift or leeway and current. If in our example we experienced a combined set in the direction, say, 135° at approximately 0.5 knots, then our terminal entry in our table would have been a C of 135° and D of 12'.

Traverse sailing problems can also be handled by polar coordinates. However, in the writer's opinion, no method proves superior to the simple trigonometric treatment given above.

GREAT-CIRCLE SAILING

Early in his study of navigation one learns that on the earth's surface the shortest distance between two points is a great-circle course. On the other hand, the routine chartwork is generally done on a Mercator chart where the shortest distance line is a rhumb line. Unless the rhumb line is drawn due north and south, it gives a distance line greater than that of a great circle. For short distances the difference between these two course lines matters little; but for long distances, especially on the east-west axis, it is desirable insofar as possible to approximate a great-circle course.

There are projections to a flat chart surface upon which great circles are represented by straight lines. The gnomonic great-circle chart is one of these. It is made by projecting the earth's surface onto a tangent plane.

In Figure 9.3 great-circle courses are plotted on gnomonic and Mercator charts. Both plots show that the course is constantly changing, intersecting each meridian at a slightly different angle. Although the gnomonic chart can be used for picking out coordinates for a great-circle track, it is not a good working chart for plotting fixes and daily runs. For general use the Mercator chart is preferred. And to use one, the navigator must rely upon supplementary aids to determine the great-circle track and distance.

At the outset we should be reminded, however, that the cruising navigator is not likely to be bound by a rigid adherence to the great-circle course. For one thing, it may be necessary to tack in order to make good a course toward the destination. And for another, the cruising sailor is likely to be relying on a limited crew, a self-steering device, and the convenience of good sail trim. Consequently, he might be quite casual about keeping course on an open passage.

Nevertheless, it is essential that the navigator know his courses. Prior to sailing, it is customary for him to plot both the rhumb line and the great-circle courses. And since he can do this with recourse only to plotting sheets and his calculator there will be no need for the small-scale charts which on a small chart table become unmanageable.

Great Circle Sailing by Calculator

The hand calculator has made it easy for us to calculate bearings and distances in the celestial triangle. And since that triangle has its counterparts on the earth's sphere, it is easy for us to transform our operations in finding altitude Hc and azimuth angle Z into those finding great-circle distance and course. In the PZM nautical triangle, P is the pole, Z is the zenith position of the observer, and M is the location of the celestial body. If we replace PZM with PXY in which X and Y are points of departure and destination on the earth's surface we construct a spherical triangle analogous to the familiar nautical triangle, Figure 9.4.

If we let X correspond to our zenith Z and Y to the body M, then L'x which corresponds to zenith distance will be the complement of the latitude of X; i.e., L'x = 90 − Lx.

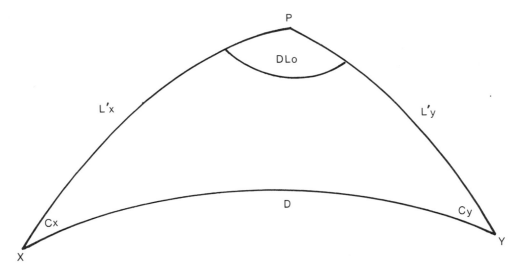

Figure 9.4   Great-circle triangle

Other correspondencies are developed as in Table 9.2.

Table 9.2

Correspondencies between Nautical Triangle and Terrestrial Great-Circle Sailing

Nautical Triangle	*Terrestrial Triangle*
Vertices	
P, celestial pole	Pn, terrestrial pole
Z, zenith	X, departure
M, body	Y, destination
Sides	
d', codeclination	L'y, colatitude Y
L', colatitude	L'x, colatitude X
h', coaltitude	D, great-circle distance
*Angles**	
Z, azimuth angle	Cx, course angle, departure
θ, parallactic angle	Cy, course angle, destination
HA, meridian or hour angle	DLo, difference longitude X, Y

Let us begin the discussion of computations by restricting ourselves to the quantities Cx, Cy, and D (initial course, final course, and overall distance) and leave until later the matter of determining intervening distances and points of change in course. Consider a passage from San Diego (32°43'N, 117°11'W) to Nuku Hiva, Marquesas islands (8°56'S, 140°05'W). Let us determine Cx, Cy, and D.

---

*Note that the two course angles Cx and Cy, like the angles Z and θ, are interior angles of the triangle and need to be converted to true course.

The three formulae we are to adopt for terrestrial use are:

$$\sin Hc = \sin d \sin L + \cos d \cos L \cos HA \qquad \text{(Formula 5.1)}$$

$$\cos Hc' = \sin Hc$$

$$\cos Z = \frac{\sin d - \sin L \sin h}{\cos L \cos h} \qquad \text{(Formula 5.2)}$$

$$\cos \theta = \frac{\sin d - \sin d \sin h}{\cos d \cos h} \qquad \text{(Formula 5.2')}$$

Formula 5.2' is analogous to 5.2 with θ being the parallactic angle in the celestial triangle.

For their terrestrial applications, we write:*

$$\cos D = \sin Ly \sin Lx + \cos Ly \cos Lx \cos DLo \qquad \text{(Formula 9.7)}$$

$$\cos Cx = \frac{\sin Ly - \sin Lx \cos D}{\cos Lx \sin D} \qquad \text{(Formula 9.8)}$$

$$\cos Cy = \frac{\sin Lx - \sin Ly \cos D}{\cos Ly \sin D} \qquad \text{(Formula 9.8')}$$

For our initial date we have:

Lx $= 32°43'N = 32.72'$
Ly $= 8°56'S = -8.93°$
DLo $= 140°05' - 117°11' = 22.90°$

And solving the appropriate formulae, we have:

D $= 47.02° = 2,821.2'$
Cx $= 148.30°, Cxn = 360° - 148.30° = 211.70°$
Cy $= 26.58°, Cyn = 26.58° + 180° = 206.58°$

when Cxn, Cyn are the true courses. (Note: if latitude of destination is different in name from latitude of departure enter as a negative value.)

With proficiency on the calculator, the great-circle courses and the distance can be readily computed with reference only to the coordinates of departure and destination. Often this is the only information the cruising navigator will require. In the above example, the difference between the initial and final courses is only 5°. Obviously no great attention need be paid to course change. This is because of the north-south axis of the course.

On the other hand, on a transoceanic voyage with a course more nearly on the east-west axis, it will be necessary to make course changes from time to time. Therefore, we need to establish a set of intervening points, each with its great-circle course and distance. To accomplish this, we first establish the vertex of the great-circle course, and from this strike off a set of intervening points, each at a regular interval.

---

*The difference in analogy between Formulae 9.7 and 5.1 is due to the fact that h is analogous to D', the complement of D. Hence we substitute: $\cos D = \sin D'$ and $\sin D = \cos D'$.

The *vertex* of the great-circle course is the point of highest latitude through which the great circle of the great-circle course passes. Graphically this point can be found by dropping a meridian from the nearest pole perpendicular to the great-circle course line however extended.* In Figure 9.5 the arc PnV is a segment of a meridian intersecting the arc XY at V. Since this is a meridian, the arc L'_v is the colatitude of the point V. And Dvx is the distance to V from X. Our terrestrial triangle is now divided into two right spherical triangles and we can make an accurate determination of the vertex by solving the following equations (in which L and L' are complementary arcs, L being latitude and L' being colatitude):

$$\sin L'_v = \sin L'_x \sin C_x \qquad\qquad\qquad \text{(Formula 9.9')}$$
$$\cos L_v = \cos L_x \sin C_x \qquad\qquad\qquad \text{(Formula 9.9)}$$

$$\sin D_{vx} = \frac{\tan L'_v}{\tan C_x} = \frac{1}{\tan L_v \tan C_x} \qquad\qquad \text{(Formula 9.10)}$$

$$\cos DLo_v = \cos D_{vx} \sin C_x = \frac{\tan L_x}{\tan L_v} \qquad\qquad \text{(Formula 9.11)}$$

Once the vertex is established then it is a simple matter to establish other points at regular intervals in the great-circle track. Knowing these points we can then solve for the intervening courses and distances. In short, our tactic here is to sail a set of chords cutting the great-circle course at regular intervals.

In Figure 9.5, PnVX and PnVY are both right triangles being made so by dropping the perpendicular PnV to the arc XY. To find some intervening point Xi between X and V, we arbitrarily select one with a specified difference in longitude DLo_{vx} with respect to the vertex V. The great circle PnX_i will be the meridian passing through X_i with DLo_{vx} being the difference of longitude between X_i and V. The latitude of point X_i will be given by the formula:

$$\tan L_{xi} = \cos DLo_{xi} \tan L_v \qquad\qquad\qquad \text{(Formula 9.12)}$$

The usual practice is to take a set of values DLo_{xi} at regular intervals, say 10° or 15°, to either side of V, and compute the associated set of points $\langle L_{xi}, \lambda_{xi}\rangle$

Example: Great-circle sailing with a set of intervening points, departing from Cape Charles Lt. (37°07′N, 75°54′W). Determine great-circle course, distance, and intervening points at 15° intervals to destination at Gibraltar (36°08′N, 5°21′W).

$$L_x = 37.12°$$
$$L_y = 36.13°$$
$$DLo = 75.9° - 5.35° = 70.55°$$

Solving for total great-circle distance, using Formula 9.7, we have:

1. $\cos D = \sin 36.13 \sin 37.12 + \cos 36.13 \cos 37.12 \cos 70.55$
     $D = 55.23° = 3,313.8'$

---

*The vertex of a great-circle course may or may not fall within the arc from departure to destination. On east-west trajectories it generally will fall within the arc. On a north-south trajectory it likely will not.

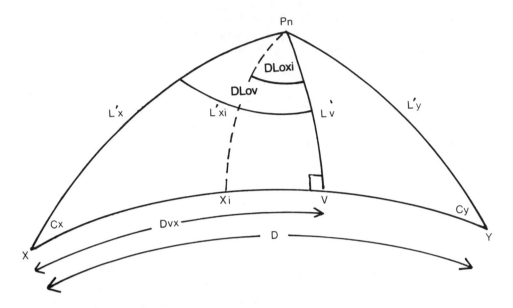

Figure 9.5   Great-circle triangle and vertex

Solving for the initial course C_x, Formula 9.8:

2. $\cos C_x = \dfrac{\sin 36.13 - \sin 37.12 \cos 55.23}{\cos 37.12 \sin 55.23}$

    $C_x = 67.99°$

Solving for the final course, with Formula 9.8':

3. $\cos C_y = \dfrac{\sin 37.12 - \sin 36.13 \cos 55.23}{\cos 36.13 \sin 55.23}$

    $C_y = 180° - 66.24° = 113.76°$

(Note that C_y as computed is the interior angle 66.24°; the true course is $180° - 66.24°$.)

Now we determine the vertex of our great-circle course with Formulae 9.9, 9.10, and 9.11:

4. $\cos L_v = \cos 37.12 \sin 67.99$
    $L_v = 42.33' = 42°20'N$

5. $\sin D_{vx} = \dfrac{1}{\tan 42.33 \tan 67.99}$

    $D_{vx} = 26.35° = 1{,}581'$

6. $\cos DLo_v = \cos 26.35 \sin 67.99$
    $DLo_v = 33.82° = 33°49'$

The coordinates for the vertex are therefore:

$V = (42°20'N, 42°05'W)$

where the longitude of the vertex is the longitude of the departure minus DLo_v.

And now determining the coordinates of the intervening points in multiples of 15° from the vertex V, via Formula 9.12:

7. $V + 15°$:
$$\tan L_{x1} = \cos 15 \tan 42.33$$
$$L_{x1} = 41.34° = 41°20'N$$
$$\lambda_{x1} = 42°05' + 15° = 57°05'W$$

8. $V + 30°$:
$$\tan L_{x2} = \cos 30 \tan 42.33$$
$$L_{x2} = 38.27° = 38°16'N$$
$$\lambda_{x2} = 42°05' + 30° = 72°05'W$$

9. $V - 15°$:
$$\tan L_{x3} = \cos 15 \tan 42.33$$
$$L_{x3} = 41.34° = 41°20'N$$
$$\lambda_{x3} = 42°05' - 15° = 27°05'W$$

10. $V - 30°$:
$$\tan L_{x4} = \cos 30 \tan 42.33$$
$$L_{x4} = 38.27° = 38°16'N$$
$$\lambda_{x4} = 42°05' - 30° = 12°05'W$$

This great-circle course passes near the Azores. If Pta. Negra Lt. (39°40'N, 31°07'W) were to be considered the most northerly point of the islands, how far north of the light will the great-circle course pass?

At 31°07'W longitude, $DLo_{vx} = 42°05'W - 31°07'W$ or 10°58'. Solving for the latitude at that point on the great-circle course we have:

$$\tan L = \cos 10.97 \tan 42.33$$
$$L = 41.80° = 41°48'N$$

The distance north will be the difference of latitude at the point where the great-circle course is due north of the light. Hence,

Dist. $= 41°48' - 39°40' = 128$ miles

MERCATOR SAILING

It is convenient at times to compute the rhumb line course and distance for an ocean passage without recourse to a small-scale Mercator. Once the navigator determines his initial course then for an oceanic passage he can easily develop a sequentially ordered set of charts on universal plotting sheets.

Mercator sailings differ from plane sailings in that the chart is not a simple square grid with an equal-distance measure over all latitudes. A graphic unit of distance at higher latitudes is not the same as it is at the equator. A difference of longitude at the equator can be directly converted to distance, one degree equalling sixty nautical miles. But the same DLo in mid-latitude represents a shorter distance. To handle trigonometric relations on the expanding Mercator, one needs a table of meridional parts (see *Bowditch*, Vol. II, Table 5). If a meridional part is 1' of arc on the equator then for every degree of ascending latitude on a Mercator chart there will be an expanding number of meridional parts.

For Mercator sailings and the use of meridional parts we need to expand the triangle that we introduced in the discussion of plane sailing. In Figure 9.6 we incorporate the triangle for plane sailing (Figure 9.1) and also show the relationships of meridional parts. Note that l, p, and D are in units of nautical miles, whereas those of DLo and m are appropriate to meridional parts. Note also that C is course angle within the triangle to be labeled N or S, E or W, according to the direction quadrant; for C labeled SE, for example, the true course TC will be $180° - C$.

With recourse to meridional parts the essential formulae for Mercator sailings are as follows. For course:

$$\tan C = \frac{DLo'}{m} \qquad\qquad \text{(Formula 9.13)}$$

where m is the difference in meridional parts between latitudes of departure X and destination Y, and DLo′ is the difference of longitude in total minutes. In effect, the

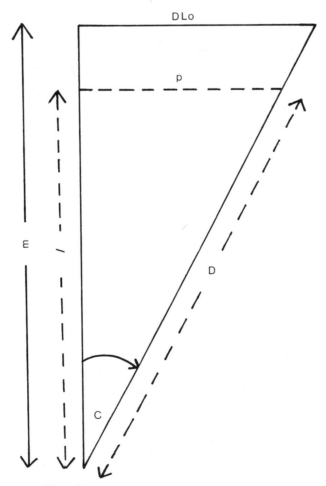

Figure 9.6   Mercator sailing

tangent of the course angle is the ratio of longitudinal to latitudinal differences as appropriately adjusted for meridional parts.

For distance, just as in the case of plane sailing:

$$D = \frac{l}{\cos C}$$ (Formula 9.14)

where l is difference of latitude in total minutes.

Example: For the great-circle problem above, Cape Charles to Gibraltar, find the equivalent rhumb line course and distance.

		Latitude	Meridional Parts*
		37°07′ N	2,387.3
		36°08′ N	2,314.2
l	=	59′,	m = 73.1

$$DLo' = 75°54' - 5°21' = 70°33' = 4,233'$$
$$C = S89.01E; \ TC = 180° - C = 90.99°$$
$$D = \frac{59'}{\cos 89.01} = 3,414.8'$$

Between the great-circle course Cape Charles-Gibraltar and the rhumb line course there is a difference of about 100 miles (i.e., 3,414 vs. 3,314).

For the earlier problem, San Diego to Nuku Hiva, the great-circle distance was found to be 2,821.2′. Computing the rhumb line course gives us:

		Latitude	Meridional Parts*
		32°43′ N	2,066.7
		8°56′ S	534.6
l	=	41°39′,	m = 2,601.3

$$DLo' = 22°54' = 1,374'$$
$$C = \tan^{-1} \frac{1,374'}{2,601.3} = S27.84°W; \ TC = 207.84°$$
$$D = \frac{2,499'}{\cos 27.84} = 2,826.1'$$

Since the course is more southerly than westerly there is very little difference between the great-circle and the rhumb line course.

Again for the cruising sailor, the matter of conforming to the great-circle track may be a bit academic. Except for a long passage on the east-west axis, the distance saved may not compensate for the inconvenience of adhering to a preplotted track. Nevertheless the computations outlined here can be quite useful. For example, from any midpassage position, say, the noonday fix, one can readily compute the course and remaining distance to destination without recourse to unwieldy charts.

---

*From *Bowditch*, Vol. II, Table 5.

COMPASS CHECKS

It is standard practice among navigators on large ships to check the compasses daily, if possible, by celestial bearings. Although the cruising sailor need hardly be so compulsive, it is good practice to check the compass periodically.

To check the compass at sea one needs a pelorus, or if his compass is so equipped, he can use the shadow pin to good effect. Consider first the case of checking the compass by its shadow pin. The shadow line cast by the pin will be 180° from the direction of the sun. Suppose there is no deviation whatsoever in the compass for a particular heading. The compass card will of course be deflected by the amount of the local variation, giving an accurate magnetic heading. Now, knowing the true azimuth of the sun at the time of observation enables us to calculate what the shadow pin bearing (SB) should be. That is:

$$SB = (Zn \pm V) - 180° \qquad \text{(Formula 9.15)}$$

If Zn were 110°, variation 15°E, then our SB should be 95° − 180°, or 275°.

(Figure 9.7 presents that relationship of the two bearings MSB and CSB that gives us the deviation of the compass. This deviation is the difference between magnetic north MN and compass north CN. Visualize the sun casting a shadow from the pin along the broken line. The shadow intercepts the compass rose at $\odot'$ with a reading equal to CSB. Since we can determine MSB by virtue of Formula 9.15, the difference between MSB and CSB gives us our deviation. If CSB is greater than MSB the deviation is west; if CSB is less than MSB the deviation is east.)

Suppose, however, the shadow intercepted the compass at the 278° mark. The compass on this heading is reading 3° more than it should be. Thus the deviation is 3°W and the correction in making course on this heading would be +3° (*cf.* Note 9.1).

Although taking the bearing of the sun by compass shadow pin is a simple matter when the sun is low on the horizon the more traditional method involves taking a bearing by a pelorus. In the latter case, one aligns the pelorus along the fore and aft line of the vessel and takes a relative bearing on the sun (or other celestial object). At that instant he reads his compass and notes the time. From a knowledge of the sun's true azimuth Zn and its relative bearing RB, one can determine the true course TC. Applying a correction for variation and comparing the magnetic course with the actual compass heading will give us compass deviation.

In this case the fundamental relation is:

$$TC = Zn \pm RB \qquad \text{(Formula 9.16)}$$

where the true course of the vessel is the true bearing of the sun plus or minus the relative bearing of the sun from the vessel's axis. See Figure 9.8.

Determining Azimuth
The fundamental formulae for the azimuth of any celestial body are:

$$\cos Z = \frac{\sin d - \sin L \sin Hc}{\cos L \cos Hc} \qquad \text{(Formula 5.2)}$$

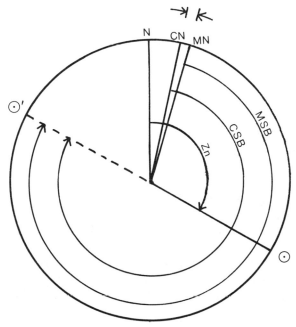

Figure 9.7   Deviation by shadow bearing

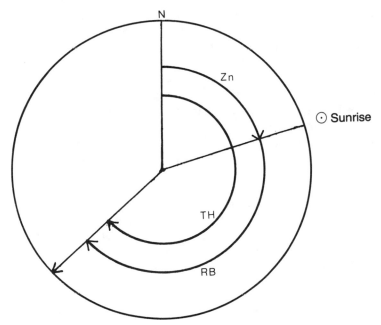

Figure 9.8   True heading by relative bearing at sunrise

$$\sin Z = \frac{\sin HA \cos d}{\cos Hc} \qquad \text{(Formula 5.3)}$$

Here Z is azimuth angle within the celestial triangle and true azimuth of the body must be determined on the basis of the observer's latitude L and hour angle HA, whether east or west. We repeat the rules for obtaining true azimuth or bearing from knowledge of azimuth angle:

$$HA$$

	West	East
N lat.	$Zn = 360° - Z$	$Zn = Z$
S lat.	$Zn = 180° + Z$	$Zn = 180° - Z$

Bearing of a Body on the Prime Vertical

Due to the pitch and roll of a sailing vessel it is much easier to obtain sighted bearings on an object when it is near the horizon than when it is high in the heavens. Perhaps the simplest of compass checks is to sight the body when it is on the prime vertical.

The *prime vertical* is the vertical circle passing through the observer's zenith and the east and west points on his horizon. Thus when the body is on the observer's prime vertical, its azimuth angle will be either 90° or 270°, and for the sun, at least, the body will appear relatively low in the horizon. From our fundamental Formula 5.1 for altitude the product term involving cos Z drops out since cos 90 or 270 is zero. Hence, when the body bears due east or west:

$$\sin Hc = \frac{\sin d}{\sin L} \qquad \text{(Formula 8.14)}$$

Thus knowing our own latitude and the body's declination, we can determine the exact moment when the body will bear due east or west. Say our latitude is 35°N and the sun's declination is 15°N, the Hc by virtue of Formula 8.14 is 26.82° (26°49.2′). We will continue to observe the sun until its altitude is 26°49′. At that time, it will bear due east or west according to whether it is rising or setting. At such an altitude we are likely to get a good sighting or shadow projection.

The procedure, then, for checking the compass is first to predetermine Hc for the time when Z = 90 or 270. We then take sextant observations until Ho = Hc. At that instant, we read our compass and obtain a bearing on the sun either by shadow pin or pelorus. We then proceed to find our compass error as outlined above.

Body, Rising or Setting.

A visible body will touch the observer's prime vertical only if latitude and declination are the same name, and L is greater than d. Therefore, for six months of the year, at least (the winter months), the sun will not reach the due east or west horizon points. A more general method for sighting the sun involves our sighting it just at sunrise or sunset.

Azimuth angle at sunrise or sunset is simple to calculate. We first proceed to compute the hour angle of rising or setting. In an earlier chapter we found that when the altitude of the body is zero:

$$\cos HA = -\tan L \tan d \qquad \text{(Formula 7.1)}$$

Since altitude at the time of rising or setting is zero, then Formula 5.3 gives us:

$$\sin Z = \sin HA \cos d \qquad\qquad \text{(Formula 9.17)}$$

and Formula 5.2 gives:

$$\cos Z = \frac{\sin d}{\cos L} \qquad\qquad \text{(Formula 9.18)}$$

Suppose again our observer is at $L = 35°N$, with the declination of the sun $15°N$. Then HA for sunrise (by Formula 7.1) will be $100.8°E$ and Z by either Formula 9.17 or 9.18 will be $71.6°$.

A relative bearing on the sun at sunrise or sunset will thereby afford us a determination of our true course and a check on the compass.

Use of Formula 9.18 to find the true bearing of the sun at rising or setting is based on the simplifying assumption that the altitude of the sun is zero at the time of our observation. However, on closer inspection there are observational and geometric factors that combine to make that assumption false. As a result, we will find that the true altitude is slightly less than zero at the time of our taking the bearing.

The four factors are:

1. Dip (D), the difference between the visible and the celestial horizons.
2. Refraction (R), which at the horizon is about $35'$.
3. Irradiation (J), the apparant enlargement of a light figure against a dark background, or about $0.6'$ for the sun.
4. Parallax (HP), which is only $0.1'$ for the sun (but varies between $54'$ and $61'$ for the moon).

The first three factors are subtractive; the last is additive. Thus, when the sun is observed as bisected by the visible horizon its true altitude ht is:

$$ht = -D - R - J + HP$$

Let us now reconsider the example above and incorporate ht into the standard Formula 5.2 for azimuth angle. The value of ht is the arithmetic sum of:

$$
\begin{aligned}
R &= -35' \\
D &= -3' \text{ (observer's eye 9.5 ft. above sea level)} \\
J &= -0.6' \\
HP &= +0.1'
\end{aligned}
$$

Thus:

$$ht = -0°38.5' = -0.64°$$

Computing azimuth angle (equal to true azimuth, in this case) we have, by Formula 5.2:

$$Z = \cos^{-1} \frac{\sin 15 - \sin 35 \sin -0.64}{\cos 35 \cos -0.64}$$

$$= 71.1°$$

Since in taking bearings fractional degree accuracy is elusive, the difference between using the more accurate Formula 5.2 and using the more convenient Formula 9.18 is negligible. As a rule, then, the cruising navigator may get by very well by using 9.18 to determine azimuth angle at rising or setting. At higher latitudes, say, above 45°, he should resort to Formula 5.2, as above.

Amplitude

Traditionally the determination of the true bearing of the sun at sunrise or sunset is treated as a matter of amplitude. The amplitude of a body at rising or setting is the arc-angular distance of the body above or below the observer's east-west axis (i.e., angular distance between the vertical circle through the body and the observer's prime vertical circle). It is labelled east or west according to rise or set and north or south according to declination. Thus, for a body with amplitude of N15°E at rise, its true azimuth is 75° (or the complement of amplitude). If its amplitude is S15°E, its true azimuth is 105°, and so on.

Values of amplitude are tabulated in *Bowditch* for selected values of latitude and declination. Table 27 (*Bowditch*, Vol. II) gives the amplitude of a body whose true altitude (i.e., altitude above the celestial horizon) is zero. Since for the N-E quadrant amplitude is the complement of azimuth angle, the values of Table 27 (*Bowditch*) provide the correction factor that we apply to the main amplitude as we adjust our observation of rising or setting to the visible horizon.

These tables are quite easy to use, but since data are tabulated only for selected values of declination and latitude, interpolation will be required. In the writer's opinion, for the lower latitudes in which most cruising takes place, use of Formula 9.18 to compute azimuth angle, hence the true azimuth, will provide sufficient accuracy. If greater accuracy is required resort to Formula 5.2. One caution, however: in higher latitudes it is imperative to have accurate knowledge of latitude in computing the azimuth of the body at rising and setting.

There is yet another method for checking compass error while underway—the equal altitude method. It has a venerable ancestry and avoids all computation of azimuth (*cf*. Note 9.3).

COURSE AND DISTANCE CHECKS

The usual procedure for the cruising navigator is to determine position by noonday fixes or, less regularly, by star fixes. On the other hand, he might well rely upon individual course and distance lines of position. A course line is any LOP that is plotted parallel to the true course of the vessel. Therefore, its true azimuth, as determined by azimuth angle of the nautical triangle, must be at a right angle to that course. A distance line, on the other hand, cuts the course at a right angle. Therefore, the true azimuth in its plot is parallel to the true course. Furthermore, an earlier line can be advanced to the time of a later one to give a running fix, which for sun observations will serve as well as the noonday fix.

The trick here is to predetermine the time for taking observations for the appropriate course and distance lines. Looking at the nautical triangle this is done by determining the hour angle that will yield the desired azimuth angle. However, azimuth angle is not a simple function of hour angle (prior knowledge of Hc would be required). In fact there is no simple computation giving HA for the given Z. Nevertheless, there is a ready means for approximating the required HA by referring to a set of sight reduction tables, such as $H.O. 249$.

Presumably we have a fair idea of the DR position for the time of our prospective observations. Then entering the tables for the approximate (nearest degree) latitude and declination of the body, we locate the desired azimuth angle and read across to the local hour angle. Applying hour angle to DR longitude will give us the GMT for our observation.

Example: On May 17, 1982, our early morning DR position is 30°05′N, 119°25′W, on a true course of 215°. Determine GMT for a course and distance LOP on the sun. For the course line LOP, take Zn = TC − 90°. Hence:

$$Zn = 215° − 90° = 125°$$

Since HA is east and we are in north latitude, Zn = Z. On May 17, 1982 (see Figure 3.7), the sun's declination to nearest named figure is 19°N. Consulting $H.O. 249$, Vol. II we find for entry Lat. = 30° and Declination = 19°, same name, that Zn will be the sought-for 125° when the LHA will be 345°. An LHA of 345° gives an HA of 15°E. Since GHA = λ ± HA,

$$GHA = 119°25′ − 15°$$
$$= 104°25′$$

Consulting the specimen pages of the *Almanac* for May 17, 1982 (Figures 3.7, 3.8), we would find that the sun will be at a GHA of 104°25′ at approximately 1854 GMT. (A sufficient approximation of GMT can be had by dividing the GHA by 15 and adding 12 hours.)

For a distance LOP that crosses the course at right angles we require that Zn = TC. Thus consulting $H.O. 249$, Vol. II, with Lat. = 30° and Declination = 19°, same name, we find that the LHA of the sun will be 008° to give the desired Zn = 215°. Thus:

$$GHA = 119°25′ + 8° = 127°25′$$

From the *Almanac* we would find that the sun is at a GHA of 127°25′ at approximately 2026 GMT.

These are reasonable approximations of times when sun shots will give course and distance LOP's. A longitude of 119°25′W places our navigator in the local time zone 8 hours slow on Greenwich. His local times of observation will, therefore, be 1058 for the course line and 1226 for the distance line. Note that under these conditions observations are approximately 1½ hours apart. Between the two times of observation in this example a latitude line could also be taken. From our specimen *Almanac* pages, the reader should verify that for meridian transit assuming a longitude of 119°25′W for a morning position, the navigator would start shooting the sun shortly before local zone noon.

On balance it would seem that the navigator would be wise to incorporate course and distance checks into his noon position fix. However, it is not always the case that the course and distance lines can be taken so nearly together in time. If the true course is on any of the cardinal headings, N, S, E, or W, then time between observations of the sun may be on the order of several hours.

NOTES

Note 9.1

Every navigator should periodically check his compass for deviation on all headings even though he may leave to experts matters of compass adjustment.

The standard procedure for taking bearings on the sun is to precompute a curve of azimuths against GMT, and then maneuver the boat to get bearings on the sun at 15° intervals. If a pelorus is used, relative bearings are taken. If the compass shadow pin is used, compass bearings are taken directly. Reviewing the procedures for relative bearings,

$$TH = TB \pm RB$$
$$TH - (CH \pm \text{variation}) = \text{compass error}$$

With a shadow pin, the shadow falls at a point 180° from the direction of the object. Thus for shadow bearing SB:

$$(TB - 180) - (SB \pm \text{variation}) = \text{deviation}$$

If the compass bearing (or compass heading) is more than it should be, the compass is deflecting to the west (west deviation); if less than it should be, it is deflecting to the east (east deviation).

In morning or evening the rate of change of azimuth is less than at noon. That is also the time when bearings are most easily obtained. A quick check on compass error can be obtained by having the vessel ready to run its headings as the sun approaches the prime vertical; i.e., when the Ho approaches Hc with:

$$Hc = \sin^{-1} \frac{\sin d}{\sin L}$$

In the latitude range of 30° to 50° one can expect Zn to hold at 90° or 270° for a period of at least four minutes (longer in the lower latitudes). With one person at the helm taking the headings and another reading the shadow bearings or pelorus, the two should easily run the headings within a ten-minute period. The procedure could be repeated morning and evening if need be.

For the pelorus and shadow pin, sun altitudes between 15° and 30° tend to give fair results. One can plot an azimuth curve against time by using any one of the formulae for azimuth angle: 5.2, 5.3, or 5.4.

However, in the case of plotting a curve of true azimuths for a given latitude and longitude, Formula 5.4':

$$Z = \tan^{-1} \frac{\sin t}{(\cos L \tan d) - (\sin L \cos t)} \qquad \text{(Formula 5.4')}$$

is preferred. Since only hour angle t, latitude L, and declination d are required, one does not first have to compute altitude as is required in Formulae 5.2 and 5.3. In using 5.4' above if the value of Z as computed is negative then azimuth angle Z is the supplement of the computed value.

Note 9.2

The formula used to compute the main data in Table 27, Vol. II of *Bowditch* is derived from Napier's rules for right spherical triangles:

$$\sin A = \frac{\sin d}{\cos L} \qquad \text{(Formula 9.19)}$$

Comparing Formulae 9.19 and 9.18 we see that:

$$\sin A = \cos Z$$

hence amplitude A and Z are complementary angles. Table 27 therefore presents amplitudes for the moment the center of the sun is on the celestial horizon (i.e., h = 0).

Table 28 offers corrections we must apply to the main data of Table 27 if in fact the sun is observed as intersecting the visible horizon. In effect, then, the entries of Table 28 are simply the differences between azimuth as computed by Formula 9.18 and azimuth as computed by Formula 5.2 (see the text). In computing the entries of Table 28, R, J, and HP are as before, but the standard value for dip, at 41 feet above sea level, is $-6.2'$. Note, however, that if one utilizes Formula 5.2 as we have done in the text, there is no need to utilize tables of amplitude. If we apply these procedures to taking a bearing on the moon at moonrise or moonset the factor of parallax HP will be considerable, ranging from $+54'$ to $+61'$ throughout the year, daily values being given in the *Nautical Almanac*. Thus at the moment the moon is observed to intersect the visible horizon its true altitude with respect to the celestial horizon will be greater than zero. There are rules for applying the tables of amplitude to moonrise and set but it is simpler to compute azimuth angle directly, Formula 5.2.

Finally, the reader should note that sunrise and sunset as derived for the tabular data of the *Almanac* are different from those which we utilize in taking bearings. In the first case rise or set is at the moment the upper limb of the sun coincides with the visible horizon. In the second case, rise or set is at the moment the center of the sun is at the visible horizon. For the former, ht as used in Formula 5.2 is given by:

$$ht = -R - D - J - SD + HP$$

For the latter, the factor of semidiameter SD is omitted.

Note 9.3

There is yet another method for checking the compass while underway, that involving double or equal altitude observations. This method goes back to the sixteenth century when navigators and hydrographers first used it to determine magnetic variation. Now that values of magnetic variation are well plotted for all seas, we may readily adapt the method to determine compass deviation. Its advantage is that it requires no detailed computations.

Consider first the implications of diurnal equal altitudes. The sun rises, reaches its maximum altitude at meridian passage, and then descends on its path to sunset. Hence for every ascending AM altitude, there is an equal descending PM altitude. What is important here is that for every pair of equal altitudes of the sun the corresponding true azimuths at a given location will sum to 360°. Thus if for some given AM altitude the true azimuth is ZnA and for the equal PM altitude the true azimuth is ZnP then:

$$ZnA + ZnP = 360°$$

and

$$(ZnA + ZnP) \div 2 = 180°$$

This follows from the fact that the two celestial triangles for the AM and PM equal altitude observations will be congruent, differing only in the direction of their hour angles. Thus, in north latitudes, $ZnA = Z$ and $ZnP = 360° - Z$, as follows from the rules for converting azimuth angle Z to true azimuth Zn.

Suppose, now, there is no substantial change in latitude or declination between two equal altitude observations. The average of the corresponding true azimuths should be 180°. We may now check the accuracy of our compass for a given compass heading by comparing the average of true bearings, derived from compass bearings, against the expected value of 180°.

The relation of true bearing TB to magnetic bearing MB is simply:

$$TB = MB \pm \text{variation}$$

and of magnetic bearing to compass bearing CB:

$$MB = CB \pm \text{deviation}$$

Combining the lot enables us to write:

$$\text{Dev.} = \left(\frac{CBA + CBP}{2} \pm \text{Var.} \right) - 180° \qquad \text{(Formula 9.20)}$$

Now a compass bearing is simply:

$$CB = CH + RB$$

where the relative bearing RB is measured clockwise from the fore and aft axis of the vessel. Hence we have the working result:

$$\text{Dev.} = \left[\frac{(RBA + RBP)}{2} + (CH \pm \text{Var.}) \right] - 180° \qquad \text{(Formula 9.21)}$$

(Note: If the sum of the relative bearings is greater than 360°, subtract 360.)

Our procedure then is as follows:

1. For some arbitrary time in the AM observe the sun's altitude HA while maintaining a given compass heading CH. At the same time obtain a relative bearing on the sun, RBA, being careful to maintain a constant compass heading, CH.
2. Observe the sun as it descends from meridian passage to the instant the afternoon altitude HP equals HA. At that moment obtain a relative bearing on the sun, RBP, being sure to maintain the constant heading CH (as in the AM).
3. Compute compass deviation by virtue of Formula 9.21.

Example 1:   On a broad reach out of Chesapeake Bay bound for Bermuda, our navigator is maintaining a compass heading of 130°. Approximately four hours before local noon he observes the altitude of the sun giving an AM HA of 32°41'. At that time a relative bearing RBA on the sun is 335°. Approximately four hours after local noon at the instant the sun again reaches the altitude of 32°41', a relative bearing RBP is 143°. Again, a compass heading of 130° is maintained. If the variation throughout is 13°W, what is the compass deviation? Applying Formula 9.21 we have:

$$\text{Dev.} = \left[\frac{(335 + 143)}{2} + (130 - 13) \right] - 180$$

$$= (59 + 117) - 180$$
$$= -4°$$

On a heading of 130° our compass has an error of −4°, which is to say that it is reading 4° less than the actual magnetic heading. Therefore, deviation is east. Recall that in tracking one goes from CH ± Dev. to MH ±Var. to TH. Therefore, east deviation and variation are added whereas west deviation and variation are subtracted. In setting course one goes from TH to MH to CH. This is the case when "east is least"—east deviation and variation are subtracted—whereas those west are added.

Example 2:   Our navigator is sailing out of Russell, N. Z., bound for New Caledonia on a compass heading of 320°. About three hours before local noon he observes the sun at 29°47' at which time he obtains an RBA of 083°. About three hours after noon, when the sun is again at an altitude of 29°47' and with the compass heading of 320°, RBP is 337°. The variation throughout is 15°E. Find compass deviation.

Applying Formula 9.21 we have:

$$\text{Dev.} = \left[\frac{(83 + 337)}{2} + (320 + 15) \right] - 180$$

$$= 545 - 180$$

Note that the bracketed value is greater than 360°. We subtract 360°, getting:

Dev. $= 185 - 180 = +5°$

Thus our deviation is 5°W indicating that on a course of 320° our magnetic heading is 315°. With 15°E variation our true heading is 330°.

The above procedure is well adapted to sailboat navigation where latitude of the observer and deviation of the sun are not likely to change appreciably between the AM and the PM observations. For commercial vessels steaming at a good clip along the north-south axis, the true azimuths of equal altitude observations will not sum exactly to 360°.

The procedures outlined here require taking relative bearings with a pelorus. Should the navigator's compass be equipped with a shadow pin, then he may work directly with CB, compass bearing, and use Formula 9.20. However, in working with shadow pins, whether on the compass or on a pelorus, the shadow bearing reads 180° from the actual bearing; that initial correction must be made.

CHAPTER TEN

Navigational Practice

We have assumed that you, the reader of this book, have been schooled in the details and routines of pilotage and dead reckoning. Doubtless as part of your training you have been encouraged to keep a tidy log book replete with hourly entries and to complement the bookkeeping with immaculate charts unbesmirched but for the crisp pencil-work worthy of a draftsman. And doubtless you have been encouraged to anticipate a cozy navigator's nest surrounded as it would be by arrays of instruments, dials, catchall cubbyholes, and neat shelves of almanacs, charts, pilots, sight reduction tables and lists, and lists of government publications: lights, radio beacons, and tide tables.

Alas, the truth is that few cruising boats are sufficiently spacious to maintain an inviolate navigator's station. And few are sufficiently staffed to carry a bona fide full-time navigator with the leisure to sharpen his pencil. Consequently, work in the log book may be rather skimpy, some perfunctory scratch on the way off-watch. Detailed entries, those tales of gale encounters, are likely to be recorded long after the tempest has passed. We have all seen facsimile pages reproduced from the logs of a circumnavigating sailor. These pages are notorious for their illegibility. There is good reason for this. A smallish boat on a robust sea is not a likely place to practice penmanship.

In substance the indispensable element of navigational practice is good chartwork. In fact the working chart or plotting sheet can carry all of the important information: wind, temperature, pressure, sea conditions, and sightings, as well as the routine plots, DR and LOP's. The log, of course, presents a record and document of the boat's passage. Therefore, the minimal record should be kept. But as for the contemplative details and the diary of the passage, the cruising sailor might well rely upon a small cassette recorder where both the recording and the playback can be done at comparative leisure.

OCEANIC PASSAGE

For the routine of passage-making let us consider a trip from San Diego (32°43'N, 117°11'W) to Nuku Hiva (8°56'S, 140°05'W), one of the two ports of entry for those splendid Marquesas islands.

Preparation
By way of preparation we determine both a great-circle course and a rhumb line course with the courses and distances being precalculated as in the earlier discussion of sailings.

In the preceding chapter we found the following:

San Diego to Nuku Hiva

Great circle:	2,821.2'
Initial Course	211.7°
Final Course	206.6°
Rhumb line:	
Distance	2,826.1'
Course	207.8°

We should not count on a rigid adherence to either one or the other of these courses. Suppose the passage is being made in April. Initially out of San Diego we might expect NW winds in the afternoons and evenings, otherwise light and variable. If we are steering by wind vane as we are likely to be doing, or if we are trading off at the helm, we'll vary the tack of the boat to keep it moving and steering with a minimum of fuss. Departures of 15° and more from that intended track are not out of the ordinary.

Eight hundred or so miles down the track, about opposite Cabo San Lucas (22°52'N, 109°53'W), we can expect to pick up the northeast trades. Since our pre-calculated track is now close to direct downwind, we again foresee the need to tack. As most cruising sailors report, direct downwind sailing is difficult, hazardous (because of jibes), and comparatively uncomfortable (due to roll). Therefore, we might expect to broaden out on our course and plan to change tacks every day or so. Thus, we'll not be overly concerned should we stray 50 miles or so from our midpassage track.

By referring to the appropriate *Pilot Charts* for the months of April and May, we note that winds generally are in the Beaufort force four to five range. No Mexican west coast hurricanes are found this early in the year. Doldrums are encountered about 7°N latitude to 5°S. However, in this area, the intertropical convergence zone, we may expect to encounter the short-term gales associated with line squalls.

Finally, at around 3° to 5°S latitude we may expect to emerge into the zone of southeasterly trades, which, at this time of the year, promise to be more fitful than the northeasterlies. As a matter of tactics it may be to our sailing advantage to be well west of our rhumb line track as we enter the SE trades. This will give us a broader slant on these lighter winds.

In effect, our preparation involves our foreseeing the voyage, anticipating sailing conditions, and having in mind such information as variation, zone time changes, weather, currents, air and sea temperature zones, and possible storm tracks. Here the *Pilot Charts* for the Pacific Coast and South Pacific are most helpful. Also, the renowned *Ocean Passages of the World*, published by the British Admiralty, can be of great assistance.

Navigational Routine
Conceivably one could sail, as a character in a Nevil Shute novel did, from San Francisco to Hawaii by following the contrails of jetliners. It is not, however, a procedure to be recommended—clouds obscure the skies for long periods of time, and airliners do not fly to all points in the world that may attract the cruiser's interest. To be sure, there are navigators who head out on a DR track with a rather cavalier attitude about celestial checks. On the other hand, if one has ever had the occasion to call a naval or a commercial vessel at sea for a position check, he has doubtless been impressed at how

quickly the position report comes back. The ship's navigator is always aware of his position. And so should the cruising sailor be.

Navigational routine on an open passage is a quite straightforward combination of dead reckoning and position check. In reckoning, the patent log and compass are essential. But more, the experienced navigator develops a keen sensitivity to position, a kind of working intuition as if some computer in the unconscious is continually keeping him informed. He has a sense of the course made good and of the distance run without constantly attending to log and compass. Still, to make things right over the long run, he relies on celestial checks.

The hallowed tradition in celestial navigation is the taking of the noonday fix. Typically a morning LOP on the sun is advanced to the time of the latitude LOP taken at local noon. Together, these two LOP's generate the noonday fix that is the basis for determining the boat's 24-hour run. The older tradition of taking a time sight can still be of use, especially after a meridian transit observation clearly establishes the observer's latitude. Also course and distance lines taken when the sun's true azimuth permits offer ongoing checks of DR. Since their respective azimuths are approximately at right angles, the one, say, a course line, can be advanced to the time of the other, say, the distance line, to give a good running fix.

To be sure, one cannot always count on seeing the sun. Passages have been made from the tropical fingers of Hawaii to sunkissed California without the navigator's once getting a noonday sight. The navigator must be prepared to take his observation when he can get it, and on any identifiable body.

In the writer's experience few cruising navigators make a practice of taking moon shots. There are several reasons for this: one, the interpolations and corrections are a bit more fussy than they are for any other body; two, during the moon's gibbous state or earlier there may be uncertainty as to which limb should be observed; and three, for nocturnal shots the moon's reflection tends to generate a false horizon below the real one. However, the taking of daytime shots of the moon during the gibbous state is to be commended. At this time the moon's azimuth is nearly at right angles to that of the sun, thereby giving a good series of LOP's for a fix. The observer will have a daytime horizon to work with at the same time the moon's image will be easy to pick up in the eyepiece of the sextant.

Although star observations are highly recommended, the twilight hours generally are busy ones for the boat's crew. Often this is when watches are being changed, meals are being fixed, and preparations are being made for the new day or the night ahead. However, as the destination is approached and course-keeping must be tightened up, star and planet observations become very important.

If the destination is an unfamiliar one, the navigator should plan his arrival for daytime—heave to, shorten sail, or extend his track by tacking if need be. This is especially true of South Pacific cruising. Navigational aids, with a few exceptions, are nonexistent. The lee shores of atoll islands are nearly indetectable during the dark of the moon, and the harbors are usually surrounded by reefs. The many boats that have been lost on the shores of the Tuamotus are matched by those lost to the misreading of the few lights to be found off the outlying reefs of Fiji. The arts of heaving-to in the offings, especially with a lively trade wind blowing, are valuable ones to master.

PLOTTING LOP'S AND FIXES

Plotting LOP's by the azimuth-intercept method is preferred to all other position line techniques. Every observation duly processed by sight reduction will yield an LOP. Some give information on course or distance, some on latitude or longitude, and any one of them can be incorporated into a fix. Regardless of whether the observation is to be processed by tabular sight reduction or by the calculation of basic formulae, all work should be checked. Obvious errors are easy to pick up. If the plotted LOP is inconsistent with all reasonable estimates of position, then there is good reason to believe an error has been made. However, the error that may be painful is the one which results in a position line that neatly satisfies our expectations. As every observer has experienced, he may sometimes warp his interpretation, or distort an observation, to support some preconception. (One of the fine old ketches of the West Coast was lost on a San Diego beach simply because the skipper, eager to escape the fog, mistook the beacons of one jetty for those of his destination 6 miles away.) The obvious safeguard is to check both observation and computations and distrust what students of problem-solving call "premature closure." Things can be too good to be true, so check and double-check.

We have discussed the Marcq St. Hilaire LOP in which the straight line segment of a circle of equal altitude is constructed at a right angle to the azimuth line. From an assumed position and computed altitude, we can tell by observation if we are away or toward the position of the body.

Since a single LOP does not pinpoint a position, we need to cross one LOP with another in order to obtain a fix. The cruising navigator utilizes two types—the simultaneous fix and the running fix. In the one case, the observations are taken so close together that for practical purposes they are considered simultaneous, e.g., star fixes. In the other case, the observations may be taken an hour or more apart, and one LOP must be advanced (or regressed) to the time of the other, thereby giving a running fix.

True azimuth of the observed body is all-important, for regardless of which kind of fix is involved, we seek a crossing of LOP's at angles that will minimize error effects. Accordingly, in two LOP fixes, we seek observations where the true azimuths of the bodies differ by 90°. This gives a 90° cut in the LOP's. For three LOP fixes, we seek observations on bodies whose true azimuths differ by 120°, four star fixes by 90°, etc. There is, however, good reason for the 120° azimuth figure rather than 60° which would give an identical pattern of cuts among the LOP's. We cover this in the context of plotting errors.

ERRORS IN THE PLOTTING OF FIXES

Observational Errors

These are of three types: (1) instrument error, (2) personal error, and (3) random error. Instrument error such as the index error can easily be determined and adjusted for by applying a systematic correction to the initial hs. In the same way, if we know that the observer tends consistently to misread the horizon so as to overestimate or underestimate altitude a constant correction factor may be applied. Random error, on the other hand, is not constant. It is a variable error which averages out to zero after constant error is removed. Still, on any given observation a random component of error is possible. The only thing we can do here is to know its range of magnitude and to reduce that range as much as possible through practice.

Plotting Error and Azimuth

In Figure 10.1 the solid lines are the actual plots of two intersecting LOP's, the broken lines the limits of random error ("probable error"). Thus we can expect our position to be anywhere within the boundary of the four broken lines. If one were to compute the possible range of error he would find that range greater in the situation of Figure 10.1b than that of Figure 10.1a.

Figure 10.2a shows a proper three-star fix composing an approximate equilateral triangle, the true azimuths of the stars differing by 120°. Figure 10.2b is identical except the true azimuths differ by 60°. Since it is seldom that the navigator will get three LOP's to intersect at a common point, such being the nature of random error, it is the usual practice to bisect the interior angles of the triangle and obtain their intersection P as definition of the fix.

Suppose now, in Figure 10.2a, that there has been an unforeseen systematic error so that actual sextant readings have had a constant error, +C', i.e., each LOP is C minutes closer to the body's GP than it should be. If we correct the LOP's for C we would get an expanded triangle, i.e., that of the broken lines, but the intersection of the bisectors would not change. Figure 10.2b, on the other hand, shows that the error C introduces a real displacement of position.

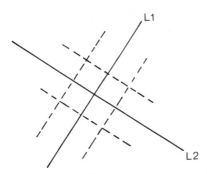

Figure 10.1a   Error range

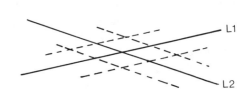

Figure 10.1b   Error range

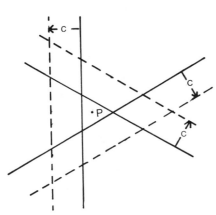

Figure 10.2a   Zn's differing by 120°

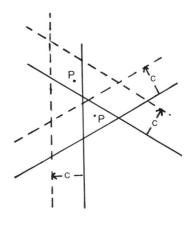

Figure 10.2b   Zn's differing by 60°

Generally, the navigator will have prior knowledge of any systematic errors in his observations and will therefore make the necessary corrections before plotting his LOP's. Random errors, on the other hand, cannot be anticipated. To be sure, with rough seas and an unstable observational platform one might expect the random error to increase. But if the component of error is truly random the navigator is able to make no more than a probable inference as to the direction of the error. In such cases, the triangle of the plotted fix may be quite large. The simplest strategy here is to bisect the interior angles of the triangle and take the intersection of the bisectors as the location of the fix.

On the other hand, there may be occasions when an unforeseen systematic error may enter the picture. For example, under unusual atmospheric conditions the visible horizon may be refracted downward thereby resulting in sextant altitudes being too high. Or, under heavy sea conditions there may be a tendency to pick up a false horizon on the crests of the swell intervening between the observer and his true geographic horizon. In such cases, the observations tend to read too low.

One of the best indications of the intrusion of systematic error into one's observations is an inordinate increase in the size of the plotted fix. As in the case of random error the best strategy is to bisect the interior angles of the triangle of a three-LOP fix. However, in the event the azimuths on a three-body fix are all within a span of 180°, as in Figure 10.2b, then the bisectors of the angles made by any two LOP's should be drawn in the direction of the average of their two azimuths. This may entail bisecting angles that are exterior to the triangle of the fix.

In Figure 10.3 the azimuths of the three LOP's are:

$Z1 = 210$
$Z2 = 260$
$Z3 = 170$

The mean of the azimuths for L1 and L2 is 235° so the bisector of the angle between L1 and L2 is in that direction. The bisector of L1 and L3 is drawn in the direction of 190°,

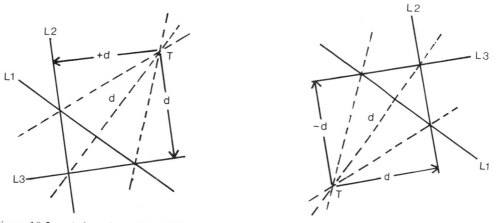

Figure 10.3a   Azimuths within 180°: +*d* error   *Figure 10.3b*   Azimuths within 180°: −*d* error

and that between L2 and L3 toward $215°$. The difference between the two figures rests in the fact that, in Figure 10.3a, a systematic error of $+d$ units has been introduced and in Figure 10.3b a systematic error of $-d$ units has been introduced. Should we incorporate *corrections* of d units (minus in Figure 10.3a and plus in Figure 10.3b), the corrected LOP's would intersect at the respective true points T.

One of the simplest ways to distinguish between systematic and random error is to plot a fix as in Figures 10.3a, b and see by trial and error if some systematic correction, $\pm d$, will bring the adjusted LOP's to converge at the intersection of the bisectors. Indeed, taking a three-body fix with azimuths in the same semicircle is a good way to discover if there is a consistent personal error operating in one's sextant observations.

When there is sufficient ambient horizon many navigators will prefer the four-star fix to any other. Figure 10.4 shows the reason why the LOP's L1 and L2 have azimuths that are diametric to one another, as do the lines L3 and L4. Bisectors of the interior angle at the rectangle offer the best fix. But if there is a systematic error operating, the rectangle will understandably assume the shape of the square as in Figure 10.4. Thus the plot of a square fix as opposed to a rectangular fix is a fair indication of systematic error. In the case of Figure 10.4 the systematic error is $-d'$. Therefore, a correction of $+d'$ added to all observations will result in the LOP's intersecting at T.

Plotting Error and the Running Fix
In addition to random and systematic errors there are those implicit in the advancing of

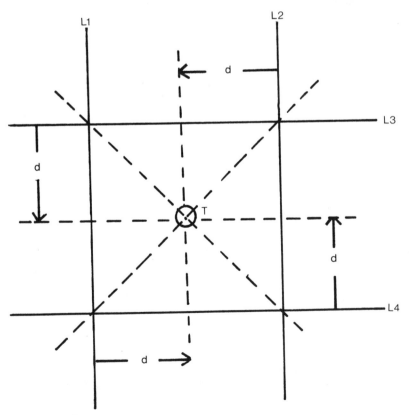

Figure 10.4   Square fix

LOP's as running fixes. The bearing or LOP at the earlier time T1 is carried forth to the time of a second bearing or LOP at T2. The carrying forth is done by advancing the LOP according to course and distance over the intervening period. Obviously, then, any error that we make either as to course or distance will be distributed to the running fix. Since the cruising sailboat is not likely to be covering large distances between the times T1 and T2, the errors due to faulty computations of course or distance may not be substantial ones. However, a precaution is in order. The effects upon advancing course and distance lines depend upon the type of error. Figure 10.5 illustrates the effects of distance error in advancing an LOP. In both figures, E is the error; 10.5a shows the effect on course line, 10.5b shows the effects on a distance line. Such effects can be given a rigorous treatment (cf. Note 10.1).

In similar fashion Figures 10.6a and b illustrate the effects of course error E upon advanced course and distance lines. In both sets of illustrations the broken line presents what should be the true position of the advanced LOP.

In general, we can say that distance errors in advancing LOP's have less effect on course lines than on distance lines. And vice versa, course errors have less effect on distance lines than on course lines. If our uncertainty is in distance more than in course, as the case is likely to be, then the course line should be advanced or regressed to the time of the distance line.

Timing Errors
It is frequently said that a four-second error on the observer's chronometer will result in

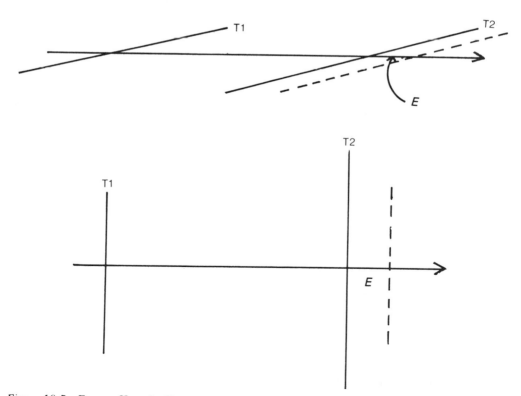

Figure 10.5   Error effects in distance

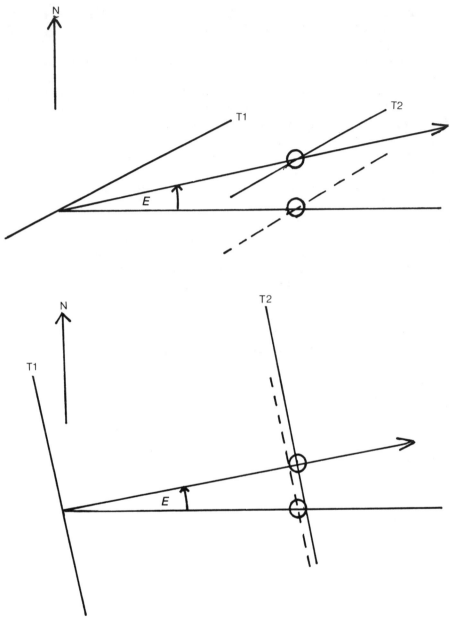

Figure 10.6   Error effects in course

a one-minute (hence one nautical mile) error with respect to the computed altitude. This, however, is only true at the equator. The overall effect of timing error on the computing of Hc is expressed in Formula 10.1:

$$\text{Error minutes of Hc} = \text{error seconds of time} \times \frac{\cos L \sin Z}{4} \qquad \text{(Formula 10.1)}$$

Therefore, the effects of chronometer error are a function both of the observer's latitude and the azimuth of the body. For example, if L = 90° or Z = 180° or 360° (i.e., upper or lower transit) the effects of chronometer error are zero. Correspondingly the effects will be greatest when the body is on the prime vertical. Consequently with timing uncertainty or unreliability of the chronometer one can expect greater error in the altitudes computed for morning or evening shots than for those taken near noon.

SUMMARY

What then can be said apropos of navigational practice for the cruising sailor?

First, we begin with the prepassage preparations: after consulting a world chart for the large-scale geographic details, we lay out great-circle and rhumb line courses on our working Mercator charts. Both large Mercator sheets and the smaller universal plotting sheets can be used. As often as not it will take more than a single chart to cover the track of the passage. In such cases the techniques covered in Chapter 9 on the sailings can be used to determine intermediate coordinates. Along with these coordinates we should plot intermediate distances and ETA's for points along the way. It may also be helpful if we transpose to the working chart weather and current information obtainable from the *Pilot Charts*.

Second, we should anticipate the kind of observations and computations we will be using. Obviously we need to have on hand the essential references, calculator, and plotting tools. We should be prepared to make the following kinds of observations:

1. Course and distance sun shots, noting the expected local times for these as required by the particular course.
2. Latitude and longitude sun shots, again anticipating the local times. The latitude shot is, of course, at local noon.
3. Noonday fix, the running fix with morning and afternoon LOP's advanced or regressed to noon.
4. Traditional time sights to determine longitude where knowledge of latitude is considered reliable.
5. Prime vertical shots for checking compass and computing longitude.
6. Sun-moon daytime fixes when azimuths of the two differ between 45° and 135°.
7. Twilight shots: stars and planets to obtain twilight fixes, and Polaris shots to establish latitude.

Sooner or later the navigator gets locked into a comfortable routine, doubtless preferring some types of observations to others. The good navigator invariably values redundancy and continuous updating. He will not be satisfied with the daily noon fix. In times when overcasts prevail he must be prepared to get an observation at the first opportunity.

Finally, there are matters of judgment. Navigation is both science and art. The science rests on the foundations of nautical astronomy. The art comes in the practice of the observational skills and taking into account the uncontrolled factors that may affect the track of the boat or vessel. In this latter respect we have stressed the need for the navigator to be constantly aware of position, relying, as it were, upon his mind as a subliminal mental computer that enables him to make quick estimates of course, distance, speed, and leeway. Let it be emphasized, however, that a navigator's intuition may prove very unreliable without those checks offered through standard navigational practice: taking observations, plotting, and updating his position.

So, back to our working navigator who has just set his anchor after a long passage. The log book may not resemble a tidy, densely packed ledger, but the essential information will be there. And the chart, however smudged and crumpled, will show the track in detail, the fixes, the tacks, and those "random walks" through exhausting gales. That chart may also record a question mark here and there to call attention to some piece of information inconsistent with expectation or knowledge of what has gone before. Alas, to check and to question one's own work is surely the sign of good navigational judgment.

NOTES

Note 10.1

There are occasions when error in advancing an LOP will result in substantial error in the accuracy of a running fix. For the cruising sailor, such error is likely whenever unforeseen current or leeway affects the track of the vessel.

Error in Distance Run: Consider the effect upon a running fix of a distance error in advancing one LOP to the time of a second LOP.

Figure 10.7 presents a situation in which the distance run in advancing an LOP has been overestimated. L1 is the first or prior LOP, L2 is the second LOP to which L1 is advanced, $L'f$ is the erroneously advanced prior LOP and $L't$ is that prior LOP as correctly advanced. D, therefore, is the distance error in advancing the prior LOP as marked off along the track C.

The intersection of L2 and the advanced LOP gives us the running fix. Therefore T, the intersection of L2 and $L't$ is our true position; F, the intersection of L2 and $L'f$, is the false position created by the error in advancing the prior LOP; and e is the actual error in distance between our true and false positions. It can be shown that

$$e = D \times \frac{\sin \phi}{\sin \theta} \qquad \text{(Formula 10.2)}$$

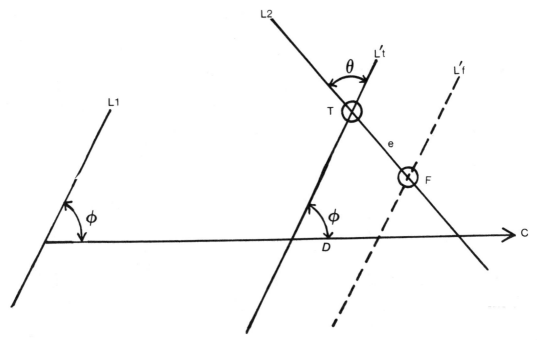

Figure 10.7   Distance error

where ϕ is the angle between our track C and the prior LOP L1, and θ is the angle between L1 and L2. Thus, for example, if D, our error in distance run, is 10 miles, ϕ is 60°, and $\theta = 70°$, then e by Formula 10.2 is 9.2 miles.

From Formula 10.2, it follows that if angle ϕ were relatively small, as it would be if L1 were a course line, then e would be comparatively small; but if angle ϕ were large, as it would be if L1 were a speed or distance line, then e would be comparatively large. Furthermore, other things being equal, the magnitude of e will be minimal when the angle between L1 and L2 is 90°.

Error in Course: Consider next the effect of a course error in advancing the prior LOP to give a running fix.

In Figure 10.8, L1 is advanced along a course line. Ct is the point along the true track to which L1 should be advanced and Cf is the point along the false track to which L1 is actually advanced. D is the distance run along both tracks. As before L'f is the erroneously advanced prior LOP and L't is that LOP correctly advanced. F and T again represent the false and true positions obtained from the advanced LOPs.

There are now three angles to consider. Angle ϕ and angle θ are as before, but, in addition, angle α represents error in course. By radian measure g, the geographic distance between Ct and Cf is given by:

$$g = .017\,D\alpha \qquad\qquad\qquad \text{(Formula 10.3)}$$

(from whence, incidentally, comes the familiar rule that for every 60 miles run with a course error α of 1°, the distance off course g will be one nautical mile).

It can now be shown the error between the true and false running fixes is:

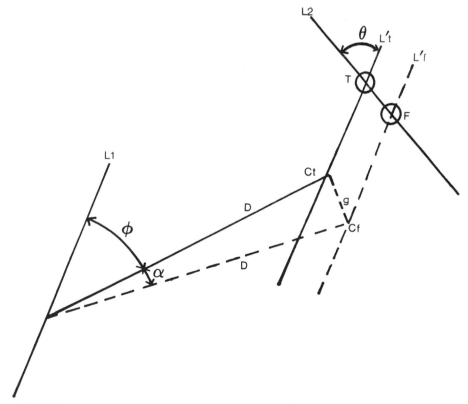

Figure 10.8   Course error

$$e = .017 \, D\alpha \, \frac{\cos \phi}{\sin \theta} \qquad \text{(Formula 10.4)}$$

Suppose, for example our course error α is 10°, distance run between L1 and L2 is 30 miles, ϕ is 45°, and θ is 60°. Our error e by virtue of Formula 10.4 is thereby 4.2 miles. Note that as ϕ approaches 90° the value of e diminishes toward zero and, other things being equal, e becomes minimal when ϕ is 90°.

In general, then, for running fixes, distance errors have maximal effects upon advancing distance lines and course errors have maximal effects upon advancing course lines. Should there be both distance and course errors, the resultant error effects will be additive.

An excellent treatment of navigational errors can be found in Charles H. Cotter, *The Complete Nautical Astronomer*.

Appendix A: Some Computational Formulae

I. CELESTIAL ROUTINES

For the following formulae, these abreviations apply.

Hc	= altitude
L	= latitude
λ	= longitude
t	= meridian angle (hour angle)
HA	= hour angle
LHA	= local hour angle
d	= declination
Z	= azimuth angle
Zn	= true azimuth
SD	= semidiameter
HP	= horizontal parallax
GHA	= Greenwich hour angle

A. Altitude, Hc

1. General:

$$Hc = \sin^{-1} (\sin L \sin d) + (\cos L \cos d \cos t) \qquad \text{(Formula 5.1)}$$

2. Meridian Transit:

$$Hc = \sin^{-1} (\sin L \sin d) + (\cos L \cos d) \qquad \text{(Formula 8.9)}$$
$$= \sin^{-1} \cos (L - d) \qquad \text{(Formula 8.10)}$$

3. Prime Vertical Observation:

$$Hc = \sin^{-1} \frac{\sin d}{\sin L} \qquad \text{(Formula 8.14)}$$

B. Azimuth Angle

1. General:

$$Z = \cos^{-1} \frac{\sin d - (\sin L \sin Hc)}{(\cos L \cos Hc)} \qquad \text{(Formula 5.2)}$$

$$Z = \sin^{-1} \frac{\sin t \cos d}{\cos Hc} \qquad \text{(Formula 5.3)}$$

$$Z = \tan^{-1} \frac{\sin LHA}{(\cos L \tan d) - (\sin L \cos LHA)} \qquad \text{(Formula 5.4)}$$

2. *At Sunrise, Sunset:*

$$Z = \sin^{-1} (\sin t \cos d)$$ (Formula 9.17)

$$Z = \cos^{-1} \frac{\sin d}{\cos L}$$ (Formula 9.18)

C. Latitude
 1. *By Meridian Transit Observation:*
 a. d and L same name, $d > L$

$$L = \sin^{-1} - \cos (d + h)$$ (Formula 8.6b)

 b. all other cases, including all lower transit

$$L = \sin^{-1} \cos (d - h)$$ (Formula 8.6a)

 c. the above from

$$L = \sin^{-1} (\sin d \sin h) \pm (\cos d \cos h)$$ (Formula 8.5)

 2. *By Polaris:*

$$L = \text{Ho of Polaris} - (90 - d) \cos \text{LHA Polaris}$$ (Formula 8.20)

 3. *By Double Altitude:*

$$L = \tan^{-1} \frac{(\cos H2 \cos Z2) - (\cos H1 \cos Z1)}{(\sin H1 - \sin H2)}$$ (Formula 8.22)

D. Longitude
 1. *By Time Sight:*

$$t = \cos^{-1} \frac{\sin h - (\sin L \sin d)}{\cos L \cos d}$$ (Formula 8.11)

$$\lambda = \text{GHA} \pm t$$ (Formula 8.12)

 2. *By Prime Vertical Observation:*

$$t = \sin^{-1} \frac{\cos [\sin^{-1} (\sin d \div \sin L)]}{\cos d}$$ (Formula 8.16)

$$\lambda = \text{GHA} \pm t$$

E. Prime Vertical Observations, Hc and t

$$Hc = \sin^{-1} \frac{\sin d}{\sin L}$$ (Formula 8.14)

$$t = \sin^{-1} \frac{\cos h}{\cos d}$$ (Formula 8.15)

$$t = \cos^{-1} \frac{\tan d}{\tan L}$$

F. Rising and Setting
 1. *Any Body, Other Than Sun, Moon (Ho = −0°34'):*

$$t = \cos^{-1} - \frac{\sin L \sin d}{\cos L \cos d}$$

$$t = \cos^{-1} - (\tan L \tan d) \qquad \text{(Formula 7.1)}$$

2. Sun:

$$t = \cos^{-1} \frac{\sin -0.83 - (\sin L \sin d)}{\cos L \cos d} \qquad \text{(Formula 7.2)}$$

3. Moon:

$$t = \cos^{-1} \frac{\sin (-34' - SD + HP) - (\sin L \sin d)}{\cos L \cos d} \qquad \text{(Formula 7.9)}$$

4. Azimuth Angle:

$$Z = \sin^{-1} (\sin t \cos d) \qquad \text{(Formula 9.17)}$$

$$Z = \cos^{-1} \frac{\sin d}{\cos L} \qquad \text{(Formula 9.18)}$$

G. Twilight
   1. Nautical, AM:

$$t = \cos^{-1} \frac{\sin -12 - (\sin L \sin d)}{\cos L \cos d} \qquad \text{(Formula 7.3)}$$

   2. Civil, AM:

$$t = \cos^{-1} \frac{\sin -6 - (\sin L \sin d)}{\cos L \cos d}$$

   3. Order of 1. and 2. Reversed for PM

H. True azimuth Zn from Azimuth Angle Z

	HA is E	*HA* is W
N lat.	Zn = Z	Zn = 360° − Z
S lat.	Zn = 180° − Z	Zn = 180° + Z

II. THE SAILINGS

For the following formulae, these abbreviations apply.

D	= distance
C	= course angle
D. Lat.	= difference of latitude, also l
P	= departure, horizontal distance
DLo	= difference of longitude
Lm	= mid-latitude
M	= meridional parts *(Bowditch)*
L	= latitude of destination
x_i	= intervals along great-circle track

A. Plane and Parallel Sailing

$$D = \frac{D. \text{ Lat.}}{\cos C} \qquad\qquad (\text{Formula } 9.1)$$

$$C = \tan^{-1} \frac{p}{D. \text{ Lat.}} \qquad\qquad (\text{Formula } 9.2)$$

$$D. \text{ Lat.} = D \cos C \qquad\qquad (\text{Formula } 9.3)$$

$$p = D \sin C \qquad\qquad (\text{Formula } 9.4)$$

$$DLo = \frac{p}{\cos L} \qquad\qquad (\text{Formula } 9.5)$$

$$p = DLo \cos L \qquad\qquad (\text{Formula } 9.6)$$

$$p = DLo \cos Lm \qquad\qquad (\text{Formula } 9.6')$$

B. Mercator Sailing

$$C = \tan^{-1} \frac{DLo'}{M} \qquad\qquad (\text{Formula } 9.13)$$

$$D = \frac{D. \text{ Lat.}'}{\cos C} \qquad\qquad (\text{Formula } 9.14)$$

C. Traverse Sailing

Course	Dist.	D. Lat.		p	
		N(+)	S(−)	W(+)	E(−)
		(entries)			
Subtotals		_____	____	____	___
Net		_____		_____	

$$D. \text{ Lat.} = D \cos C \qquad\qquad (\text{Formula } 9.3)$$

$$p = D \sin C \qquad\qquad (\text{Formula } 9.4)$$

$$DLo = \frac{p}{\cos L} \qquad\qquad (\text{Formula } 9.5)$$

D. Great Circle Sailing

x = departure
y = destination
x_i = interval points
v = vertex of great circle

$$D = \cos^{-1} (\sin Lx \sin Ly + \cos Lx \cos Ly \cos DLo) \qquad\qquad (\text{Formula } 9.7)$$

$$Cx = \cos^{-1} \frac{\sin Ly - (\sin Lx \cos D)}{\cos Lx \sin D} \qquad\qquad (\text{Formula } 9.8)$$

$$Cy = \cos^{-1} \frac{\sin Lx - (\sin Ly \cos D)}{\cos Ly \sin D} \qquad \text{(Formula 9.8')}$$

$$Lv = \cos^{-1} (\cos Lx \sin Cx) \qquad \text{(Formula 9.9)}$$

$$Dvx = \sin^{-1} \frac{1}{\tan Lv \tan Cx} \qquad \text{(Formula 9.10)}$$

$$DLov = \cos^{-1} \frac{\tan Lx}{\tan Lv} \qquad \text{(Formula 9.11)}$$

$$= \cos^{-1} (\cos Dvx \sin Cx)$$

$$Lxi = \tan^{-1} (\cos DLoxi \tan Lv) \qquad \text{(Formula 9.12)}$$

Appendix B: Glossary

Aberration An optical effect due to the earth's orbital motion relative to light from a stellar source.

Altitude Angular distance of a celestial body above the observer's true horizon. Also the arc distance on the observer's vertical circle between the horizon and the observed body.

Aphelion Point in a planetary orbit where the planet is farthest from the sun, the source of gravitational attraction.

Apparent magnitude Brightness of a celestial body as established by psychological parameters as opposed to physical scaling.

Apparent sun The true sun as opposed to the fictitious mean sun.

Arc distance Distance between two points on a great circle, where on the earth's surface one minute of arc converts to one nautical mile.

Arc measure One minute of arc on the earth's surface is equal to one nautical mile (by convention, 6,076.1 feet); an angle of one minute at the earth's center subtends an arc of one minute on its surface.

Aries, first point of Point at which the sun passes from south to north declination; the vernal equinox; also that point on the equinoctial which is the reference for locating the hour circles of stellar objects (i.e., SHA and RA).

Artificial horizon Any device for giving a horizon reference identical except for dip to that of an observer at sea.

Assumed latitude (aL) Latitude of the assumed position AP as adopted for setting up the navigational triangle.

Assumed longitude (aλ) Longitude of the assumed position AP as adopted for setting up the navigational triangle.

Assumed position (AP) Position, usually DR, that is assumed for setting up the navigational triangle in computing a celestial line of position.

Astrolabe Early instrument for measuring the altitude of a celestial object.

Astronomical twilight The period when the sun is from 0° to 18° below the horizon.

Augmentation Apparent increase in semidiameter of sun or moon as the body approaches culmination due to the fact that the body is nearer to the observer at culmination than at rising or setting.

Autumnal equinox Point at which sun moves from north to south declination.

Average deviation The mean of all deviations of individual observations from the mean, the magnitude of all deviations being treated as positive.

Azimuth angle (Z) Angle within the nautical triangle between the observer's meridian and the vertical circle through the body. Gives the bearing of the body from the observer.

Backstaff An early device for measuring altitude whose observational principles fall between those of the cross-staff and the modern sextant.

Bubble sextant Sextant that levels upon the horizon by centering a bubble in its chamber rather than by sighting on the visible horizon.

Cartesian coordinates A two-coordinate geometry in which a point is located on an x, y grid whose axes are mutually perpendicular (akin to latitude and longitude on a Mercator chart).

Celestial equator The equinoctial, that equatorial band made by projecting the earth's equator onto the celestial sphere.

Celestial poles Projection of the terrestrial poles onto the celestial sphere.

Celestial triangle   Triangle projected onto the celestial sphere with the celestial pole, the observer's zenith point, and the celestial position of body as the vertices, and codeclination, coaltitude of the body, and colatitude of the observer's zenith as its sides. (Used interchangeably with the navigational triangle.)

Chronometer   A clock designed to keep accurate time.

Circle of equal altitude   The locus of points on the earth's surface from which identical altitude observations of a given body will be obtained.

Circle of uncertainty   A circle within which the navigator would locate his position granting an allowance for error.

Circumpolar body   A celestial object visibly rotating about the pole, thereby never dipping below the horizon.

Civil twilight   The period when the sun is from 0° to 6° below the horizon.

Clearing the distance   Correcting the apparent angular distance between the moon and another celestial object to its true angular distance as measured at the center of the earth.

Coaltitude   The complement of altitude (i.e., 90° − altitude).

Coast Pilot   A book containing detailed information on coastal waters, harbors, currents, weather, etc., for the guidance of the mariner.

Codeclination   The complement of declination (i.e., 90° − declination).

Colatitude   The complement of latitude (i.e., 90° − latitude).

Compass error   The difference between true heading or direction and compass heading.

Computed altitude (Hc)   Altitude as computed by methods of sight reduction, for comparison with observed altitude in determining a celestial LOP.

Conjunction   The alignment of bodies such that they are located on the same celestial meridian.

Course line   An LOP parallel to a vessel's course, hence the true azimuth Zn cuts the course at a right angle.

Cross-staff   Early instrument for measuring the altitude of a celestial object based on the principle of a shadow astrolabe, with a sliding crosspiece indicating altitude along a horizontal staff.

Culmination   The point at which a celestial body reaches its maximum altitude for the given observer. Also *transit, meridian passage.*

d correction (d)   An interpolated correction due to the inconstancy of hourly change in declination.

Dead reckoning (DR)   Determining position from a knowledge of heading, speed, and drift.

Declination (Dec. or d)   Angle at the center of the celestial sphere between the equinoctial and a parallel of latitude through a celestial body. Corresponds to the latitude of a celestial body.

Departure (p)   A term used in plane sailing to indicate difference of longitude along a given parallel of latitude, the difference being expressed as distance in nautical miles.

Dip (D)   The angular difference between the geometrically true and the apparent or visual horizon.

Distance line   An LOP that cuts the course at a right angle, hence the true azimuth Zn parallels the course.

Diurnal motion   The apparent daily motion of a celestial object; its track in a twenty-four-hour period.

Double altitude   Method of determining latitude from the altitude observations at different but proximal times.

Eclipse   The obscuring of one body by the interposition of another vis-à-vis the observer.

Ecliptic   Apparent path of the sun through the stellar sphere as generated by the earth's axial orientation and orbit of revolution about the sun.

Elongation   Arc-angle between two celestial objects as measured from the earth.

Ephemeris   Astronomer's almanac of celestial information.

Equation of time   The difference in arc, translated into time, between the true sun and the fictitious mean sun.

Equatorial plane   Plane perpendicular to polar axis, midway between the North and South poles; enscribes the great circle of the equator on the earth's surface.

Equinoctial (Q)   Celestial equator as projected by the earth's equatorial plane.

Equinox   Nodal point at which the ecliptic crosses the equinoctial (the spring and autumnal equinoxes).

Euclidean space   Our conventional three-dimensional space, making use of Euclid's geometry.

Ex-meridian   Methods involving the computation of rates of change in altitude as a function of differences of time between meridian passage and the time of an actual observation.

Geocentric parallax   The difference of altitude of a body as measured at the center of the earth and as measured at a point on the earth's surface.

Geocentric system   A hypothetical celestial system placing the earth at the center of the celestial sphere (as in traditional celestial navigation).

Geodesic   A line in some designated space that represents the shortest distance between two points (on the earth's surface, a great circle).

Geographic position (GP)   Position on the earth's surface directly under a celestial body. Point at which the body's altitude is precisely 90°.

Gibbous moon   State of moon when less than full but more than half.

Gnomon   A vertical pin whose shadow, projected on a horizontal base, indicates the altitude of the sun.

Gnomonic chart   A chart constructed by projecting the earth's surface onto a plane tangent at some given point. Sometimes known as a great-circle chart, since a great circle will appear upon it as a straight line.

Great circle   Circle inscribed on a sphere made by passing a plane through the center of the sphere. (On the earth's surface all meridians are great circles, as is the equator).

Great-circle course   The great circle, or shortest distance line between a departure and a destination.

Great-circle sailing   Determining courses and distances along the great-circle track.

Greenwich hour angle (GHA)   Hour angle between the prime meridian of Greenwich and an hour circle through a celestial object, the angle measured westerly through 360°.

Greenwich hour angle of Aries (GHA♈)   Hour angle between Greenwich and the first point of Aries measured westerly through 360°.

Greenwich mean time (GMT)   Also Greenwich civil time. Time as measured from the lower branch of Greenwich meridian to the hour circle of the mean sun. Also local apparent time at Greenwich, England. Now reported as *Coordinated Universal Time*.

Greenwich meridian   Meridian through the Royal Observatory, Greenwich, England; the standard reference for longitude and Greenwich time.

Haversine   A trigonometric function, $(1 - \cos) \div 2$, whose advantage in early navigational practice was to eliminate angular ambiguities inherent in ordinary trigonometric functions.

Heliocentric system   A hypothetical celestial system placing the sun at the center of the celestial sphere.

Horizon   The plane at right angles to the zenith-nadir axis that theoretically intersects the center of the earth, that plane subtending a great circle on the celestial sphere.

Horizon, apparent   Horizon as seen at sea unobscured by intervening waves. The difference between the true and the apparent horizon will be due to the factor of *dip* and in the case of the moon, both dip and *parallax*.

Horizon glass   The fixed mirror of a sextant, half of which is clear glass permitting direct viewing of the horizon.

Horizontal parallax (HP)   The maximum value of parallax when the moon is on the horizon.

Hour angle (HA)   Angle between any two hour circles or between a meridian of longitude and an hour circle in the celestial sphere, generally measured westerly through 360°, as in LHA. If hour angle is measured east or west through 180°, it is identical with meridian angle, t.

Hour circle   Celestial meridian made by projecting meridians of longitude onto the celestial sphere.

Index arm   The movable arm of a sextant.

Index error   Instrumental error due to imperfect alignment between the horizon and index mirrors. If the error is "on the arc" the instrument reads too high and the correction is subtracted; "off the arc," vice versa.

Index mirror   The mirror attached to the movable index arm.

Inferior planets   Mercury and Venus, the two planets whose orbits lie inside the earth's orbit; only Venus is used for navigational observations.

Instrumental error A constant or fixed error due to imperfections in an instrument such as a sextant.

Intercept Difference in minutes of arc between the observed altitude Ho and the computed altitude Hc, labelled toward (T) or away (A) as Ho is greater or smaller than Hc.

International date line Lower branch of the meridian passing through Greenwich; requires advancing a clock twenty-four hours in crossing from W to E, or retarding it twenty-four hours in crossing E to W.

Inverse of a trigonometric function The angle for which the given trigonometric function holds.

Irradiation An illusory error generated by the contrast of a bright sky against a dark horizon; its effect is to depress the apparent horizon and slightly increase the apparent diameter of the sun.

Isomorphic relationship Congruence of terrestrial and celestial position in navigational astronomy.

Kamal An ancient Arabian device used to measure altitude, whereby the observer sights on the base and top of a rectangle while holding the rectangle at a determined distance from the eye.

Latitude (L) Angle at the center of the earth between the equator and a point on the earth's surface as measured north or south of the equator along the meridian passing through the point.

Latitude by meridian passage Finding latitude by observing the altitude of a body at transit.

Law of cosines, spherical triangle The cosine of any side is equal to the product of the cosines of the other two sides plus the product of the sines of those two sides times the cosine of their included angle; e.g., $\cos x = \cos y \cos z + \sin y \sin z \cos X$.

Law of sines, spherical triangle
$$\frac{\sin x}{\sin X} = \frac{\sin y}{\sin Y} = \frac{\sin z}{\sin Z}$$
where x, y, and z are the arc sides opposite the angles X, Y, and Z.

Limb Upper and lower points of tangency on the circumference of the sun or moon.

Line of position (LOP) Locus of points all of which are consonant with an observer's observation. In celestial observation the LOP is a segment of a circle of equal altitude.

Local apparent noon (LAN) Moment at which the true sun crosses the upper branch of an observer's meridian.

Local hour angle (LHA) Hour angle between an observer's meridian and an hour circle through an observed body, *measured westerly through 360°.*

Longitude (λ) Angle at the center of the earth between the prime meridian through Greenwich and a meridian through a point on the earth's surface, as measured east or west through 180°.

Lower branch of a meridian The half of a body's or observer's meridian between the poles which intercepts its antipodal location.

Lower limb Point on the circumference of the sun or the moon yielding the least altitude from the horizon.

Lower transit Transit of celestial body at the lower branch of an observer's meridian.

Lunar distance The angular difference between the moon and another celestial body (usually the sun) as measured at the center of the earth.

Magnetic bearing Bearing relative to magnetic north.

Marcq St. Hilaire method Determines an LOP by comparing an observed altitude (Ho) and a computed altitude (Hc) and striking the difference (the intercept) along the true azimuth (Zn) of the body.

Mean The arithmetic average of a set of observations obtained by dividing the sum of all such measures by the total number of observations.

Mean sun Fictitious sun projected to move along the equinoctial at a constant rate, and completing its circle in one solar year.

Mean time Time as measured relative to the motion of the mean sun.

Mercator chart Chart made by the projection of the earth's surface onto a cylinder tangent to the earth usually at its equator.

Mercator sailing Methods for computing course and distance on a Mercator chart where the measure of distance is a function of latitude.

Meridian A great circle made by passing a plane through the polar axis. Meridians on the earth's surface constitute lines of longitude.

Meridian angle (t) Hour angle, the angle

between the observer's meridian and the hour circle through a celestial object, measured east or west to 180°.

Meridian passage   Meridian transit.

Meridian transit   The moment when a celestial body intersects the observer's meridian. Also *meridian passage,* and *culmination.*

Meridional part (M)   One minute of arc on a meridian at the equator as represented on a Mercator chart. *Meridional parts* will be the number of such units required to measure the expansion of latitude on a Mercator chart.

Mid-latitude sailing   Method of computing the departure (p) of plane sailing by assuming a latitude midway between that of a vessel's geographic departure and its destination.

Moonrise   Local mean time at which the upper limb of the moon is seen to emerge above the true horizon.

Moonset   Local mean time at which the upper limb of the moon is seen to disappear below the true horizon.

Nadir   Point on the celestial sphere opposite the observer's zenith.

Nautical Almanac   An ephemeris of celestial and navigational data published jointly by Great Britain and the United States.

Nautical astronomy   That aspect of astronomy which concerns the determination of position on earth from observations of celestial bodies.

Nautical mile   One minute of arc on a great circle inscribed on the earth's surface, visualized as a perfect sphere; by convention a distance of 1,852 meters, or 6,076 feet, or 1.15 statute miles.

Nautical triangle   The navigational triangle as generalized both for celestial sight reduction and great-circle sailing.

Nautical twilight   The period when the sun is from 0° to 12° below the horizon; the period when most observations of stars and planets are made by the navigator.

Navigational planets   Those for which navigational data are provided in the *Nautical Almanac,* namely, Venus, Mars, Jupiter, and Saturn.

Navigational triangle   Spherical triangle with zenith (Z), pole (P), and geographic position of the body (GP or M) as its vertices, and codeclination, coaltitude, and colatitude as its sides.

Nodal point   Point of intersection between two or more celestial tracks.

Node   The intersection of two or more tracks, such as the ecliptic and the equinoctial or the moon's celestial track and the ecliptic.

Normal   The line of sight or direction at right angles to the plane of a mirror.

Observed altitude   The sextant altitude corrected for systematic and personal factors of error.

Occultation   The obscuring of a body by the bright background of a larger body, as for example when Jupiter's moons pass between the observer and Jupiter itself.

Parallatic angle (θ)   One of the angles of the navigational triangle, viz., that between the meridian through the celestial body and the vertical circle from the body to the observer's zenith.

Parallax   The difference in angle between altitude as measured at the center of the earth and as measured at the surface of the earth.

Parallel of latitude   That circle passing through all points of a given latitude and inscribed on the earth's surface by a small circle parallel to the equator.

Pelorus   An instrument for sighting relative bearings.

Perihelion   Point in a planetary orbit where the planet is nearest the sun, the point of gravitational attraction.

Personal error   Error due to bias or idiosyncrasy in a particular observer's observations.

Pilot Chart   Chart providing information on ocean currents and temperatures, wind, storm tracks, magnetic variation, and other items of interest to the mariner.

Plane sailing   Method of finding course and distance by trigonometric means when a small section of the earth's surface is regarded as a simple plane.

Polar axis   The axis of the earth's rotation between the true North and South poles.

Polar coordinates   A two-coordinate geometry in which position from an origin is specified by direction and distance, for instance, course and distance on a Mercator chart.

Polar distance   The arc measure between a celestial object and the nearest pole. Same as codeclination of the body.

Polar-equatorial system   The celestial hemisphere as defined by the polar axis and the equinoctial.

Polyconic projection   A map or chart that is constructed by projecting the earth's surface onto one or more cones placed tangent to the earth's surface.

Precession   Change of direction of the axis of a rotating body due to applied torque.

Prime meridian (G)   The meridian passing through Greenwich, England, which serves as a standard for measuring longitude and Greenwich time.

Prime vertical circle   Vertical circle intersecting the observer's geographic east and west.

Prime vertical sight   Determining when a body is due east or west by comparing observed altitude with a precomputed altitude.

Radian   Arc subtended at the center of a circle equal to the radius of the circle, there being 2π radians in a circle.

Random error   Error that is not systematic in nature, i.e., that which is due to unpredictable fluctuations in the accuracy of observation.

Rate of change   Change per unit of time.

Refraction   The deflection of linear light as it passes between media of differing densities. Upon entering the earth's atmosphere the light from a stellar source is refracted toward the earth's surface resulting in an apparent or observed altitude greater than the true altitude.

Relative bearing   Bearing between two objects as seen from an observer's point of reference; bearing relative to the fore and aft axis of a vessel.

Retrograde motion   Reversal in direction of a planet's apparent motion against the stellar background.

Revolution   The orbital motion of one body about another.

Rhumb line   A line constructed to cut all meridians of longitude at a constant angle; a straight line on a Mercator chart.

Right ascension   Hour angle between first point of Aries and the hour circle through a body, measured easterly through 360° and converted to time.

Rotation   The circular motion of a body about the polar axis.

Running fix   A positional fix established by advancing or regressing one or more

LOP's to the time of a base LOP.

Sailing Directions   Publications containing information useful to the mariner in coastal pilotage and navigation. For the U. S. coast, the U. S. publications are known as *Coast Pilots*.

Sailings   Methods for computing courses and distances, latitudes and longitudes, by trigonometric means.

Semidiameter (SD)   Half the diameter of a stellar body such as the sun or moon; the *magnitude* of semidiameter is the correction applied to a sextant observation of the upper or lower limb of these bodies.

Sextant altitude (hs)   The altitude actually observed on a sextant prior to introducing corrections for systematic, personal, and instrument errors.

Shadow bearing   The bearing of the sun determined by a shadow pin. For the magnetic compass the shadow bearing will be the compass bearing plus 180°.

Shadow pin   Vertical pin at the center of a compass card designed to cast a linear shadow on the compass rose.

Sidereal day   Duration of one rotation of the earth with a fixed stellar point as reference, namely, the first point of Aries.

Sidereal hour angle (SHA)   Hour angle measured westerly from first point of Aries to the hour circle through a particular star.

Sidereal period   A rotational or orbital period of time with a fixed stellar point taken as reference.

Sidereal year   Time of one orbital revolution of the earth about the sun, with a fixed stellar object as reference.

Sight reduction   Procedure of computing altitude and azimuth angle of a celestial object for an assumed position. More generally, the process of determining a line of position from a celestial observation.

Sight reduction tables   Tables of solutions of the navigational triangle, giving computed altitudes and azimuths on entry information of latitude, declination, and hour angle.

Small circle   Circle inscribed on a sphere by passing a plane through the sphere but not intersecting its center. (On the earth's surface all parallels of latitude except for the equator are small circles.)

Solar time   Time based on the rotation of the earth relative to the sun.

Solstice   Points of maximum declination,

north and south, reached by the sun on the path of the ecliptic.

Spherical trigonometry   The application of trigonometric principles and relations to spherical triangles. The mathematical foundations of nautical astronomy.

Standard deviation   A statistical measure of variability; the square root of the mean of squared deviations.

Statute mile   A traditional unit of distance in Great Britain and the United States equal to 5,280 feet, or .869 nautical mile.

Sumner line   An LOP, a segment of a line of equal altitude computed by assuming a set of different latitudes and then determining corresponding longitudes compatible with the latitudes and the given altitude.

Sunrise   Local mean time at which the upper limb of the sun is seen to emerge above the true horizon.

Sunset   Local mean time at which the upper limb of the sun is seen to disappear below the true horizon.

Superior planets   Those planets whose orbits lie outside the earth's orbit; Jupiter, Mars, and Saturn are the navigational planets.

Swinging the arc   Rocking the image in the sextant view piece so as to assure perpendicularity of the sextant.

Synodic period   Period of time required for two successive conjunctions of celestial objects, usually the sun and another planet.

Theory of error   The statistical treatment of errors of observation.

Time diagram   Circular diagram plotting the location of objects with respect to the Greenwich meridian using time and angular measures interchangeably.

Time sight   Method of determining longitude by computing the hour angle between an observation at meridian transit and a later observation.

Traverse sailing   Tracking courses and distances over a set of short tacks by the method of plane sailing.

True azimuth (Zn)   The bearing of a body from the observer measured from true north westerly through 360°.

True bearing   Bearing of an object with respect to true north; magnetic bearing corrected for variation.

Universal plotting sheets   Approximate segments of Mercator charts constructed on fixed lines of latitude but variable lines of longitude.

Upper branch of meridian   The half segment of a meridian between the poles that intercepts the observer's or the body's position.

Upper limb   Point on the circumference of the sun or moon yielding the greatest altitude.

Upper transit   Transit at the upper branch of the observer's meridian.

v *correction*   An interpolated correction due to the fact that hourly increment for GHA of a body such as Venus or the moon is not constant.

Vernal equinox   The first point of Aries; the point at which the sun moves from south to north declination.

Vertex   Point of highest latitude through which the extended great-circle course passes.

Vertical circle   Great circle passing through the observer's zenith and nadir.

Zenith (Z)   Point on the celestial sphere directly over the observer's head.

Zenith distance   The complement of latitude (i.e., 90° − latitude); the distance of the zenith from the elevated pole.

Zenith system   The celestial hemisphere as defined by the observer's zenith and horizon.

Zodiac   The region straddling the ecliptic, 16° in width, which includes the orbits of the visible planets.

Zone time   Greenwich mean time adjusted on the basis of one hour of difference for each 15° time zone, the prime Greenwich time zone being from 7.5°E to 7.5°W longitude.

References

American Air Almanac. Washington, D. C.: U. S. Goverment Printing Office, semiannually.

Bowditch, Nathaniel. *American Practical Navigator.* Washington, D. C.: U. S. Government Printing Office, 1966.

Cotter, Charles H. *The Astronomical and Mathematical Foundations of Geography.* New York: American Elsevier Publishing Co., 1966.

————. *The Complete Nautical Astonomer.* New York: American Elsevier Publishing Co., 1969.

————. *A History of Nautical Astonomy.* New York: American Elsevier Publishing Co., 1968.

Dutton's Navigation and Piloting. Edited by G. D. Dunlap and H. H. Shufeldt. 12th ed. Annapolis, Md: Naval Institute Press, 1969.

————. Edited by Albert S. Maloney. 13th ed. Annapolis, Md.: Naval Institute Press, 1978.

Gatty, Harold. *The Raft Book.* New York: G. Grady Press, 1943.

May, W. E. *A History of Maritime Navigation.* New York: W. W. Norton & Co., 1973.

Mills, H. R. *Positional Astronomy and Astro-Navigation Made Easy.* New York: John Wiley and Sons, 1978.

Nautical Almanac, Washington, D. C.: U. S. Government Printing Office, annually.

Sight Reduction Tables for Air Navigation, Pub. No. 249. 3 vols. Washington, D. C.: U. S. Government Printing Office, 1981.

Slocum, Joshua. *Sailing Alone Around the World.* New York: Macmillan (Collier Books), 1970.

Taylor, E. G. R. *The Haven-Finding Art.* New York: American Elsevier Publishing Co., 1968.

Waters, D. W. *The Art of Navigation.* New Haven, Conn.: Yale University Press, 1958.

Index

Entries followed by an asterisk are defined in the Glossary, pp. 208-14.

A
Aberration,* 159
Air Almanac, 41
  Polaris correction in, 146, 158
  star chart from, 18-19
Altitude*
  computed,* 60, 71, 78, 154
  double, 187-88
  ex-meridian, *147-49
  observed,* 61
  sextant,* 61
Altitude corrections, 100-11
  for moon, 110
  for planets, 110-11
  for stars, 110-11
  for sun, 109-10
Amplitude, 184
  tables of, 184
Aphelion,* 25
Apparent magnitude,* 138-39
Apparent motion
  and time, 32-34
  factors influencing, 48
  history of, 24
  of Mars, 25-26
  of moon, 17, 28
  of planets, 17, 20
  of sun, 17, 24-25, 48
  of Venus, 26
Apparent sun,* 34, 37, 48, 132
Arc distance,* 53, 67-68
Arc measure,* 67-68
Aries (♈), first point of,* 13, 55
Artificial horizon,* 118
Assumed latitude (aL),* 81
Assumed longitude (aλ),* 81
Assumed position (AP), G, 53, 60, 62
Astrolabe,* 112
Astronomical twilight,* 130
Astronomy
  nautical, 4
  positional, 4

Augmentation,* 110
Autumnal equinox,* 48
Average deviation,* 117
Azimuth angle,* 58-60
  ambiguity of, 72
  and true azimuth, 76-78
  computation of, 72, 76, 180-84
  law of sines solution of, 72
  at sunrise and sunset, 183

B
Backstaff,* 115
Bearing
  celestial, 16-17, 111
  line, 9-11
  relative, 111, 180-81
Big Dipper, 127
Bowditch, 6
  amplitude, 184
  ex-meridian latitude, 147
  horizon distance, 100
  meridional parts (M), 179
Brahe, Tycho, 41, 112
Brightness, 138-39. *See also* Relative magnitude
Bubble sextant,* 116

C
Calculators, 86
Cartesian coordinates,* 7
Celestial equator,* 11
Celestial fix, 66-67
Celestial triangle,* 54-59
  and terrestrial triangle, 173
Charts
  gnomonic (great-circle), 22
  Lambert's polyconic, 22
  Mercator, 20-22
  requirements of, 20
  star, 16-19
Chartwork 190
Chronometer,* 47-48, 52